Dutch Explorers, Traders, and Settlers
in the Delaware Valley
1609-1664

Other Books by C. A. Weslager

Delaware's Forgotten Folk, 1943

Delaware's Buried Past, 1944

Delaware's Forgotten River, 1947

The Nanticoke Indians, 1948

Brandywine Springs, 1949

Indian Place-Names in Delaware, 1950
    (in collaboration with A. R. Dunlap)

Red Men on the Brandywine, 1953

The Richardsons of Delaware, 1957

Dutch Explorers, Traders and Settlers in the Delaware Valley

1609-1664

by

C. A. Weslager

in collaboration with

A. R. Dunlap

University of Pennsylvania Press

Philadelphia

Commemorating the 350th anniversary
of Henry Hudson's third voyage, which
brought him to Delaware Bay

Foreword

The present study was undertaken with the aim of commemorating, in 1959, the three hundred and fiftieth anniversary of Henry Hudson's "discovery" of Delaware Bay. Initially it was conceived as a joint production of the two authors whose names appear on the title page, each to contribute different chapters based on his own research. But because of the press of official duties, one of the writers found it necessary to reduce himself to the status of a collaborator and to leave the bulk of the writing to to the other. This change in procedure naturally delayed the completion of the manuscript, with the result that the finished book, which still technically commemorates the Hudson voyage, is a full two years behind itself. The three hundred and fiftieth year of Hudson's visit to American waters, one regrets to say, passed with only casual notice in the public press. It is hoped, therefore, that the publication of this volume comes not too late to do timely honor to one of the great navigators of the seventeenth century.

As the book now stands each chapter, by design, is a separate entity, as originally planned. A certain continuity has, nevertheless, been observed, and the reader will find that although he can turn to a chapter of specific interest without necessarily reading what precedes or follows, he can also start at the beginning and read straight through without being aware of any unnatural transitions. For example, Chapter 6, which deals with Dutch maps and geographical names, is a chapter unto itself, yet it ties in with material presented in earlier chapters. This chapter, incidentally, is the only one for which the collaborating author is wholly responsible, but he also supplied all the new translations of Dutch documents into English.

An account of the seventeenth century Dutch settlements on the Delaware has been given before, as an incidental part of the history of New Netherland (e.g., by O'Callaghan in 1848), or of New York (e.g., by Brodhead in 1853). The subject has also been treated with authority, but incompletely, by historians primarily concerned with New Sweden (e.g., by Amandus Johnson in 1911), or with Delaware (e.g., by Scharf in 1888). But there has never before been a separate and independent volume dealing with the Dutch on the Delaware, and one has long been needed to enable the student to see in full perspective the history of both New Netherland and New Sweden, as well as the English efforts to command the area. The need has become even more critical since the translation and publication, in 1925, by A. J. F. van Laer of the so-called *Van Rappard Documents*. Although of utmost importance in the story of the Dutch on the Delaware, the significance of these documents, found in Holland, has not been generally recognized.

The center of political and social life in New Netherland in the seventeenth century was on Manhattan Island, where, as most schoolbooks have it, Peter Minuit supposedly made the noted purchase from the Indians which gave ownership rights to the Dutch and permitted the founding of their colony. On the basis of evidence now available, the present study shows that the Dutch originally intended a "beautiful" or "high" island in the Delaware River to be the seat of New Netherland two years before Manhattan Island was purchased by Minuit — if, indeed, he were the purchaser. The account of that Delaware island settlement is given here in as full detail as the limited data permit, including an identification of the island in terms of today's geography.

The reader will observe that a new translation of Henry Hudson's contract with the directors of the East India Company (1609) appears in full in the opening chapter. This is a key document in the history of New Netherland, for it set in motion a series of events leading to the "discovery" of Delaware Bay, the formation of the West India Company, and the founding of the short-lived community on the "beautiful" island in the Delaware River, prior to the settlement on Manhattan Island.

This volume also tells the *full* story of the efforts of the Dutch patroons to found a whaling colony at Swanendael (present Lewes, Delaware), and to establish a sister colony in New Jersey on the opposite shore of the bay. In *Appendix A*, for the convenience of the student, are brought together, from scattered sources, all the known major documentary references to the ill-fated Swanendael colony, later called the Hoeren-kil. Among these documents is a new English translation of a passage in *Kort Verhael van Nieuw-Nederlants Gelegenheit* (1662), which has heretofore been only partially translated; the transcript of a patent to Francis Jenkins for 600 acres of land (1672), and a deposition by Philemon Lloyd about the burning of the settlement at the Hoeren-kil in 1673.

Other documents not previously published are a full translation of the secret instructions issued to Peter Minuit (1637); an account of Andries Hudde's purchase of lands from the Indians at the site of present Philadelphia (1646); and a deposition by James Way, concerning both English and Dutch settlement efforts on the Delaware (1684). These all contribute to a better understanding of the story of New Netherland from the southern point of vantage, i.e., the South River, and bring into sharper focus the significance of Fort Nassau and the erection of Fort Beversreede, which preceded the shift of Dutch strength to Fort Casimir, later called Fort Amstel, and still later, New Castle.

Writers in the field of history inevitably build upon the works of their predecessors, and this volume is no exception. The very considerable indebtedness owed to other writings that have come before is, it is hoped, thoroughly enough acknowledged in the footnotes to obviate repetition here. There are, of course, others to whom grateful appreciation for assistance, advice, and encouragement is due, even though they are not named. Special thanks should be accorded, however, to the staffs of the Enoch Pratt Free Library, the Historical Society of Delaware, the Historical Society of Pennsylvania, the Memorial Library of the University of Delaware, the New York Public Library, the Public Archives of the State of Delaware, and the Wilmington Institute Free Library for courteous and valued assistance. Thanks are also due to the Faculty Research Committee of the University of Delaware for encouragement and financial aid.

Important Dates in Dutch Chronology
on the Delaware

August 1609   Henry Hudson anchors in Delaware Bay.

1610–1620   Dutch navigators explore Delaware River.

1621   West India Company formed in Holland.

1624   The Company sends a group of Walloons to settle on an island in the Delaware.

1625   The Company sends Willem Verhulst as " provisional governor " of New Netherland, instructing him to have his usual residence on High Island in the Delaware and to strengthen the Delaware colony.

1626   Walloon and Dutch settlers withdrawn from the Delaware to Manhattan Island, which becomes seat of New Netherland. Fort Nassau built as a post for use in Indian trade.

1631   Patroons establish a whaling colony called Swanendael at site of present Lewes, Delaware.

1632   Settlers at Swanendael massacred by the Indians.

11

1634	Party of English brought by Thomas Yong settle at *Arrowamex* (Fort Nassau) but are removed by the Dutch.
1638	Peter Minuit brings Swedish expedition to the Delaware and builds Fort Christina.
1640–1641	Swedes extend limits of New Sweden from Schuylkill River to the falls at Trenton. Peter Ridder buys land for Swedes from Raccoon Creek to Cape May.
1641	Group of English from New Haven settle at *Watcessit* on the Varckens Kill (Salem River) on the east side of the Delaware.
1642	English from Watcessit attempt to settle on Schuylkill, but are driven off by the Dutch.
1644	Englishmen from Boston enter Delaware, intending to found a settlement, but are turned back by Dutch and Swedes.
April 1648	The Company builds Fort Beversreede.
1651	Stuyvesant builds Fort Casimir, and Fort Nassau and Fort Beversreede are abandoned.
May 21, 1654	Swedish Governor Rising captures Fort Casimir and renames it Fort Trinity.
September 1, 1655	Dutch recapture Fort Casimir, and seize Fort Christina, taking control of the Delaware from the Swedes.
December 19, 1656	Ownership of Fort Casimir transferred from the West India Company to the Burgomasters of the City of Amsterdam,

who change name to New Amstel. Documents covering sale signed April 12, 1657.

1659   " The Company's Fort " built at Swanendael, now called the Hoerenkil.

1659   Col. Nathaniel Utie, member of Maryland Council, comes to New Amstel and orders Dutch to leave. Stuyvesant sends Augustine Herrman and Resolved Waldron to Maryland for discussions ; they find a flaw in Lord Baltimore's charter.

1663   The City of Amsterdam acquires all of the Delaware River territory from the Company. Cornelis Plockhoy founds a colony of Dutch Mennonites at the Hoerenkil under auspices of the City.

October 1644   New Amstel surrenders to Sir Robert Carr ; name changed to New Castle ; Carr destroys Plockhoy's colony at the Hoerenkil ; all the Delaware territory now falls under control of the Duke of York.

August 8, 1673   New Netherland, including New Castle and Delaware territory, again seized by Dutch.

Xmas Eve, 1673   Lord Baltimore's soldiers burn all the houses at the Hoerenkil to prevent their falling into the hands of the Dutch.

February 19, 1674   New Castle, the Hoerenkil, and all the Delaware territory returned to the English under the Treaty of Westminster.

Abbreviations Used in Footnotes

Albany Recs.

Early Records of the City and County of Albany and Colony of Rensselaerswyck, trans. Jonathan Pearson, rev. A. J. van Laer, Albany, 1916, 4 vols.

BASD

Bulletins, Archaeological Society of Delaware, Wilmington.

Brodhead

J. R. Brodhead, *History of the State of New York, 1609 - 1664,* New York, 1858.

Campanius

Thomas Campanius, *A Short Description of the Province of New Sweden,* Memoirs, Historical Society of Pennsylvania, Philadelphia, 1834, vol. 3.

Colls. N.Y. Hist. Soc.

Collections of the New York Historical Society.

Del. History

Delaware History, Delaware Historical Society, Wilmington, semiannual.

Doc. Hist. N.Y.

E. B. O'Callaghan, *The Documentary History of the State of New York,* Albany, 1819, 4 vols.

Dunlap & Weslager, 1950

A. R. Dunlap and C. A. Weslager, *Indian Place-Names in Delaware,* Archaeological Society of Delaware, Wilmington, 1950.

Dunlap, 1956

A. R. Dunlap, *Dutch and Swedish Place-Names in Delaware,* University of Delaware Press, Newark, 1956.

Dunlap & Weslager, A. R. Dunlap and C. A. Weslager, "Topon-
    1958   omy of the Delaware Valley as Revealed
                    by an Early Seventeenth Century Dutch
                    Map," *Bulletin,* Archaeological Society of
                    New Jersey, Nos. 15 and 16, 1958.

DYR   *The Duke of York Record,* Sunday Star,
                    Wilmington, 1903.

Iconography   I. N. P. Stokes, *The Iconography of Man-
                    hattan Island,* New York, 1915 - 1928, 6
                    vols.

Inst. for Printz   *The Instruction for Johan Printz,* trans.
                    Amandus Johnson, Swedish Colonial
                    Society, Philadelphia, 1930.

Lindeström   Peter Lindeström, *Geographia Americae,*
                    trans. Amandus Johnson, Swedish Colonial
                    Society, Philadelphia, 1925.

NYCD   *Documents Relative to the Colonial History
                    of the State of New York,* ed. E. B. O'Cal-
                    laghan, Albany, 1856 - 1857, 15 vols. Vol.
                    12 is entitled *Documents Relating to the
                    Dutch and Swedish Settlements on the
                    Delaware River,* ed. B. Fernow.

Narratives, Hall   *Narratives of Early Maryland, 1633 - 1684,*
                    ed. C. C. Hall, New York, 1910.

Narratives, Jameson *Narratives of New Netherland, 1609-1664,*
                    ed. J. F. Jameson, New York, 1909.

Narratives, Myers   *Narratives of Early Pennsylvania, West
                    New Jersey and Delaware, 1630 - 1707,* ed.
                    A. C. Myers, New York, 1909.

PA   *Pennsylvania Archives,* 1st Series, ed.
                        Samuel Hazard, 1852 - 1856 ; 2nd Series,
                        ed. John B. Linn and Wm. H. Egle, 1874 -
                        1890.

Penna. Magazine   *The Pennsylvania Magazine of History and
                        Biography,* Historical Society of Pennsyl-
                        vania, Philadelphia.

Scharf   J. T. Scharf, *History of Delaware 1609 -
                        1888,* Philadelphia, 1888, 2 vols.

Swedish Settlements   Amandus Johnson, *The Swedish Settle-
                        ments on the Delaware,* New York, 1911,
                        2 vols.

Van Laer   *Documents Relating to New Netherland
                        1624 - 1626,* trans. and ed. A. J. F. van
                        Laer, in the Henry E. Huntington Library,
                        San Marino, Calif., 1924.

VRB   *Van Rensselaer Bowier Manuscripts,* ed.
                        A. J. F. van Laer, Albany, 1908.

Winsor   Justin Winsor, *Narrative and Critical His-
                        tory of America,* Boston, 1884 – 1889, 8
                        vols.

CONTENTS

Dutch Explorers, Traders, and Settlers
in the Delaware Valley
1609-1664

I

Henry Hudson

" Land! Land!" The shout came from a Dutch sailor hugging the topmast with one arm, his eyes shaded against the midday sun by a calloused palm held to his forehead. Almost at the same time a cry was heard below him on the foredeck, where an English sailor with a leaded line was taking soundings. " Five fathoms—three fathoms—two fathoms—," he called out. Then came the captain's command from the poopdeck in English, repeated in the Dutch language by the first mate, also in the stern. " Drop anchor! Haul in main topsail! Lower sprits!" The little vessel shuddered as her bottom timbers scraped into the sandbank, her masts bending as the wind billowed her sails and fought to push her free from the hidden barrier. Before the captain's command could be obeyed, a strong gale carried her off the bank and well beyond into deeper and safer waters as suddenly as she had run aground.

Tacking this way and that to avoid stranding again, the vessel, actually a yacht of 60 tons burden although her silhouette resembled the shallow-bottomed Vlie boats seen in the Zuider-Zee, luffed slowly into the estuary that as yet had no European name. So came Henry Hudson in the *Half Moon* on August 28, 1609 to Delaware Bay. He anchored after reaching a place described in the ship's log as " the Point," which may have been present-day Cape Henlopen. The sand bars, visible above the surface of the water, and the shoals, which suddenly appeared in what seemed to be deep water, made a course upstream too dangerous to pursue further without a shallop to lead the way. Furthermore, Hudson was soon convinced that the objective of the voyage did not lie within this shoaly waterway whose current pressed outward to the sea. He steered the vessel southeast again, rounded the opposite cape, and set his course north in the Atlantic, the banners of Holland and the East India Company streaming in the wind from her masts.

How did Henry Hudson, an English navigator, come to be sailing a Dutch ship? How did a voyage that had started in a northerly direction from Holland more than seven months before bring him to these as yet uncharted New World waters? What was the purpose of the voyage? Why had it taken seven months to reach Delaware Bay? In the answers to these questions lies an exciting story of adventure, daring, and intrigue that has been told before but which bears telling again in the year that marks the 350th anniversary of the voyage.

The quest during the sixteenth and seventeenth centuries for a shorter all-water route to the riches of the East Indies — its gold, gems, ivory, spices, and fabrics — excited interest in Holland, then one of the world's greatest sea powers, as it did among the other leading maritime nations of Europe — England, Portugal, France, Spain, Sweden, and Denmark. Among the early navigators who sought this all-water passage were Christopher Columbus, John Cabot, and Giovanni da Verrazano, in the employ respectively of Spain, England, and France. Instead of finding a new trade route to the Indies, they, and other explorers, discovered new lands in the western world over which a struggle for possession by the European nations would be waged for many years to come. It was the quest for the undiscovered route that brought Hudson to Delaware Bay. He had made two previous voyages in search of it, one in 1607 and the second in 1608, under the auspices of businessmen in England, the country of his birth. He had sailed to the 81st degree of north latitude in the polar region, where few, if any, sea captains had been before. He had not found the passage to the East, but he had won a reputation as a brave and skillful mariner who had faced and conquered the dangers of the arctic seas.

Based on Hudson's third voyage, Holland, or the United Netherlands, to use a more inclusive word,[1] would lay claim to lands in America from Cape Cod to and including Delaware Bay and River. Although this claim would be made for many years to come, it is now certain that Hudson was actually not the " discoverer " of these regions. In the words of one of Hudson's biographers, Hudson River, Hudson Bay, and Hudson Straits had "repeatedly been visited and even drawn on maps and charts long before he set out on his voyages."[2] Such a statement could not be made about Delaware River and Bay, since there are no maps or charts made prior to Hudson's visit on which this waterway is unmistakably delineated. It is likely—but by no means certain—that the explorer Verrazano in 1524 may have visited Delaware Bay,[3] but the so-called " Velasco Map " of 1610 is the earliest map extant on which Delaware Bay is shown, and this was made after Hudson's voyage. Ironically the " Velasco Map " is an English, not a Dutch, map; furthermore, it is

---

[1] People of Dutch, Walloon, and Flemish or Belgian ancestry lived in the seventeen provinces called the Netherlands or Low Countries. In 1576, the ten Walloon and Flemish provinces abandoned the struggle against Spain, and were thereafter known as the Spanish Netherlands. The remaining seven Dutch provinces, viz., Holland, Zeeland, Guelderland, Utrecht, Overyssel, Friesland, and Groningen, joined together by compact in what became known as the Union of Utrecht. They renounced Spanish allegiance and declared themselves an independent nation called the United Netherlands. The terms " Dutch " or " Netherlands " used in this volume apply to this united nation.

[2] G. M. Asher, *Henry Hudson, the Navigator*, Hakluyt Society, London, 1860.

[3] For discussion of Verrazano's discoveries, see *Winsor*, 4 : 6. A translation of Verrazano's account of his voyage appears in *Colls. N.Y. Hist Soc.*, 2nd Series, 1 : 41-67.

but a copy of the missing original.[4] The map proper was made in 1610 by an anonymous surveyor (possibly John Daniel); the copy is called the " Velasco Map " because it was acquired and sent to Spain by the Spanish ambassador in London, Alonzo de Velasco. By good fortune it was preserved in the Spanish National Archives.

Hudson's employment in the interests of the United Netherlands was solely a business proposition so far as the Dutch were concerned. Certain Dutch merchants, who in 1602 had formed a trade monopoly in Holland with their enormously wealthy East India Company and its six branches or Chambers, learned of Hudson's experience and daring and saw in him a man who might serve their commercial purposes. The directors of the Amsterdam Chamber invited him to come to Holland for an interview. After hearing the account of his two previous arctic voyages from his own lips and listening to his theories about the certainty of a northern route, they engaged him for his third voyage, placing under his command *de Halve Maen* (" the Half Moon"), one of the Company's many vessels. His crew consisted of sixteen or eighteen Dutch and English sailors.[5]

Hudson was in Holland for about four months conferring with the directors. Conversation was of necessity carried on through interpreters ; Hudson's native tongue was English and he never mastered the Dutch language. A contract was drawn up, supplementary written instructions prepared, and the *Half Moon* rigged and provisioned for a voyage to what is now the Arctic Ocean in further search of a northeast route to the Orient. Negotiations

---

[4] *Iconography*, 2 : C. Pl. 22 and C. Pl. 22A. A partial reproduction showing Delaware Bay appears in H. G. Richards, *A Book of Maps of Cape May*, Cape May N.J., 1954, p. 8. A full reproduction is in Alexander Brown, *The Genesis of the United States,* 1890, 1 : opp. p. 456.

[5] Lambrechtsen, who had access to West India Company papers, now missing, said there were sixteen in the crew (*Colls. N.Y. Hist. Soc.,* 2nd Series, 1 : 85). Van Meteren, a contemporary of Hudson, said there were " 18 or 20 men " in the crew,

were no sooner brought to a head and the contract readied for execution than intelligence reached the Amsterdam merchants that Pierre Jeannin, Minister of Henry IV of France, was making approaches to Hudson to enter French service on a similar mission. The brevity of the contract and its general tone suggests an element of haste on the part of his Dutch sponsors to forestall the efforts of their competitors to engage the navigator. The contract with Hudson was signed by only two members of the Amsterdam Chamber. Normally, the other Chambers would all have been represented before such an important instrument was made official, but the situation evidently demanded prompt action to block the French from engaging Hudson. The decisive action taken by the directors indicates that Hudson's abilities were considerable and that those with whom he came in contact recognized these qualities. The Amsterdam merchants were hard-headed business men, and they doubtless subjected Hudson to close questioning, and carefully examined his record, before engaging him.

On April 6, 1609, Hudson sailed under Dutch colors through the strait called the Texel into the open sea, never again to be seen in Holland. He returned from the voyage, to be sure, after an absence of about eight months, but pressure from a discontented crew took him to England instead of Holland. On November 7, 1609, he brought the *Half Moon* to anchor in the English port of Dartmouth. During his absence he had initially gone north as instructed toward Novaya Zemlya, two arctic islands now owned by the Soviet Union. There, on May 14, he found ice blocking his passage, whereupon, and contrary to what is known of his written instructions, he reversed his course and turned westerly toward Newfoundland, finally touching a point of what is now the Maine coast. Then he sailed south to Cape Cod, where he made a landing, and from there he continued south to the coast of present-day Virginia and the mouth of Chesapeake Bay. He did not, however, stop at the Virginia settlement to see his countrymen, although he must have known exactly where they were. This would indicate he did not want his presence in American waters to be known to the English. From the Chesapeake he sailed to Delaware Bay and finally went up along the seacoast to the Hudson River, which he explored with sufficient thoroughness to convince him that it, like the shoal-filled Delaware, was not the passage to the Orient he sought.

After anchoring at Dartmouth on his return, he sent a message to Holland, notifying the directors of his presence in England and proposing to them that he " go out again for a search in the northwest, and that, besides the pay and what they already had in the ship, fifteen hundred florins should be laid out for an additional supply of provisions. He also wanted six or seven of his crew exchanged for others and their number raised to twenty. . . ."[6] In terms of attaining the stated objective, the voyage was a failure, but Hudson was now convinced more than ever that success lay through one of the waterways crossing the land mass of the New World.

Meanwhile, the English authorities forbade Hudson and the English members of the crew to return to Holland or to continue in Dutch service. Keen rivalry existed between England and Holland, not only to find new trade routes, but to control existing markets. The authorities saw the inconsistence of allowing a mariner with Hudson's experience to serve the interests of a principal competitor. Furthermore, Hudson now had very valuable information in his possession ; viz., an account of his voyage, with navigation courses detailed and reference to the lands he had visited, as well as charts and maps which he had drawn.

Before departing, Hudson had contracted with the directors to " give over his journals, courses, charts and all that he encounters on the voyage, without holding anything back," and they were anxious to receive these data. But Hudson's detention

---

[6] Van Meteren in *Narratives, Jameson,* p. 8.

in England prevented him from laying his accounts and reports before his employers. Evidently he was able to send a " brief summary " to Holland of his discoveries on the voyage, perhaps accompanied by a rough draft of a map, but it was well known in diplomatic circles that the Dutch had not received their full due from the Englishman. A Spanish diplomat wrote secretly to his king from Brussels on December 2, 1611, " Juan Hudson who some time ago was sent from there by our East India Company to the north, and has since arrived here in England and did not give a full report to his employers."[7]

Hudson's journal eventually fell into Dutch hands, but it no doubt had also been scanned by the English. Moreover, the voyage must have been talked about by the English members of his crew and the details disclosed to English authorities long before the directors of the East India Company heard the full story. Since there is no record of Hudson's map in contemporary Dutch references, it is possible that the completed map never reached Holland.

Hudson made a final voyage to America in 1610, under English auspices, in the vessel *Discovery*—this is usually termed his " fourth " voyage. He was still searching for the northern passage. On this voyage his crew mutinied, setting Hudson, his son John, and seven others adrift in a small boat in what is now Hudson Bay. Neither he nor his companions were ever heard of again.[8]

This, in brief, is the story of Henry Hudson's quest for the passage, beginning in 1607 with his appearance on the pages of history as a captain in the employ of the English Muscovy Company, and ending in 1610 with his tragic disappearance, again in English service. Between these two dates occurred his third

---

[7] *Iconography,* 2 : 44.
[8] For an account of the trial of the mutineers, see Llewlyn Powys, *Henry Hudson,* New York, 1928, p. 193.

voyage, an adventure which is extremely important in the history of New Netherland. In the very brief period of three years Henry Hudson played so prominent a role on the stage of world history that his name lives on as one of the great seventeenth-century navigators and explorers. There is every reason to believe that his fame is well deserved ; that within him burned the flame of a true explorer ; that he was fired with zeal to broaden man's horizons; that his adventures influenced world history long after his death. He was not a mere adventurer, but a thoughtful student of geography well versed in the latest cartographical knowledge of his time.

Information about the third voyage must be obtained from the writings of others, since the whereabouts of Hudson's own account is still not known. In 1625, when he wrote his history of the New World, Johan de Laet had access to it, from which he quoted several passages verbatim, but none of these applies directly to Delaware Bay. De Laet describes in his own words Hudson's entry into Delaware Bay ; the possibility exists that this information may be a paraphrase of Hudson's journal :

Running thence to a northward they again discovered land in latitude 38° 9', where there was a white sandy shore, and within it an abundance of green trees. The direction of the coast was north-northeast and south-southwest for about eight leagues, then north and south for seven leagues, and afterwards southeast and north-west for five leagues. They continued to run along the coast to the north, until they reached a point from which the land stretched to the west-northwest, and there was a bay into which several rivers discharged. From this point land was seen to the east-northeast, which they took to be an island ; but it proved to be the main land, and the second point of the bay, in latitude 38° 54'. Standing upon a course northwest by north, they found themselves embayed, and, encountering many breakers, stood out again to the south-southeast. They suspected that a large river discharged into the bay, from the strength of the current that set out, and caused these sands and shoals.[9]

The logbook of the elderly, cynical Robert Juet of Limehouse, one of the mates on the *Half Moon* on two earlier voyages (and a ringleader in the mutiny on the *Discovery*), was first published in 1625. It contains an account of the third voyage, including the earliest description of Delaware Bay written in the English language. Juet wrote as follows :

The eight and twentieth [of August, 1609] faire and hot weather, the winde at South South-west. In the morning at sixe of the clock wee weighed, and steered away North twelve leagues till noone, and came to the Point of the Land ; and being hard by the Land in five fathomes, on a sudden wee came into three fathomes ; then we beare up and had but ten foot water, and joyned to the Point. Then as soon as wee were over, wee had five, six, seven, eight, nine, ten, twelve, and thirteene fathoms. Then wee found the Land to trend away North-west, with a great Bay and Rivers. But the [Delaware] Bay wee found shoald ; and in the offing wee had ten fathomes, and had sight of Breaches and drie Sand. Then wee were forced to stand backe againe ; so we stood backe South-east by South, three leagues. And at seven of the clocke wee Anchored in eight fathomes water ; and found a Tide set to the Northwest and North North-west, and it riseth one fathome and floweth South South-east.

And hee that will thoroughly Discover this great Bay, must have a small Pinnasse, that must draw but four or five fotte water to sound before him. At five in the morning wee weighed and steered away to the Eastward on many courses, for the Norther Land is full of shoalds. Wee were among them, and once we strooke, and wee went away ; and steered away to the South-east. So wee had two, three, foure, five, sixe, and seven fathomes, and so deeper and deeper.[10]

[9] Excerpts from de Laet are quoted in *Narratives, Jameson,* pp. 36-60.

[10] Samuel Purchas, *Hakluytus Posthumus or Purchas His Pilgrimes,* James Mac Lehose & Sons edition, Glasgow (pub. Macmillan Company, New York, 1906), 13 : 359-360.

So far as is now known, only two other contemporary published works made reference, all too briefly, to Hudson's third voyage : a 1611 supplement of a history by Emanuel van Meteren and the so-called *Hudson Tract* of 1612 - 1613, published by Hessel Gerritsz, the official cartographer of the East India Company.[11] Both appeared shortly after Hudson's fourth and final voyage when it was hoped he was still alive. The latter discloses an important item of information : during his negotiations with the directors of the Amsterdam Chamber, Hudson requested of Peter Plancius, Flemish theologian and an outstanding geographer, then living in Amsterdam, and received from him, a copy of the manuscript journal of George Weymouth containing an account of that Englishman's two New World voyages, one in 1602 and the other in 1605.

The van Meteren history also adds an item of significance : the author states that before Hudson departed on the third voyage he had come into possession of " letters and maps which a certain Captain [John] Smith had sent him from Virginia and by which he indicated to him a sea leading into the western ocean by the north of the southern English colony." Neither in John Smith's own writings nor in other contemporary sources is there positive evidence that Smith had been in direct personal contact with Hudson. However, such contact between the two men could have occurred prior to Smith's departure for Virginia, December 20, 1606. As of that time, which was three years prior to Hudson's negotiations with the Dutch, Smith had no data from personal experience since he had not yet been in America. Of course, the executives of the London Virginia Company were possessed with

---

[11] H. C. Murphy, *Henry Hudson in Holland,* with notes by Wouter Nijhoff, The Hague, 1909. Nijhoff introduces what he states is the original Latin version of that part of van Meteren's history relating to Hudson. There were at least two Dutch and two Latin editions of the history. For an English translation of pertinent passages, see *Narratives, Jameson,* pp. 6-8. Excerpts from the Hudson Tract of Gerritsz are also given by Nijhoff.

the thought of a northwest passage to the Indies via the New World. This idea intrigued Smith as it did Hudson, Thomas Hood, and other English navigators and geographers of the period, and was doubtless a subject of much discussion among navigators.[12]

In 1608, Smith, who was then in Virginia, had forwarded to the Treasurer and Council of Virginia in London a letter and drafts of a " Mappe of the bay and rivers." On September 10, 1608, Don Pedro de Zuniga sent secretly to Philip III of Spain from England a copy of a map of Virginia which had come into his possession through a leak in English communications. The historian Brown states that he is convinced Hudson had a copy of this chart with him before he went to Holland.[13] As van Meteren wrote, Smith may have been in communication with Hudson, and this could have occurred through messengers who returned from Virginia some time after Smith's arrival there in the spring of 1607, possibly Captain Newport or Captain Francis Nelson. One thing is certain : Smith could not have given Hudson any information about the Delaware—he evidently didn't know of its existence ; never explored it ; never showed it on his maps.

The authors have been unable to find in Smith's writings any positive statement of acquaintanceship with Henry Hudson ; this does not mean they were strangers. Smith makes the following reference to Hudson in his "The Description of New England," which suggests he held him in high regard : " Beyond whose bounds, America doth stretch many thousand miles ; into the frozen partes whereof, one Master Hutson an English Mariner,

---

[12] In the *Instructions of 1606,* issued by the London Virginia Company, it is urged that the leaders seek out a safe port on a navigable river, and in choosing a river, " make choice of that which bendeth most toward the North-west for that way you shall soonest find the other sea." (*Smith's Travels,* Arber-Bradley, 1910 edition, 1 : xxxiii).

[13] Brown, op. cit., 1 : 183-184 ; see also Ben C. McCary, *John Smith's Map of Virginia,* Williamsburg, 1957.

did make the greatest discouerie of any Christian I know of, where he vnfortunately died."

Van Meteren was in a position to obtain accurate information ; he was the Dutch consul in London and wrote in England his account of Hudson within two years after the third voyage. Some of the dates and places mentioned in his history could only have been obtained from a member of the crew, possibly from the first mate, a Dutchman. The fact that Hudson had in his possession communications and a map from Smith, as well as the Weymouth journal, all dealing with America, when he sailed from Holland, is of significance because his contract with the directors obligated him to sail *north*. Later in the voyage he turned the prow of the *Half Moon* westward toward the New World, which was not even mentioned in the contract. From the little that is known about the written instructions given him, which are also missing, nothing was said in them about his going to America. Indeed, there is reason to believe that these instructions expressly directed him to think of discovering no other routes except the one in the north, and if this could not be accomplished, another route would be the subject of consideration for a *later* voyage upon his return from the north.

Despite the contract and the written instructions, Hudson had prepared himself for a sortie in another direction. This is further illustrated by a note in the aforementioned *Hudson Tract* which states that he had left a copy of *his* map in Plancius' possession. On this map, we are told, Hudson had plotted a route to the west in pursuance of the theory that there was an opening through the lands of the New World to the southern seas. He apparently believed that entrance to this water passage was either immediately above the London Company Virginia colony, in the vicinity of the 40th parallel, or still farther north near the 60th parallel at the entrance of present Hudson Straits. His third voyage took him to the region of the 40th parallel without attaining his goal ; his fourth and final voyage saw him entering the straits and bay which now bear his name, and there being cast adrift and deserted by a mutinous crew.

It can be argued that Hudson did not deliberately disobey his instructions or disregard the contract, but that when ice prevented his reaching Novaya Zemlya he exercised a shipmaster's discretionary power to employ his vessel and crew to the best advantage of the owners, consistent with the original aim of the voyage. The record of events proves that, with or without the knowledge and consent of his employers, Hudson was fully prepared for a voyage to the New World, even though his contract directed him to go elsewhere. The sequence of events suggests a number of questions for which there are no ready answers. Was Hudson guilty of deception by using the facilities of the Dutch to pursue his own theories of geography? Did the Dutch intend him to go to the New World, but, in order to conceal the true aims of the voyage from both the English and Spanish, deliberately phrase a misleading contract? Was the contract drawn up in good faith, but did the directors of the East India Company have an understanding with Hudson that permitted him to sail westward if he could not pass eastward through the arctic waters?

To Hudson's credit it must be said that he was mindful of the interests of his Dutch employers. The 1613 edition of the *Hudson Tract* states that he exchanged merchandise in the New World for animal pelts " in order that he might get some profit for our country and the directors." Does not the fact that Hudson had merchandise to trade with the Indians indicate that the directors had supplied him with goods for this purpose? Or would he have carried the same kind of merchandise for trade in the Orient in the event of his finding the northern passage? The disclosure by Hudson on his return that the lands he had visited abounded in fur-bearing animals was of especial interest to the Dutch merchants. This was certainly one of the tangible accomplishments of the voyage, and within a short time certain of the merchants would organize companies for the sole purpose of exploiting this new avenue of commerce. Still later, a West India Company would be formed (patterned after the East India Company) which would turn its attention to the New World to exploit the fur trade and to lay down commercial colonies. This organization would use as a basis for its claim to lands in America the argument that it had inherited the " discoveries " from an English navigator in Dutch employ. For years to follow, the Dutch would refer to Hudson when pressed by other nations, particularly the English, to justify their commercial activities in America as though his third voyage gave them inalienable land rights.

At the time Hudson embarked from Holland no one realized that this would be the first step in the founding of a New Netherland in America. This was a consequence not planned or anticipated ; in fact, had Hudson faithfully followed the letter of the written contract he would not have sailed westward to America but would have returned to Holland after encountering ice in northern waters. Thus, the United Netherlands' claim to New World lands might have been preëmpted by others ; the Dutch fur trade would never have got its start ; the New Netherland would never have existed, and an early chapter of America's political and cultural history, including that of the Delaware Valley, would have been entirely different.

*   *   *   *   *

The contract that follows, translated from a copy of the missing original, was found by Henry Cruse Murphy, United States minister at the Hague, during a search of the records of the Dutch East India Company in the Royal Archives. It was appended to an unpublished history of the company written by Pierre van Dam, legal counselor from 1652 until his death in 1706. Murphy translated the contract into English and published it at the Hague in 1859 in a booklet which is now rare. In 1909, on the occasion of the 300th anniversary of the year of Hudson's third voyage, the booklet was reprinted at the Hague under the title *Henry Hudson in Holland,* with notes and documentation by Wouter Nijhoff.[14] To date, Murphy's has been the only English translation of the contract, and the 1909 edition is almost as scarce in America as the 1859 printing.

It seems appropriate that the contract should be retranslated, reprinted, annotated, and reassessed in light of information that has become available since 1909. The new English translation by Dunlap does not differ substantially from Murphy's, thus strengthening certain conclusions that Murphy drew, to which reference will be made. Any account of the Dutch settlements on the South River[15] — or on the Hudson for that matter — has its beginning with Hudson's voyage, and an examination of the contract is a logical introduction to the chapters to follow containing data on the New Netherland not available to Murphy at the time he made his translation. In the light of these newer data, the Hudson contract stands out in sharper perspective today than ever before. It is not the contract alone that is of such importance, but rather the series of events it set in motion, culminating in the Dutch settlements on the Hudson and Delaware Rivers.

On this day the 8 January in the year of our Lord one thousand six hundred and nine the directors of the East-India Company of

---

[14] A. J. F. van Laer reviewed this publication in the *American Historical Review,* 15 (January, 1910), 418-419. He stated without reservation that Murphy's 1859 booklet " stands as the best treatise on Hudson's third voyage and the circumstances which led to the exploration of the Hudson River. " Another excellent discussion of Hudson and his voyage is John Meredith Read, Jr., *A Historical Inquiry Concerning Henry Hudson,* Albany 1866.

[15] The Delaware was so called by the Dutch, not because it coursed south, " but because it is the most southerly river of New Netherland " (*PA,* 2nd Series, 5 : 151).

the chamber of Amsterdam of the ten-year calculation on the one hand, and Mr. Henry Hudson, Englishman,[16] assisted by Jodocos Hondius[17] on the other side, are in accord with one another and agree in the manner following after. To wit : that the aforesaid directors in the first place shall equip a small ship or yacht of about thirty lasts,[18] with which the aforenamed Hudson shall sail, about the first of April, well provided with crew members,[19] provisions, and other necessities, in order to seek passage via the north, around to the north of Nova Sembla,[20] and so following along the [line of] longitude that he shall be able to sail south-ward to the height [latitude] of sixty degrees, and to obtain as much

---

[16] Dutch writers used several versions of Hudson's name, which often gave the impression that he was a Dutchman. De Laet, for example, in his 1625 history calls the mariner *Hendrick Hutson.* " Ten year calculation " means that the charter permitted stockholders to withdraw capital at the end of a ten-year term.

[17] Hondius, a Fleming by birth, had previously lived in London and had learned to speak English. He was a capable artist and an engraver of maps. Perhaps he had met Hudson in England. In their discussions preparatory to the voyage, Hudson doubtless gave him information about his previous voyages which Hondius used on his map of the polar regions. It is ironical that no portrait or likeness of Hudson is known, although his friend Hondius had executed bronze statues and engraved pictures of many prominent persons of his time. Hondius also gave Hudson an English translation of a Dutch version of old Norse sailing directions to guide him ; see B. F. De Costa, *Sailing Directions of Henry Hudson Prepared for Use in 1608 from the Old Danish of Ivar Bardsen,* Albany, Joel Munsell, 1869.

[18] In Francis Burke Brandt's *The Majestic Delaware,* Philadelphia, 1929, p. 52, appears an engraving of 1604 showing a battle between six Spanish and seven Dutch vessels, one of which is believed to be the *Half Moon.* Brandt states that in 1909 a replica of the *Half Moon,* built by the people of Holland according to existing plans for her sister ship, the *Hope,* was presented to the Hudson-Fulton Celebration Committee.

[19] Only two of the names of the crew on the third voyage are known, Robert Juet and John Colman. The latter, a mate on former voyages, was killed by the Indians in the Hudson River ; cf. Chapter 5.

[20] The two islands then called Nova Sembla, or Nova Zembla (" New Land "), or as they are called today by the Russians, Novaya Zemlya, contain respectively 20,000 and 15,000 square miles. They were uninhabited until about 1877. Hudson had landed here on his second voyage (Purchas, *op. cit.*).

familiarity with [the] lands as may come to pass without noticeable loss of time, and is, if feasible, to return speedily,[21] in order to make to the directors [an] exact report and account of his voyage, and give over his journals, courses, charts and all that he encounters on the voyage, without holding anything back. For which projected voyage the directors shall pay the aforesaid Hudson, as much for his providing for the aforesaid voyage as for support of his wife and children, the sum of eight hundred guilders,[22] and in case (there may God prevent) he should not in a year arrive back here or in these parts, the directors shall pay besides to his wife[23] two hundred guilders current, and in that case not further be held by him and his heirs, unless he thereafter still might arrive, or within the year should come, and had found the passage so good and convenient that the company should again make use of it, in which case the directors should make recompense to the aforenamed Hudson at their discretion for his hazards, troubles and skill, wherewith the

---

[21] Murphy translates this as, " and if it is possible return immediately, etc." We believe that "speedily" is more precise than "immediately," although " afterwards, " " directly, " " in the near future " could have been meant. The shade of meaning is important, because the words " if feasible " could have given Hudson certain freedom to explore elsewhere.

[22] The sum of 800 guilders may seem inadequate when measured against today's standard of value, since it represents only about $320. However, in 1626, Isaac de Rasière, as secretary of the New Netherland colony, a position of importance and responsibility, was paid an annual salary of 100 guilders, plus a commission of one stiver (about 2c) for each beaver and otter skin that passed through his hands (*van Laer*, p. 191). Gerrit Fongersz, assistant commis, was paid 288 guilders a year (*ibid.*, p. 199). In 1642, Johannes Megapolensis was paid 1000 florins (same as guilders) for three years employment as pastor at Rensselaerswick (*Narratives, Jameson*, p. 165). All things considered, the amount paid Hudson does not seem inconsiderable.

[23] Hudson's wife's name was Katherine, and they had three sons, Oliver, the eldest, John, and Richard. Oliver was married and had a daughter at the time the contract was signed (Read, *op. cit.*). John was his father's companion on his travels, and on the fourth voyage was one of the party set adrift. Three years after Hudson's disappearance, Katherine applied to the East India Company to aid the youngest son, Richard. He was employed and rose high in the Company's service. He died in 1648, leaving several children (Powys, *op. cit.*, p. 187).

aforenamed Hudson is [to be] content.[24] And in case the directors think fit at that time to pursue and continue such voyage, it is agreed and contracted by the aforenamed Hudson that he shall here take residence with [his] wife and children, and allow himself to be employed by no one other than the company,[25] and this at the good judgment and discretion of the directors, who also for the same further service promise to satisfy and content him in all fairness and reasonableness. Everything without deceit or fraud. In knowledge of the truth two contracts of one tenor are hereof made, and undersigned by both parties, likewise by Jodocus Hondius, as interpreter and witness. Date as above.

Was signed : Dirck van Os, I. [Jan] Poppe,[26] Henry Hudson ; lower stood : by me Jodocus Hondius, as witness.

---

[24] The amount of the promised award is not stated, but a bounty of 80,000 livres was offered by the States General to the first discoverer of the northeast passage (see Jeannin's letter, Murphy, *op. cit.*).

[25] This clause was apparently inserted to prevent Hudson from accepting employment in French or any other service provided the Dutch wanted his service to continue.

[26] Dirck van Os was one of the organizers of the first Dutch expedition to the East Indies. He, Jan Poppe, and seven other merchants were associated in a firm called the Company of Foreign Parts, which had established a fort at Amboyna before the Dutch East India Company was organized. An engraved portrait of van Os appears as a frontispiece in the original Murphy edition of 1859. Van Os, Poppe, and Arent ten Grotenhuys were commissioned to write the contract (Murphy, *op. cit.*, p. 142).

II

The First Expedition

Knowledge of the first Dutch settlements in America is still far from complete, largely because the letters, reports, and other papers belonging to the old East and the later West India Companies, of a date prior to 1700, were bundled up and sold as waste at public auction in Amsterdam in 1821. What eventually happened to these records is unknown ; some of them were reportedly damaged by dampness and vermin prior to the time of sale ; others may have purposely been destroyed soon after ; still others were " lost." The historian lives in hope that such " lost " records will eventually be found to broaden his knowledge of the past. In 1910, such a windfall occurred ! Six documents, written in old Dutch script and pertaining to the New World, came to light in Amsterdam and were purchased and preserved by a collector who sensed their historical value.

The *Van Rappard Documents,* as these manuscripts came to be called, passed through several hands, finally coming into the possession of Henry E. Huntington, who had them translated into English and published in 1924.[1] They shed new light on the Dutch efforts to found a *southern* colony in New Netherland, although their full significance in this particular connection has

[1] Referred to herein as *van Laer.* In preparing this chapter the author (C.A.W.) visited the Henry E. Huntington Library and Art Gallery in San Marino, Calif., and examined the original Mss. He also examined other Dutch documents owned by the library and obtained a list of titles of those pertaining to New Netherland, through the courtesy of Miss Norma B. Cuthbert, librarian, a copy of which he deposited in the Historical Society of Delaware.

been overlooked. These documents, as well as other seventeenth-century Dutch records which can now be reinterpreted in a new light, are the basis for the discussion in this and the following chapter.

In considering Dutch exploration and settlement in America, let us first dispose of a report made in 1644 in Holland to the effect that the Dutch Greenland Company as early as 1598 built forts on both the Hudson and Delaware Rivers as winter shelters for use in the fur trade.[2] Proof is entirely lacking to support this claim, made at a time when, to counter the English, it was advantageous for the Dutch government to push back the date of occupancy by their countrymen to the earliest possible time. No record has been found of Dutch exploration of either the Hudson or Delaware prior to Hudson's 1609 voyage. Following Hudson's return from this voyage, Dutch traders sailed to America and made further explorations, leading to the formation in 1614 of the New Netherland Company by opportunistic Amsterdam and Hoorn merchants. This company was given the right to make four voyages during a three year period, to any lands and places in America discovered by them between the 40th and 45th degrees of latitude — a region which, for the first time, was then called New Netherland. After the charter expired in 1618, voyages continued to be made to New Netherland while negotiations were in progress to form a West India Company, modeled after the East India Company, a project that had long been advocated by a prominent merchant, Willem Usselinx.[3]

---

[2] *NYCD,* 1:149. Hendricksen's "Figurative Map" of 1616, cf. below, shows "Nassou," the fort on the Hudson, but no indication of any forts on the Delaware. Furthermore, the Northern, or Greenland Company, formed in 1613, was not chartered until 1614 (George Edmundson, *History of Holland,* Cambridge, 1922, p. 166).

[3] This background information is given in detail in many sources, one of the most authoritative being Charles M. Andrews, *The Colonial Period in American History,* New York, 1937, particularly vol. 3 entitled, "A Dutch Province and a Ducal Property."

Among the Dutch sea captains who visited American waters during the early period were Hendrick Christiaensen (also spelled Corstiaenssen), Adriaen Block, and Cornelis Jacobsen May. Their discoveries were the basis of the charter issued to the New Netherland Company. All three navigators kept journals or logs of their voyages (Johan de Laet refers to these accounts in his New World history), which are now missing. However, there can be no doubt that Cornelis Hendricksen explored the Delaware River in his yacht *Onrust* ("Restless"), for, on August 19, 1616, he submitted a brief report to the Holland merchants, claiming to have discovered " certain lands, a bay, and three rivers situated between 38 and 40 degrees." Accompanying his report was positive proof — a " Figurative Map " delineating the Delaware River system as he thought it to be. The original copy of this map is still preserved in the Royal Archives at the Hague.[4] When Hendricksen delivered this map, the Dutch authorities considered it so valuable that they would not immediately allow the new data to be used to correct existing maps. Undoubtedly they wanted to keep the geography of the Delaware River system a secret, particularly from English merchants, perhaps not knowing that the English already had access to a map, made by Henry Hudson, which had not reached Holland. Hudson's map could not have shown any of the detail of the Delaware River, because he saw only the mouth of the bay — Hendricksen's map purported to show the complete river system.

Cornelis Jacobsen May (sometimes spelled Mey) was in America at the same time Hendricksen was there, and he was reported again in American waters in 1620, making further explorations and trading with the Indians.[5] It is generally believed

---

[4] *NYCD*, 1:12, 13. The map is reproduced opposite p. 11. See also Chapter 5 below.

[5] *NYCD*, 1:12, 24. The suffix " sen " meaning " son of " occurs in various ways in Dutch surnames, sometimes " s," often " se," or " sz."

that May visited the Delaware River after Hendricksen " discovered" it, but how far upstream he sailed is still not known. His visit, or visits, were sufficiently noteworthy to warrant his name being attached to the bay, which for a time appeared on many Dutch maps as *Nieuw Port May*. Although his name did not last as a designation for the bay, May's name is still remembered in Cape May.

These early voyages did not have colonization as their objective ; they were purely for exploration or trade, but there can be no question that Dutch navigators had been going in and out of Delaware Bay and River long before any other nation attempted to explore or settle it. While the Dutch were engaged in discovery and trade in the Delaware, as well as the Hudson, the English (claiming the North American coast as a result of Cabot's discoveries) were busy colonizing Virginia and later New England. The London Company was granted the land between Cape Fear and the Potomac River ; the Plymouth Company was granted the land between Long Island Sound and the Bay of Fundy. Between these two settlements lay the area which the Dutch called New Netherland — approximately one hundred miles in width — wherein both the Delaware and Hudson systems were situated. The English crown had purposely held back this territory from both the Virginia Company and Plymouth Company as a sort of no-man's land separating them. The English were reasonably well informed about the course of the Hudson River at an early date, but the Delaware River system was only vaguely known to them prior to about 1634. However, the Englishman, Captain Samuell Argall, had anchored in Delaware Bay on August 27, 1610. He had sailed from Jamestown for Bermuda two months before in his pinnace, the *Discovery,* but storms had driven him north to

New England. His entry into the mouth of what he termed " a very great Bay," on his homeward voyage, was a circumstance of the winds, and he lay at anchor for about twelve hours before the wind shifted, permitting him to continue toward Virginia. In an account of the voyage, Argall wrote that he " felle among a great many of shoals about twelve leagues to the Southward of Cape La Warre." His description of the location of this cape leaves little doubt that it was present Cape Henlopen, and it is generally accepted that Argall had bestowed its first English name in honor of Lord de la Warre, then the governor of Virginia. Not, however, until June, 1613, in a letter written to Nicholas Hawes, did Argall specifically refer to " the De la Warre Bay," which is usually interpreted to mean that the bay took its English name from the cape.[6]

Argall evidently did not know that if he had sailed further into the bay he would have found an uncharted river system ; another Englishman was destined to make that " discovery," namely, Thomas Yong. Accompanied by his nephew and lieutenant, Robert Evelyn, Yong sailed into the bay in 1634 and continued up the river, exploring as he went. Like Henry Hudson, Yong was seeking a water passage to the Orient. He wrote that he had " purposed at my departure from England to make triall for the Passage " in " that great Bay." Imagine Yong's delight to learn from an Indian chief that the Delaware River issued from a great lake, and that about four days' journey beyond the head of the river he would find a " great mediterranean sea !" Yong thought of himself as the discoverer of the Delaware region and " took possession of the countrey for his Majesty and there sett up his

[6] Samuel Purchas, *Hakluytus Posthumus or Purchas His Pilgrimes,* James Mac Lehose and Sons edition, Glasgow (pub. Macmillan Company, New York, 1906), 19 : 73-84.

Majesty's armes upon a tree."[7] He named the Delaware " Charles River," in honor of the King. Whether or not Yong left any people to start an English colony on the Delaware is a debatable point which will be discussed further in Chapter 6.

Yong did not know that the Dutch had placed colonists on the Delaware River ten years before, as we shall soon see, and that everything he had " discovered " was already well known to the Dutch!

Cornelis Jacobsen May returned to Holland in the fall of 1620 with tales of " new and fruitful lands " *he* had discovered, and he was soon engaged by the West India Company to take a party of colonists to New Netherland. Chartered on June 3, 1621, the Company was given a monopoly for twenty-four years to trade in certain specified foreign waters, including the full sweep of the North and South American coasts. The Company was also delegated power to make alliances with native rulers, appoint governors and other officers, administer justice, and lay down colonies. Another and prime purpose was that of weakening the power of Spain — the Company was authorized to capture Spanish ships on the high seas and attack Spanish colonies!

Dr. Nicholas van Wassenaer, whose semiannual publication, the *Historisch Verhael,* was a sort of seventeenth-century Dutch current events magazine, wrote as follows under date of April, 1624 :

The West India Company being charted to navigate these rivers,

---

[7] Yong's journal appears in *Narratives, Myers,* pp. 37-49. Soon after his voyage " Charles River " appeared on a map made by John Daniel (*Iconography,* 2 : Pl. 34). Mention should be made of an English attempt to explore the Delaware prior to Yong's voyage. In September of 1632 seven or eight men were sent from Virginia in a sloop, " to see whether there was a river there, who had not returned, " according to de Vries. In 1633, Mantes Indians living on the eastern side of the Delaware were seen wearing garments taken from these Englishmen, whom they had evidently killed (*Narratives, Myers,* pp. 20-21).

did not neglect to do so, but equipped in the spring a vessel of 130 lasts called the *Nieu Nederlandt* whereof Cornelis Jacobsz May of Hoorn was skipper, with a company of 30 families, mostly Walloons, to plant a colony there. They sailed in the beginning of March.[8]

These Walloons (French-speaking Belgians) took an oath of allegiance on board the ship, March 30, 1624, leaving no doubt that they arrived in America *after* that date.[9]

In the late spring, May brought the *Nieu Nederlandt* with the thirty families into the mouth of the Hudson. Upon entering the river he found a Dutch yacht, the *Maeckereel,* lying above. She had embarked from Holland the previous year in company with another vessel, the *Pigeon,* which carried an earlier contingent of Walloons under the leadership of Jesse de Forest, to found a colony in South America, destined for failure. The *Maeckereel* had left the *Pigeon* on September 14, 1623, near the island of Madeira and sailed to the Hudson to barter with the Indians. Members of the crews of the *Nieu Nederlandt* and *Maeckereel* joined forces and drove away a French vessel, lying at anchor in the Hudson, " who would erect the Arms of the King of France there." Wassenaer wrote of this incident that the master of the French vessel " would do the same thing on the South River, but he was also prevented by the settlers there."[10] This statement is misleading because, as van Laer pointed out, the word " settlers " was incorrectly translated from the Dutch and should have read " traders," which puts a different meaning in the passage. At this date, it is unlikely that there were settlers living on the Delaware — although they would soon take up residence there. Information about them is given in two depositions by Catelina Trico, a member of the *first* (the word is hers) expedition sent to New Nether-

---

[8] *Narratives, Jameson,* p. 74 ; also *NYCD,* 1 : 149.

[9] *Van Laer,* p. xi.

[10] *Narratives, Jameson,* p. 75. Jesse de Forest's voyage and adventures are related in a journal reprinted in full in Mrs. Robert W. de Forest's, *A Walloon Family in America,* Boston, 1914, 2 vols.

land by the West India Company. In the first deposition made in 1685 she stated:

> That she Came to this Province either in the yeare one thousand six hundred and twenty three or twenty fouer to the best of her remembrance, and that fouer Women Came along with her in the same Shipp, in which ship the Governor Arian Jorissen [Adriaen Jorissen Thienpoint] Came also over, which fouer Women were married at Sea and that they and their husbands stayed about three Weekes at this place and then they with eight seamen more went in a vessell by ordr. of the Dutch Governor to Dellaware River and there settled.[11]

In 1688 she made a second deposition, part of which reads as follows:

> Catelyn Trico aged about 83 years born in Paris doth Testify and Declare that in ye year 1623 she came into this Country with a ship called ye Unity whereof was Commander Arien Jorise belonging to ye West India Company being ye first Ship yt came here for ye sd Company; as soon as they came to Mannatans now called N:York they sent Two families & six men to harford River & Two families & 8 men to Delaware River and 8 men they left att N:Yorke to take Possession and ye Rest of ye Passengers went wth ye ship up as farr as Albany which they then Called fort Orangie. When as ye shipp came as farr as Sopus [Esopus: present Kingston] which is ½ way to Albanie; they lightened ye Ship wth some boats yt were left there by ye Dutch that had been there ye year before a tradeing wth ye Indians upont there oune accompts & gone back again to Holland & so brought ye vessel up; there were about 18 families aboard who settled themselves at Albany & made a small fort; and as soon as they had built themselves some hutts of Bark . . . .[12]

---

[11] *Doc. Hist. N.Y..* 3:49-50.

[12] *Ibid.* Catelina Trico's husband was Joris Jansen Rapelje, their daughter Sarah is sometimes referred to as the first white child born in New Netherland, which Stokes said was " dubious and improbable " (*Iconography*, 4:40). The couple lived at Wallabout, Long Island (*Colls. N.Y. Hist. Soc.*, 46:19).

Mme. Trico's arithmetic is not consistent ; in her first deposition she refers to sixteen persons having gone to the Delaware,
four women and twelve men ; then in the second she says that
two families and eight men, a total of twelve, were sent. The
number is less important than the fact that persons were sent by
the West India Company to colonize the Delaware at a very
early date. Some historians have tended to question these depositions on the grounds that they were made by a woman in her
senility who had forgotten the facts — or what have generally been
believed to be the facts, i.e., that May (not Thienpoint) was in
charge of the first expedition ; that May (not Thienpoint) was
the first " governor " of New Netherland ; that the *Nieu Nederlandt* (not the *Unity*) brought the first colonists ; that they came
in 1624 (not in 1623).

Van Laer, however, recognizing that the data relating to New
Netherland are still incomplete, did not lightly put aside Mme.
Trico's testimony. He realized that it could be explained only
in one of two ways — either there was an earlier expedition to
America, or her testimony was garbled. But failing to find any
documentary support pointing unmistakably to an earlier expedition, he rationalized the question by saying that the *Nieu
Nederlandt,* under May's command, " was the first ship that
brought a properly equipped and officially organized company of
settlers to New Netherland," and that Catelino Trico must have
come over on it.[13] In the next paragraph, he cited an entry from
the *Copie-Boek* of the Consistory of the Dutch Reformed Church
of Amsterdam referring to the sailing to New Netherland of
Bastiaen Jansen Krol as *Sieckentrooster,* or comforter of the sick,
on *January 25, 1624!*[14] Since the *Nieu Nederlandt* departed in
March of 1624 it must have been preceded by another vessel if

---

[13] *Van Laer,* p. xvi ; see *Iconography,* 5 : xii.

[14] *Ibid.,* p. xvii. The term *Krankenbezoeker* was also used for this
position.

Krol left on January 25. Furthermore, if he went as comforter of the sick, a position that was sort of a combination of lay preacher and male nurse, who sometimes acted as school teacher, there must have been colonists on the same vessel with him.

Unknown to van Laer, another precious document lay buried in a sheaf of notarial papers in Amsterdam which would have lessened his perplexity. Unfortunately, van Laer did not have access to this document, later found by Professor Albert Eekhof of the University of Leyden. He translated it into English and published it in 1926. It relates that a vessel called the *Falling Nut-Tree,* owned by the West India Company, had come to America *before* the *Nieu Nederlandt* with its party of Walloons ; that it was commanded by Jan Jansz. Brouwer ; that two other vessels, the *Red Dove* and another whose name is not given — but which might have been the *Unity* — were lying in the Hudson River near present Albany when the *Nieu Nederlandt* arrived in May, 1624. Although the name of Adriaen Jorissen Thienpoint is not mentioned in the document, it is well within the realm of possibility that he was in command of the latter vessel, as Catelina Trico stated. But even if this unnamed vessel were not the *Unity,* there is every reason to believe that the *Unity* did come to America before the *Nieu Nederlandt.* Here is further evidence :

On November 3, 1623, Thienpoint, a skipper then in the employ of Pieter Boudaen Courten, a prominent member of the Zeeland Chamber and also a private trader to New Netherland, appeared at a session of the Assembly of XIX. The records of the meeting state :

There was heard also Adriaen Jorisz Thienpoint skipper of Mr. Coerten having been in the Virginnis and declaring they still have there in the rio de Montagne [Hudson River] some goods, 2 sloops and people. Requests therefore that they may have permission to make ready a yacht to trade their merchandise and bring home their people. Whereupon deliberation being had, it is resolved that those who have any goods or merchandise left there shall be dealt with fairly, in the same way as shall be done with those on the Gold Coast, for which a committee has been appointed to draft an order, with the advice of the commander.

As to bringing home the people, it is thought necessary to send a ship to the Virginias, which shall be equipped by the Chamber of Amsterdam with the necessary cargo to continue the trade, for which purpose they may also take with them 5 or 6 families of the colonists in order to make a beginning of settlement there and on that occasion bring back here the goods secured in return for the aforesaid merchandise and the people.[15]

It is significant that Thienpoint had previously been in New Netherland in Courten's interests, having left vessels there to engage in the Indian trade. Furthermore, it should be noted that the Assembly of XIX agreed that the vessels and people should be brought back ; that colonists should be transported to make the *beginning* of a settlement ; that this should be done, not privately by a merchant like Courten, but under the direction of the Amsterdam Chamber. Since it is a matter of record that Thienpoint was in the employ of the West India Company in 1624 - 1625, is it not probable that he was given the assignment he requested — but in the services of another employer who now took precedence over the first?

That a vessel was outfitted by the Amsterdam Chamber ; that it left Holland for New Netherland on or about January 25, 1624 ; that there were passengers aboard, including Bastiaen Jansen Krol as comforter of the sick, all seems very likely in light of the document found by Eekhof, reprinted below in full :

On this last day but one of July in the year XVIc seven and twenty appeared before me Palm Mathijsz, notary public, etc. in

---

[15] *Iconography,* 4.53 ; van Laer, p. xiii. Thienpoint, who lived in Seelant in the province of Zeeland, was skipper of a trading vessel that was in the Hudson in 1618 (*Iconography,* 6:5).

the presence of etc., Willem van der Hulst, dwelling in this town, about 37 years of age, has declared etc., at the request and demand of the honorable Hendrick Eelken, merchant of this town, and that it is true that he testifier has sailed, as passenger in the service of the Company, from this town in the year XVIc twenty four, with the ship named *Nieu Nederlant,* of which the skipper was Cornelis Jacobsz Meijn [May] to the Virginies, and sailing up the river named Ree de Montaingie for about a distance of forty [Dutch] miles, they came to the place called " de Maeykans " where they found a yacht anchored, called " the falling Nut-tree " [*Den omvallende Nooteboom*]" and that the principal commanders and officers of the ship, called *Nieu Nederlandt,* took into their possession the said yacht, and have lodged therein the families, which were in their ship, as they also made use of the said yacht, until they had an opportunity to land and build dwelling places, in which they afterwards lodged the said families.

Declares further, at the time they arrived at the yacht, on this yacht was already the commendary of Jan Jansz. Brouwer who with certain people were also lodged therein, in the service of the West India Company.

Declares further that they found at the same time a yacht called " The Red Dove " [*De Rooduyff*] with sail and tackle, that they used this yacht too in the service of the West India Company, sailing in it along the coast to the north and to the south and have been

---

[16] On March 21, 1626, two ship's carpenters, Gerrit Phillipss and Jan Pieterss, testified that they had sailed to New Netherland on the *Witte Duyff* (" *White Dove* "), " and that about 2½ years ago [late in 1623] when they left the Virginies, they delivered into the safe keeping of Jonathan de Necker, skipper of Willem Snel [director of Zeeland Chamber] a yacht of about 16 lasts called *d 'Omvallende Nooteboom* [the *Falling Nut-Tree*] then about 1½ years old, with masts and spars, well built of dry timber and having eight portholes, as the same had sailed to the south and to the north along the entire coast, except the sails and rigging. The deponents also declare that at the time mentioned they also delivered to Jonathan de Necker a yacht of about 8 lasts with all its appurtenances, except the anchor, cables, and munitions of war ; also a sloop, a Sardam boat and the Biscay shallop ; all of which yachts and boats have been taken over by the West India Company " (*Iconography,* 6 : 13).

trading with it in the service of the same Company ; that they also found there a biscay-sloop, which they also used in the service of the same Company.

All of which he, testifier, declared to be true, etc. Given within the aforesaid town, at the dwelling house of my notary, in the presence of Barent Jansz. and Jan Evertsen, as witnesses.[17]

Less than a year after the first colonists had arrived in New Netherland, the Company tried to get an accounting of the disposition of goods that certain of the vessels had carried, as indicated in this instruction :

And whereas Joost van den Boogaert requests permission to come over on a visit [i.e., return to Holland] he shall allow him to do so, but first have him draw up the account of his entire administration, both of the trading-goods sent with Jan Brouwer and Cornelis Jacobsz Mey and those that came over for Pieter [Boudaen] Courten, and advise us distinctly of whatever fault he may have to find with the said account.

Viewed in light of the above deposition this seems to mean that Brouwer, who may have carried colonists, definitely brought goods for the Indian trade on the *Falling Nut-Tree* ; that May also brought goods, as well as passengers, on the *Nieu Nederlandt*; and that another vessel, or vessels, also brought goods on behalf of the merchant Courten.

The directors persisted in demanding an accounting and asked Isaack de Rasière, first secretary of the province, to make a report to them, which he did in the following language :

In accordance with your Honors' instructions I have examined

---

[17] The Dutch version and an English translation are both given by Prof. Dr. A. Eekhof, *Jonas Michaëlius Founder of the Church in New Netherland,* A. W. Sijthoff's Publishing Co., Leyden, 1926, pp. 96-98. The English translation was printed in part in *Iconography,* 6 : 16, under date of " 1627, July 30. "

Pieter Barentz[18] chief-boatswain to Jan Brouwer with regard to the account of Mr. Pieter Courten. He refers to the letter or book of the son of Adriaen Jorissz [Thienpoint] and says that he can render no further account. He says that pursuant to the orders of Adriaen Jorissz they outbid one another, each trying to get hold of as many skins as possible, and, furthermore that many goods were exchanged against victuals and other things ; in short, he concludes there is nothing left and that all was used up.[19]

The role played by Adriaen Jorissen Thienpoint in this puzzle-game of fitting Dutch ships and people into their proper places is still undefined. Perhaps a missing document may some day be found which holds the key to this puzzle. What we actually know about Thienpoint can be summed up in a few sentences. The records show that in November of 1623 he was a ship's captain in Courten's employ, having been in New Netherland on trading missions. Soon thereafter, according to Mme. Trico, he was in the employ of the West India Company, commanding the vessel *Unity*, bringing colonists to settle at Fort Orange, the Connecticut, and on the Delaware. Thienpoint remained at Fort Orange all winter, after landing the colonists, and his son took the *Unity* back to Holland. During this sojourn at Fort Orange, he made a covenant of friendship with the Indians and engaged in trading with them for their furs — this, too, is taken from Mme. Trico's second deposition.

In 1625 Thienpoint was skipper of the vessel *Sea-Mew*, as the next chapter will relate ; this indicates that his tenure of office at Fort Orange was relatively short.

The above excerpt from de Rasière's report makes it evident that Thienpoint had occupied a position of authority, since he

---

[18] Barentsz, or Barentsen, was a trader, fluent in the Indian languages, who brought back valuable cargoes of furs to Holland (*Narratives, Jameson,* p. 87) ; after Crieckenbeeck's death, Minuit appointed him temporary commander at Fort Nassau (*ibid.,* p. 85).

[19] *Van Laer,* pp. 60-63. 219-220.

had issued orders to his fellow skipper, Brouwer, and others, having to do with the Indian fur trade. It may now be assumed, in light of van der Hulst's testimony regarding Brouwer, that this took place *prior* to the arrival of the *Nieu Nederlandt* under May's command. Therefore, it is possible that Thienpoint was master of a vessel which preceded the *Nieu Nederlandt* and which brought the *first* colonists to America on behalf of the West India Company, as Mme. Trico deposed. In 1625 it was written (see next chapter) that Thienpoint was " vice-director " of the settlement made at Fort Orange — a position which would have justified Mme. Trico's reference to him as the " governor " in her first deposition, even though he may have been in command only provisionally.[20] In her second deposition — which is presumed to be the more accurate and complete of the two — she refers to him as " commander " instead of as " governor."

With Thienpoint in charge at Fort Orange, May presumably took the colonists to the Delaware, and it is not unlikely that van der Hulst, whose deposition has been quoted, may have accompanied him. Someone had to guide the Walloons through unfamiliar and dangerous waters, and May had been in the Delaware before. This assumption is further supported in a statement made some years later by the Lenape chief Mattahorn in a conference with the Dutch that " one Cornelis [May] with one eye, or a film on his eye, was the first who coming here, made his dwelling on the river."[21] On account of his previous experience and familiarity with the Delaware River region, May could have been sent by the Company for the express purpose of establishing a colony on the Delaware. May did not remain on the Delaware

---

[20] *Ibid.,* p. 64. Ellis Lawrence Raesly, *Portrait of New Netherland,* Columbia University Press, New York, 1945, goes so far as to refer to Thienpoint as the first Dutch governor of New Netherland, an extremely liberal interpretation of the data. Wassenaer (*Narratives, Jameson,* p. 84) says flatly that " Cornelis May of Hoorn was the first Director there. "
[21] *NYCD,* 1:597.

very long, and after completing his assignment he sailed back to Holland. The *Nieu Nederlandt* returned home in October of 1624, and among its passengers were probably Krol and van der Hulst, about whom we will hear more in the next chapter.

The key question is : where exactly was this first Dutch settlement on the Delaware River? The answer is not given in any one source in unmistakable terms, but the place can be identified as each reference is considered in light of others. One thing seems certain : the post on the Delaware called Fort Nassau was not built to accommodate these Walloons. They arrived on the Delaware before Fort Nassau was built.[22]

An official account of conditions on the Delaware submitted by the Company to the States General in 1656 contains this passage :

> The Incorporated West India Company of this country took possession in the year 1626 among other places, of the South river situate in New Netherland, and there erected or caused to be built, two posts or fortresses ; the one and the largest called Nassau, 16 leagues up the river on the east bank, being their southern frontier ; and the other named Beversreede, down the river on the west bank, about the lands of the Schuylkill . . .[23]

Even more convincing evidence that 1626 is the correct date for the building of Fort Nassau occurs in the *Van Rappard Documents* ; a letter written from New Netherland on September 23, 1626, by de Rasière to the Amsterdam Chamber indicates that Fort Nassau was not then in existence. This is what he wrote :

> The honorable gentlemen, in their letter, submit to our consideration whether it would not be advisable to erect a small fort on the

---

[22] Various unreliable dates have been given for the building of Fort Nassau : 1623 (*NYCD*, 1 : 290) ; 1624 (*NYCD*, 1 : 149) ; " since the year 1623 " (*NYCD*, 1 : 564).

[23] *NYCD*, 1 : 587-588. See Chapter 6 below for discussion of both forts.

South River. This, according to my judgment, is not only advisable, but necessary for the following reasons :

First, to keep possession of the river, in order that others may not precede us there and erect a fort themselves.

Secondly, because, having a fort there, one could control all the trade in the river.

Thirdly, because the natives say that they are afraid to hunt in winter, being constantly harassed by war with the Minquaes, whereas if a fort were there, an effort could be made to reconcile them.[24]

De Rasière would scarcely have written such a letter if Fort Nassau had already been standing, nor would the directors have suggested in " their letter " that a fort be erected. De Rasière's letter invalidates the opinion of the historian Scharf that Dutch soldiers and sailors, accompanying the Walloons, were stationed at Fort Nassau, " hurriedly built for their protection."[25] The letter also shows that the other historians of New Netherland, most of whom give a date earlier than 1626 for the building of the fort, are in error.

Having ruled out Fort Nassau as the site of the Walloon settlement, let us examine documentary evidence which may indicate where these first settlers lived on the Delaware. To begin with, a somewhat indefinite statement by Wassenaer must be considered. He wrote that the colonists who accompanied May not only built Fort Orange but " They also placed a Fort which they named *Wilhelmus* on Prince's Island, heretofore called Murderer's Island, it is open in front, and has a curtain in the rear and is

---

[24] *Van Laer*, pp. 208-211. This 1626 reference is one of the earliest to the Minquas war against the Delaware River Indians. Several years later, Yong (1634) and de Vries (1632) both referred to this strife (*Narratives, Jameson*). De Vries was unable to obtain corn from the Delaware Indians because Minquas war parties had destroyed their crops (*ibid.*, p. 26).

[25] *Scharf*, 1 : 29.

garrisoned by sixteen men for the defense of the river below."[26]

The early maps of the Hudson and Delaware do not show an island named either Prince's Island or Murderer's Island, but *Wilhelmus* and a variant occur on at least two Dutch maps as an early name for the Delaware River : *Willems* on a map entitled *De Zuid-Baai in Nieuw-Nederland,* reproduced here as Figure 1,[27] and *Wilhelmus,* the Latinized form, on the Buchellius Chart.[28] Since fortified houses, or a trading post, built on a river named *Wilhelmus* might logically be named *Fort Wilhelmus,* the possibility exists that this island could have been one in the Delaware where the Walloons settled.

Less speculative evidence occurs in the deposition of a reliable witness, a sailor, Peter Lourenson, who came to New Netherland in 1628. Two years later, by order of the West India Company, he and seven others were sent in a sloop from Manhattan to the Delaware River. The following are his words :

> . . . where the Company had a Trading house with 10 or 12 Servants belonging to it which the Deponant himself did see there Setled and he further saith that at his Returne from Delloware River the said vessell Stopt at the hoorekill [Swanendael] where the deponant did also See a Settlement of a Brikhouse belonging to the West India Company ; and the deponant further Saith that uppon an Island neare the falls of that River and neare the west side thereof the said Company some 3 or 4 years afore had a Trading house where there were 3 or 4 familyes of Waalloons, the Place of there Setlement he saw, and that they had been Seated there, he

---

[26] *Narratives, Jameson,* p. 76. *Prince Hendricx River* was also a Dutch name for the Delaware (*NYCD,* 12 :48 ; *Dunlap, 1956,* p. 49). *Brodhead,* note K, Appendix, p. 758, discusses Murderer's Island, but fails to identify it.

[27] A facsimile is in David Pietersen de Vries, *Korte Historiael ende Journaels Acteyskeringe,* ed. H. T. Colenbrander, 's—Gravenhage, 1911, facing p. 154 ; see *Dunlap, 1956,* p. 59.

[28] *Narratives. Jameson,* frontispiece.

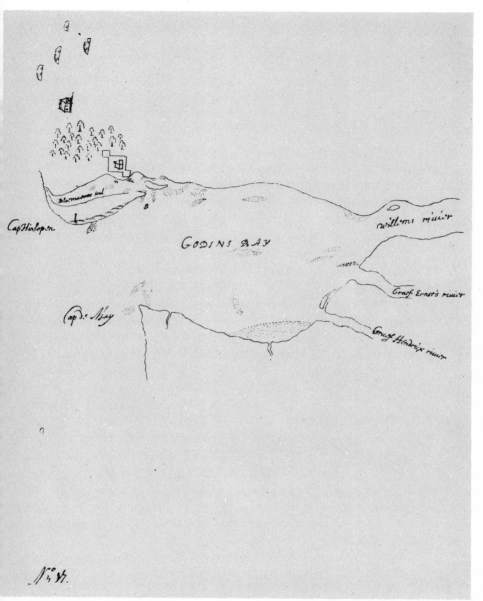

Figure 1. De Zuid Baai in Nieuw-Nederland, dating from the
1630's, shows the palisaded area at Swanendael, two European
houses, and Indian huts. The Delaware River is given as "Willems
rivier." The river of "Graef Hendricx" (Count Henry) may be
present-day Maurice River, and the river of "Graef Ernst" (Count
Ernst) may be either present-day Cohansey Creek or Salem
River. Reproduced with the permission of Algemeen Rijksarchief,
's-Gravenhage, the Netherlands.

was informed by Some of the Said Waalloons themselves when they were returned from thence.[29]

An earlier deposition made by Lourenson has recently been found and published, which gives additional details about the Dutch colonists on the Delaware. In this earlier statement he names the settlements as follows :

in the hoorekill on the West side of Dellowarre bay, where the sd West India Companie then had a Commander whose name was Gillis [Hossitt] together with 17 or 18 men more, and had built there a great dwelling house of Yellow hollande brick, together with a kooke howse alsoo of brick ; and the other settlement was made on the Eastside of Dellowarre, at a place called the *Arwamus*, where they had erected a fort called Nassau, and in it about 13 or 14 men. . . .[30]

Sifting from the two depositions the information pertinent to the settlements, it is possible to place the three sites of the earliest Dutch occupation on the Delaware. Each place is noted below and opposite is a description as paraphrased from Lourenson's depositions :

---

[29] This deposition, dated March 24, 1685, first appeared in *Doc. Hist. N.Y.*, 3 : 50. The above is a newer version found in the William Penn papers, published in *Penna. Magazine*, 80, No. 2 (April, 1956), 233-234. The deponent was the same " Pieter Lourissen " who with Wessel Gerritsen was appointed a pilot in 1655 for Stuyvesant's fleet attacking the Swedes, he and his companion "having both sailed to and from there for a long time" (*NYDC*, 12 : 95). On October 26, 1656, he offered to convey the soldier's baggage from Manhattan to present-day New Castle " if he could send there his own goods in the same vessel " (*ibid.*, p. 130). A patent for a plantation near Fort Casimir was issued to him on February 28, 1657, and a lot the following September (*ibid.*, pp. 180, 182). In 1660, there occurs reference to him and Dirck Smith seeking intelligence about pirates (*ibid.*, p. 323). On May 1, 1658, he sold his sloop *de Hoop* for " 550 merchantable pine boards " (*Albany Recs.* 4 : 42). Evidently he moved from the Delaware back to Manhattan, for on December 26, 1661, he was referred to in the records as an " inhabitant of this city " (*The Minutes of the Orphan-Masters of New Amsterdam, 1655-1663*, ed. B. Fernow, New York, 1902, p. 219).

[30] *Penna. Magazine*, 80, No. 2 (April, 1956), 233.

Fort Nassau

Built at a place called by the Indians *Arwamus*. At the time of his visit in 1631, the Company had a trading house garrisoned by thirteen or fourteen men.

Swanendael

He saw a settlement there consisting of a large dwelling house of yellow brick and a brick cookhouse, under command of Hossitt.

Unnamed island

He saw an island near the falls of the river where the Company had placed three or four Walloon families. There was also a trading house there. The place was vacant at the time of his visit, but when he returned to Manhattan he talked to some of the Walloons who had been there.

Each of these settlements warrants separate discussion, and they will all be treated fully in the chapters to follow. The oldest was that on the unnamed island in the Delaware ; let us now learn what we can about the location of the island and the circumstances attendant to the Dutch effort to colonize it.

III

The Island in the Delaware

In 1625 the West India Company sent a new commander to New Netherland — none other than Willem van der Hulst, the same testifier who had made his first voyage to America the previous year with May on the *Nieu Nederlandt*. The official title given him was " provisional director," and we will call him by the form of his surname preferred by van Laer, i.e. Verhulst. He sailed to America on his second voyage in the vessel *Den Orangeboom* ("*The Orange Tree*"), probably leaving Holland in January, 1625. The vessel brought additional colonists, as well as cattle, seeds, trees, vines, farm implements, and other suplies.[1] Accompanying Verhulst as comforter of the sick, and also experiencing his second voyage to America, was Bastiaen Jansen Krol.

Wassenaer had written the previous year, about affairs in New Netherland, " Respecting this colony, it has already a prosperous beginning ; and the hope is that it will not fall through provided it be zealously sustained not only in that place [Fort Orange] but in the South River."[2]

The instructions issued to Provisional Director Verhulst prior to his departure for America contain the following two paragraphs of utmost importance in identifying the unnamed island where Lourenson saw the remains of the Walloons' settlement :

Whereas we have received and examined a report about the

---

[1] *Van Laer,* pp. 56, 59.
[2] *Narratives, Jameson,* p. 76.

condition of a certain island to be called the High Island, situated about 25 miles up the South River, below the first falls, we deem it expedient, unless a still more suitable place be found, to settle there all the families together with the hired farmers and the cattle that will be sent thither in the ship *Den Orangeboom* and the following ship[s] since the said island is in itself a level field with a fertile soil and on both sides has much suitable arable and pasture land as well as all kinds of timber, so that a large number of families could support themselves there better than on the North River.

For this purpose, at the most suitable place at the lower end of the said island, such a provisional fortification is to be built as will best protect the people and the cattle, the dimensions to be taken rather somewhat too large than too small.[3]

Whether or not the island " to be called the High Island " is the same as the one Wassenaer called Prince's or Murderer's Island is something the documents do not make clear, but that possibility exists. The island " to be called the High Island," but still without a name to the Dutch prior to the issuance of the instructions to Verhulst, lay " below the first falls." Lourenson said that the unnamed island where the Walloons had lived was " near " the falls, which would place it south of present-day Trenton. It could not have been north of Trenton, because Lourenson arrived by sloop, and the river was not navigable to sloops as the falls were approached. (The " falls " was actually an extensive area in the bed of the river where rocks interfered with navigation. The lower area was sometimes known as " the first falls.") Lourenson refers further to the settlement being " neare the west side thereof," which is usually interpreted to mean the island was on the west side of the river. He probably meant that the settlement was on the west side of the island, which agrees with the above description in the Verhulst instruc-

---

[3] *Van Laer,* pp. 48-51.

tions of the most suitable place being the " lower [i.e., western] end of the said island."

The opening phrase, "Whereas we have received and examined a report," can only mean that someone had been on this island, and had been impressed with its resources. That person could have been May, or even Verhulst, since both had previously been in New Netherland. Furthermore, the evidence points in the direction that " the island to be called the High Island " was the site of the first Delaware settlement, and that the Walloons were still in residence there when Willem Verhulst arrived in New Netherland with additional colonists.

The instructions to Verhulst go on to say, and we have italicized the significant words :

. . . And whereas he, Willem Verhulst, is to have *his usual place of residence on the South River,* the skippers being present there are joined unto him as councillors, with whom he shall deliberate and act upon all matters of importance. . . . he . . . *shall also from time to time, as occasion may require, betake himself to the North River* to regulate matters there, leaving there in the North River in his absence Adriaen Jorissen Thienpoint as vice-director and Daniel van Cryeckenbeeck [Krieckenbeeck] as sub-commissary of trading goods, etc.[4]

There can be no question that the intent was not only to populate High Island with all the families, but to situate the " usual place of residence " of the provisional director there, which would make it a seat of the Dutch government in New Netherland. In fact, the instructions direct Verhulst, his family, and members of his council as well as " such others as he shall deem fit " to sit at one table to eat, and " rations shall be dealt out to the farmers and their families and other persons, until other arrangements therein shall be made by the company."[5]

---

[4] *Van Laer,* p. 64.
[5] *Ibid.,* pp. 74-75.

The families accompanying Verhulst were to be distributed to all occupied places, " but he shall strengthen the population of the southern colony most."[6] The significance of this phrase is evident ; the Company intended that the heaviest concentration of colonists should be placed on the Delaware River. Based on information that had been received from May, Verhulst, and others, after the return of the *Nieu Nederlandt,* the directors decided to make the main settlement of New Netherland on the Delaware, and to reinforce the other occupied places on the Hudson.

The documents do not make it certain that Verhulst settled on High Island as directed — he may have placed his colonists elsewhere, probably on Manhattan Island. Unfortunately his administration was short and information about it is meager. It was written that the colonists were " harshly ruled by Verhulst and that without any legal formality, but merely upon his own authority." It was further written that " only that was punished which offended Verhulst or his dignity, not according to law, but according to his pleasure."[7] There is one clue that faintly suggests Verhulst may have come to the Delaware. A Dutch map, c. 1629, entitled *Caert vande Sydt Rivier in Niew Nederland* has an entry " Verhulsten Island " in the Delaware River.[8] In view of the practice of attaching personal names to places discovered, visited, occupied, or otherwise associated with an individual it is possible, but by no means certain, that Verhulst had something to do with this island. Unfortunately, Verhulsten Island cannot be located with exactness on the above map nor on maps of the later Jansson-Visscher series on which it later appeared. Its general position on the c. 1629 map is approximately the same as

[6] *Ibid.,* p. 40.
[7] *Van Laer,* pp. 187, 188.
[8] *Dunlap & Weslager, 1958.*

present-day Biles Island.[9] Inasmuch as High Island was *below* the first falls, and the above map shows Verhulsten Island *above* the first falls, they must have been two different places.

Sometime after his arrival in New Netherland, Verhulst was reinforced by additional families of settlers, who left Holland in April of 1625. Wassenaer said of these reinforcements that " an extraordinary shipment was sent thither this month," stating that " country people have joined the expedition " and that stallions, mares, bulls, cows, hogs, sheep, seeds, and more agricultural implements were sent.[10] The ships in the second expedition were the *Paert, Koe, Schaep,* and *Mackerel.*

The *Mackerel* brought a second set of instructions, dated April 22, 1625, drawn up by the directors of the Amsterdam Chamber for " Willem van der Hulst, commissary and for the members of the Council residing on the rivers, islands, and the mainland of New Netherland, etc."[11] In these instructions one senses a change in the directors' attitude, apparently due to the additional reports that had reached them and of which regrettably there is no record. The directors, in the second instructions, are less certain about the South River being the most suitable locale for the seat of the colony. The new contingent of colonists are " to take up their abode on the South or North River or at such other places as may be most advantageous to the Company."[12]

Among the newcomers was Cryn Fredericksz, an engineer and surveyor, who had been given written instructions to assist Verhulst in building a fort according to detailed specifications prepared by the directors. The site of the fort was not stipulated, but Verhulst was instructed to " investigate which is the most suitable place, abandoned or unoccupied, *on either river,* and

---

[9] *Ibid. Van Laer* erred, p. 260, in identifying High Island with Verhulsten Island ; he was evidently unaware of the existence of two falls.
[10] *Narratives, Jameson,* p. 79.
[11] *Van Laer,* p. 82.
[12] *Ibid,*

there settle with all the cattle and build the necessary fortification." [13] Fredericksz was told in his special letter of instructions
that he should proceed when Verhulst and council, pursuant to
instructions, " have found a suitable place in which to establish
a settlement with all cattle." The fort was to be called Amsterdam." [14]

New settlers who reinforced the colony arrived in the late
spring of 1625 — and others followed in later vessels — but in the
fall of 1626 Willem Verhulst was on his way back to Holland in
disgrace, banished from the colony for bad conduct. The exact
nature of his malfeasance is not known, but the council tried him,
found him guilty, relieved him of his office, and sent him and his
wife back home on the ship *Wapen van Amsterdam ("Arms of
Amsterdam")* which departed from Manhattan September 23,
1626. [15]

After discharging Verhulst, the council appointed Peter Minuit
as his successor. Although of French descent, Minuit came from
Wesel, Germany, a city on the Rhine famous as an asylum for
persecuted Protestants. His name appears variously as Menuet,
Minuict, Minuyt, or Menewe — a Dutch transliteration of the
French sound — and sometimes in the Germanized forms, Minnewit or Minnewitz. Evidently he was a man of education ; he
wrote excellent Dutch although with distinctly German spelling,
and he had been an elder in the French church at Wesel, suggesting knowledge of that language. Jameson said that Minuit

---

[13] *Ibid.,* p. 106.

[14] *Ibid.,* p. 152. ·

[15] Among Verhulst's goods was his wife's coat, made of thirty-two otter
skins, and his own tabard, of sixteen beaver skins. Both garments were made
of the finest black pelts (*ibid.,* p. 244). Perhaps these were some of the skins
Verhulst took illegally from Jan Price, barber-surgeon, who later petitioned
the Company for settlement of his account, claiming that Verhulst unjustly
took possession of pelts he had earned by " bleeding the Indians "
(*Iconography,* 4 : 67). This is one of the earliest references to medical practice
among the natives.

arrived in New Netherland on May 4, 1626, taking this information from Wassenaer, who wrote that " Adriaen Joris [Thienpoint — the same skipper referred to in the previous chapter] went out there on the 19th of December of the year 1625 with the ship *Sea-mew* and conveyed Pieter Minuit aforesaid . . . . the *Sea-mew* arrived there 4th May, 1626." Wassenaer also stated that Minuit " went thither from Holland on January 9 Ano 1626."[16] This contradiction in dates caused Jameson and others to speculate that the *Sea-mew* left Amsterdam on December 19, 1625, was delayed by weather, and did not depart from the Texel until January 9, finally arriving in America on May 4. If true, this would be an unusually long time for a voyage that normally required six to eight weeks. Jameson, of course, did not have access to the *Van Rappard Documents* wherein there is information strongly suggesting that Minuit was in New Netherland prior to May 4, 1626.

For example, in the first instructions (January, 1625), Verhulst was told to have " Pierre Minuyt and others whom he shall deem fit investigate what minerals and crystals there may be both on the North River and on the South River." The same instructions order him to have " Pierre Minuyt, as volunteer, and others whom he deems competent thereto sail up the river as far as they can in any way do so, in order to inspect the condition of the land . . . ."[17] In the second instructions (April, 1625) Minuit is named as one of the members of Verhulst's council.[18]

---

[16] *Narratives, Jameson,* p. 83, fn. 1, p. 88 ; also *van Laer,* p. 260. In 1895 the Assembly of the State of Delaware appointed a committee to prepare a brief but authentic sketch of Minuit's life, resulting in a memorial service April 23, 1895, in Dover described in a pamphlet entitled *Memorial Services in Honor of Peter Minuit.* The pamphlet states that Minuit was born in 1580 ; that his name appears in the civil records of Wesel, March 5, 1619, as guardian of his deceased sister's children ; that the records show that on April 15, 1625, he " left for foreign countries."

[17] *Van Laer,* pp. 44, 75. Several years later Minuit was able to inform van Rensselaer where to find rock crystal on his lands (*VRB,* p. 198).

[18] *Van Laer,* p. 90.

If — as this evidence seems to indicate — Minuit was in New Netherland with Verhulst in 1625, and if, as Wassenaer states, he arrived in May of 1626, then he must have made two trips. There is no reason to doubt this, because some of his contemporaries in the Company's employ — Verhulst, May, Thienpoint, and Krol, for example — had been in New Netherland more than once prior to 1626.

Another item has come to light that further complicates the question of the date of Minuit's departure from Holland. The notarial records of Amsterdam contain a declaration under date of January 15, 1626, by " Peter Minuit of Wesel " who stated that some time previously he had entered into partnership with Jan Valck to buy grain at Frankfort for which Valck furnished the money ; that the grain was taken from them ; that Valck demanded of Minuit one half of the purchase money ; that he was unable to pay, and that Valck forced him to cause " his brother-in-law Geurt Raets, residing at Cleves, to become security for 600 rixdollars."[19] Obviously, Minuit could not have departed Amsterdam on December 19, the Texel on January 9 — and made a declaration before an Amsterdam notary on January 15.

One inference to be drawn from this declaration is that Minuit had been a merchant of sorts prior to his leaving for New Netherland. Having encountered heavy losses, it may have been the state of his finances that prompted him to seek employment with the West India Company as a member of the Verhulst expedition.

Apart from the question of the date of Minuit's departure from Holland, it is made clear in the *Van Rappard Documents* that he was not originally sent as governor, as so many historians have maintained. It was intended by the directors that he play a lesser role in the colony than that which circumstances forced upon him after his arrival. Nor was the purchase of Manhattan Island from the Indians — an incident for which Minuit receives credit in

---

[19] *Iconography*, 6:13.

American histories — made when he first arrived. At that time, he was not the ranking officer and as yet had no authority to make land purchases for the Company. As the reader has seen, Minuit, probably on his second visit, was advanced to become " Director-General " of New Netherland because of Verhulst's reprehensible conduct.

The brief reference to the purchase of Manhattan Island from the Indians is found in a letter written at Amsterdam November 5, 1626, by Peter Schagen, the Deputy of the States General. The letter was unknown in America until John R. Brodhead returned from Holland with a photostat of it in 1844. Prior to that date no historical work on the New Netherland that has come to attention refers to Minuit buying Manhattan Island. In fact, neither Minuit's name nor the date of the purchase is mentioned in Schagen's letter, which states in part, " Their women, also, have borne children there, they have bought the island *Manhattes* from the wild men for the value of sixty guilders, is 11,000 morgens in extent. They sowed all their grain the middle of May, and harvested it in the middle of August." [20]

Those who have said that the purchase was made by Minuit have so assumed because they inferred he was the Director-General at the time of the purchase. If there was a deed covering the sale, which would settle the question, it, unfortunately, has not yet come to light.

If Schagen meant that the colonists planted their grain on Manhattan Island in May, it can be argued that the island must have been purchased before this time. It is inconceivable that the Company would have started planting without acquiring owner-

[20] The first translation appeared in *NYCD*, 1 :xxix. A facsimile of the original letter appears opposite p. 106 in John Fiske, *The Dutch and Quaker Colonies in America*, 1903. In *NYCD*, 1 :56, a letter from the States General in 1632 stated, " having purchased from the native inhabitants and paid for a certain island also called Manathans, etc. "

ship of the land. Unless Minuit was the Director-General in May, which the information to follow will suggest is not a certainty, then it could have been Verhulst or someone else who initiated the memorable purchase. Under the erroneous impression that Minuit was sent as the first " governor," many historians interpreted Schagen's letter to mean that Minuit was in office in May, 1626, but this has not yet been established,[21] Not until November, 1626, does an entry appear in Wassenaer's account to the effect that " The Honorable Pieter Minuit is Director there at present," although de Rasière indicates he held the post earlier.

It cannot be proved that Minuit did *not* buy Manhattan Island, because it is still uncertain when he succeeded Verhulst, and the *Van Rappard Documents* do not name a specific date. An important clue, however, is found in the letter written by de Rasière on September 23, 1626, from which a passage was quoted in the previous chapter. This letter states that " on Minuyt's arrival here he was placed in command by the Council . . . ." This brings us back to the contradiction in dates concerning his arrival in New Netherland. If Minuit arrived (on a second trip) on May 4, 1626, the date given by Wassenaer, and was then placed in command by the council, it is extremely unlikely that they would have allowed five months to elapse before sending Verhulst back to Holland. Several Dutch ships moved back and forth across the Atlantic during those months, and there would seem to have been no reason to delay Verhulst's sailing until September 23, 1626. It should also be noted that the *Arms of Amsterdam* which took Verhulst back to Holland also carried de Rasière's letter, and the news about the purchase of Manhattan

---

[21] *Brodhead,* p. 164 (1853), said that Minuit bought the island for sixty guilders. The price is from Schagen's letter, but, as explained, the letter does not connect Minuit with the purchase. One of the first textbook references to his having paid the equivalent of " twenty-four gold dollars " was John J. Anderson and A. C. Flick, *A Short History of the State of New York,* 1902.

Island that Schagen covered in his letter to the States General. This leaves no doubt that Verhulst was in America at the time the island was purchased.

De Rasière's letter bears closer examination because a meaning can logically be drawn from it which, if correct, would place the events in a different sequence. He wrote that " On our arrival there [at Fort Amsterdam, July 28, 1626] we did not find Minuyt, he having gone to Fort Orange to inquire into the disaster caused by the reckless adventure of Crieckenbeeck.[22] He then goes on to inform the directors of Minuit's advancement :

On Minuyt's arrival here he was placed in command by the Council on account of the bad conduct of Verhulst, as your Honors will see from the copies of the proceedings brought against him which go over herewith.[23]

Then, in the following paragraph, he explains further that :

On Friday the 31st in the evening [July 31, 1626] Minuyt returned here, and on the 1st of August I handed him in the Council your Honors' letters, which were opened and read, etc.

Presumably the letters de Rasière delivered were intended for Verhulst and contained instructions from the directors along with other matters of business. De Rasière's phrase " on Minuyt's arrival " can be interpreted to mean when he arrived back at Fort Amsterdam from his trip to Fort Orange and not necessarily his arrival date in America. It would then follow that Minuit was placed in command at the meeting of the Council the following day attended by de Rasière, who had a voice in the proceedings. Until this meeting took place Verhulst had probably not been sentenced, for de Rasière said in his letter that he was sending the directors " a copy of the judicial proceedings which

---

[22] *Van Laer,* p. 175. This refers to the war between the Mohawk and Mohegan in which Krieckenbeeck, then in charge at Fort Orange, had foolishly become embroiled, losing his life and the lives of three of his men.
[23] *Ibid.,* p. 176.

took place in the Council *during my time*."[24] These proceedings, which are missing, included the accusations against Verhulst and his defense. In referring to the deportation of Verhulst and his wife, de Rasière repeats the plural *we* three times, leaving no doubt that he participated in the sentence. The following is his phraseology, with italics supplied :

. . . *we* are sending your Honors the person of Willem van der Hulst and his wife, together with the record of their trial and sentence, but in the haste of writing I have forgotten to state why in that sentence *we* are banishing him now and forever from the limits of your Honor's charter. This was done because he gave out here that if he were not serving the honorable gentlemen here he knew other masters who would help him and would know how to avenge himself. *We* therefore added that, so as to have cause to arrest him if he should happen to come here again in the service of the French or English, intending then in accordance with the sentence to try and sentence him and send this to the respective prince or lord for our justification.[25]

Minuit now recognized that his tenure would be permanent, and in November he sent for his wife to come to New Netherland.[26] This fact must also be considered, for had Minuit taken Verhulst's place at the time of his arrival in the colony, he probably would have sent earlier for his wife. De Rasière's letter was the first notice to the directors of the change in commanders — if Minuit had taken office as early as May it would not have been necessary for the secretary to report the incident more than five months later. The directors had good intelligence of the affairs in New Netherland, and they would have known about a change in their principal officers before the lapse of five months.

Following Verhulst's departure, all the settlers living on the

---

[24] *Ibid.,* p. 183.
[25] *Ibid.,* p. 183.
[26] *Ibid.,* p. 259.

Delaware, and the majority of those at Fort Orange, were transferred to Manhattan. Minuit played an important part in consolidating the population at Manhattan, which by 1628, according to Wassenaer, " numbered 270 souls." In November, Wassenaer wrote, " Those of the South River will abandon their fort and come hither [to Manhattan]."[27] Soon afterward he noted, " The fort at the South River is already vacated in order to strengthen the colony. Trading there is carried on only in yachts, in order to avoid expense."[28] In an entry dated October, 1628, he makes it clear that all of the settlers on the Delaware had gone to Manhattan: " Those of the West India Company have also removed *all* those who were at the South River."[29]

The records do not disclose how many colonists actually lived on the island in the Delaware, but there can no longer be any doubt that such a settlement existed ; that the West India Company sent Verhulst as the " governor " in 1625 with orders to expand the settlement ; the expansion never materialized ; Verhulst was banished from the colony ; the settlers on the Delaware were then withdrawn and sent to live under the jurisdiction of Minuit on Manhattan Island, which was destined to become New Netherland's political and economic center.

High Island and the unnamed island occupied by the Walloons were unquestionably one and the same place, but to identify this island in terms of today's geography requires documentary research in a later period. Fifty years after the Walloons had departed, another Dutch " governor " chose a Delaware island as his estate. During these fifty years, Swedes and English had both contested with the Dutch for control of the Delaware, and the Dutch had returned with a new contingent of settlers. Refer-

[27] *Narratives, Jameson*, p. 84.
[28] *Ibid.*, p. 86.
[29] *Ibid.*, p. 88. All the people from Fort Orange, except fifteen or sixteen men, were also transferred to Manhattan.

ence to the island is found in a journal of two Dutch travelers under date of November 18, 1679. The italic has been added by the authors :

The water was then rising, and we had to row against the current to Burlington, leaving the island of Matinakonk lying on the right hand. *This island formerly belonged to the Dutch governor, who made it a pleasure ground or garden, built good houses upon it, and sowed and planted it.* He also dyked and cultivated a large piece of meadow or marsh from which he gathered more grain than from any land which had been made from woodland into tillable land. *The English governor at the Manathans now held it for himself, and hired it out to some Quakers who were living upon it at present.*

It is the best and largest island in the South river; and it is about four English miles in length and two in breadth. It lies nearest the east side of the river. At the end of this island lies the Quaker village, Burlington . . . .[30]

The former Dutch " governor " mentioned in this quotation was Alexander d'Hinoyossa, a tyrannical, unprincipled man who was promoted to office in 1659, having formerly been an army officer. He was still holding his high position in 1664 when Sir Robert Carr descended on the Dutch settlement on the Delaware and seized control on behalf of the Duke of York. Carr confiscated the lands, houses, and personal possessions belonging to the Dutch officials, including d'Hinoyossa's property. Carr kept the latter for himself, " that is to say, the Governor Inniosa's island."[31] In Chapter 10 the reader will find further discussion of

---

[30] *Journal of a Voyage to New York in 1679-1680* (Danckers and Sluyter), Memoirs, Long Island Historical Society, 1 (1867), 174. The two travelers had passed five islands in the Delaware, and they observed that Matinakonk and Tinicum " are the principal islands and the best and largest " (*ibid.,* p. 177). Matinakonk and Tinnicum both derive from an Algonkian word meaning " at the island," although they are different places.

[31] *PA.,* 2nd Series, 5 : 600.

Carr's attack on the Delaware and the properties seized by him and his officers.

Sir Robert remained only for a few months on the Delaware following the attack, and after his departure the island was for a time in the custody of Captain John Carr, one of his officers, who would later become the chief English administrator at New Castle. On December 15, 1668, orders were issued to Captain John Carr directing him to surrender, to Peter Alricks, " Matinicom als [alias] Carrs Island in Delaware ryver & all the Stock Goods and other materials there upon heretofore in your care and Custody . . . . and whatever else was delivered to you there by Sr Robert Carr." [32]

Peter Alricks was a brilliant and resourceful business man who had come to New Netherland from Groningen prior to the English attack. The burgomasters of Amsterdam employed him as an official in their Delaware colony where, soon after his arrival, he acquired large land holdings. He lost these lands, as well as his other possessions, to Carr's forces in the attack. After the smoke of battle settled, Alricks became friendly with the English officials, who soon recognized that his influence and ability could be utilized to their best interests. Within a few years his position as landholder had been restored, and he not only acquired d'Hinoyossa's Island, but the English authorities confirmed the patents of two other islands to him on February 15, 1667. They were described as " scituate lying and being on ye West side of ye said River and about South West from ye Island called Matineconck." The bigger of the two islands was " formerly known by the name of Kipps Island and by ye Indian name of *Koomenakanokonck,* containing about a myle in length and half a myle in breadth and

---

[32] *Ibid.,* pp. 603-604. *Dunlap, 1956,* p. 38, lists " Inniosa's Island," but at that time was in doubt about its location.

ye other Island lying somewhat to the North of ye former being of about half a myle in length and the quarter of a myle in breadth . . . ." [33] Before the English attack, Alricks had owned another island, on which there was a plantation, in the Delaware seven miles below New Castle. [34]

This insular Dutchman was, therefore, owner at different times of *four* islands in the Delaware, of which Matinakonk was the largest and by far the most valuable. The latter island remained in his possession for about six years, and he employed others to cultivate it for him while he sought profit in other directions. In 1671 two of his Dutch servants were killed by Indians on the island " of Matiniconk in Delaware River," which provoked retaliation against the Indians by the English. [35]

In 1673, the Dutch wrested control of New Netherland from the English, and for a brief period Anthony Colve, former " captain of a company on foot," held office, having been appointed August 12 by Jacob Benkes and Cornelius Evertsen " to govern and rule these lands." In the role of Governor-General, with headquarters at New York, Colve on September 19 appointed Peter Alricks as " Commander and Schout " on the Delaware, which further attests to Alricks' executive ability, recognized alike by the English and his own countrymen. Needless to say, the former English officers on the Delaware were made extremely unhappy by this turn of events, which again gave the Dutch political control of the colony. Following the signing of the Treaty of Westminster between Holland and England, the English position was restored, and English officials resumed authority on the Delaware. Alricks then found himself in bad graces ; the English accused him of having " been too eager to work in Dutch

---

[33] *NYCD*, 12 :461. He paid four otter skins annually as quit rent ; his name is shown on the rent list of 1671 (*ibid.*, p. 492). His tract of 560 acres on St. Augustine Creek was known as Groningen (*DYR*, p. 100).

[34] *DYR*, p. 26. The English confiscated this also in 1664.

[35] *PA*, 2nd Series, 5 :629-630.

interests " during the interlude when they were out of office.[36]
Evidently it was at this time that his island property was confiscated, for on November 18, 1678, Edmund Andros, who had
succeeded Lovelace as governor, leased " Mattiniconck Island in
Delaware River unto Robert Stacey for the Term of Seven
Yeares."[37] Stacy, a Quaker from Yorkshire, had come from England in 1677, along with two hundred others of the same sect, to
settle in New Jersey, or *Nova Caesaria*. Thus, at the time of the
visit in 1679 by the two Dutch travelers the island belonged to
the English governor, and was, indeed, occupied by Quakers, as
they stated. When Stacy obtained his lease, Peter Jegoes and
Henry Jacobs had been renting the island from Governor Andros.
Jegoes name was corrupted to " Chygoe," and the island was also
known by this name for a time.[38]

In Stacy's lease, Matinakonk Island was described as being
" in delaware River towards the ffals." High Island was " below
the first falls " and the unnamed Walloon's island was " near the
falls." Furthermore, the fertility and size of High Island were
highly praised, and when this description is compared with the
statement that Matinakonk was the " biggest and best " island,
there is little reason to doubt that High Island, Matinakonk
Island, and the unnamed Walloons' island were all the same
place.[39]

The island had another name, recorded in 1633 by the Dutch
navigator de Vries, to whom later reference will be made. He

---

[36] *NYCD*, 12 : 513. For a translation of Colve's commission and information
about his appointment see William Smith, *A History of New York*, Albany,
1814, p. 59 ; the commission was later printed in *NYCD*, 2 : 609-610.

[37] *NYCD*, 12 : 614.

[38] *Ibid.*, p. 615.

[39] It is now possible to understand the unsigned, undated petition in the
New York records which heretofore has not been explained. Written in
wretched English, the petitioners ask Andros to grant them a tract of
four-thousand acres, four miles above and four miles below the falls,
including the islands. It seems evident that they were Quakers (*ibid.*, pp.
521-522).

described an island he had touched in the Delaware River in these words : " *ende raeckten met die Vlot tot het Schoone Eylandt toe.*"[40] This is translated to mean that he arrived at " the Beautiful Island." By capitalization and use of the definite article, de Vries particularized the island which suggests he was familiar with its name, possibly from a map in his possession.[41] The previously mentioned *Caert van de Sydt Rivier in Niew Nederland* has the entry *Schoon Eylandt* (" Beautiful Island ") which, if one may judge from its position, can only be the island known today as Burlington Island. Murphy, who translated and edited the journal of the two Dutch travelers who were on the Delaware in 1679, indicates that Burlington Island and Matinakonk Island were the same place.[42] The present authors are in agreement with this identification.

The following passage taken from the writings of Gabriel Thomas, a Welsh yeoman and resident of William Penn's colony of Pennsylvania in 1681, adds finality to the identification of the Walloons' island. In his account, he explains that the Indians were the first occupants of the Delaware River. Then follows this very significant passage :

The next who came there were the Dutch ; which was between Forty and Fifty years agoe though they made but very little Improvement, only built Two or Three Houses, upon an Island (called since by the English) Stacies Island . . . .[43]

There is scarcely room for doubt that Thomas was describing the site of the short-lived Walloon settlement, and he refers

[40] David Pietersen de Vries, *Korte Historiael ende Journaels Aeteyckeninge,* ed. H. T. Colenbrander, 's-Gravenhage, 1911.
[41] A map made in Minuit's time, c. 1630, shows *Schoon Eyland* and immediately above it the name *Matonancons,* another form of *Matinakonk* (*Iconography,* 2 : Pl. 39).
[42] *Journal of a Voyage,* p. 174, fn. 1.
[43] *Narratives, Myers,* p. 344.

specifically to the island as " Stacies Island." This was one of the names for Matinakonk Island—other names for the same island were High Island, *Schoon* (Beautiful Island), d'Hinoyossa's Island, Carr's Island, *Chygoes* Island, and—today's name— Burlington Island.

Due to modern dredging operations to obtain sand and gravel, the lower end of Burlington Island has been partially destroyed and any evidences of the first Dutch occupation obliterated. On April 22, 1961, the writer [C.A.W.] and several associates [a] explored the island, which now plays an important commercial role in supplying the city of Burlington with fresh water. There are five water wells having a total capacity of five million gallons daily, pumped to Burlington by submarine pipe.

The lower, or western, portion of the island formerly arose to a 20-foot elevation, and was, indeed, "high" land and ideal for house sites. The fertility of the soil, the remains of woods, the bird and animal life, and its strategic location and accessibility set it apart from other Delaware River islands. One can readily understand why the Dutch singled out this beautiful and useful location as the seat of their first Delaware colony.

---

[a] Members of the party were Dr. Walter Dew, James Hain, Lee Ward, and two New Jersey archaeologists, Charles Kier and Fred Calverley. We are indebted to George A. Schultz, officer in charge of the island, for his courtesy and co-operation. Although there are some summer residents, Mr. Schultz is the only all-year occupant.

IV

The Swanendael Tragedy

On March 28, 1628, the nineteen-member executive committee of the Dutch West India Company, known as the Assembly of XIX, representing the five Chambers and the States General, ruled that individual members of the Company could send out colonists. This directive was amended and modified on June 7, 1629, in a formal document known as the *Charter of Freedoms and Exemptions*. However, there existed a sharp difference of opinion among the stockholders and directors, some of whom felt the Company should restrict its activities to trading. They were opposed to any colonization efforts by the Company. A strong element among the members even opposed individual sponsorship of colonies ; they believed this would eventually infringe on the Company's fur trade and result in a loss of income.

The *Charter of Freedoms and Exemptions* provided for grants of land estates, or patroonships, to such members who were disposed to establish colonies at their own expense. The patroon was obliged to select and register land within certain specified limits and then to extinguish the Indian title by purchase. He could then possess the land as a sort of feudal lord with authority to place settlers, appoint officers and magistrates, collect funds from the earnings of his colonists to support a minister and teacher, and do whatever else was needed, within certain limitations, to expand his colony. He was obliged to conform to the general scheme of government framed by the Assembly of XIX, and to observe prescribed rules and regulations in his commercial conduct. Although a number of prominent members of the Company became patroons, the system was destined at the outset to fail, primarily because the Company did not give it wholehearted support. Furthermore, there were many problems in transporting colonists and supplies across the Atlantic ; the lack of experienced leaders proved to be a handicap ; once a colony was laid down, there was continuing difficulty in maintaining friendly relations with the neighboring Indians. There were also many other problems of the kind that are attendant to any system of absentee ownership.

Swanendael (" valley of swans ") was one of the first settlements made in New Netherland by patroons ; it was situated on land included within the town limits of present Lewes, Delaware. The exact site of the settlement is uncertain except that it was on the bank of the stream later known as Lewes Creek, now part of the Lewes-Rehoboth Canal, and a short distance above its mouth. The name " Swanendael " first appeared in a document executed June 1, 1629, which recorded the purchase of land from the Indians on which the settlement was founded. This document and others, which have been gathered from widely scattered sources, are given in Appendix A. One of these is a passage from *Kort Verhael Van Nieuw-Nederlants Gelgentheit–1662,* which has previously been only incompletely translated into English ; the new translation was made by Dunlap.

These documents, taken together, tell the full story from the founding of Swanendael to its tragic end. They constitute a new and convenient point of reference for use by the scholar. What now follows is the story of Swanendael, based on these documents, told in broad strokes, whereas the documents themselves reveal it in fine detail.

On January 13, 1629, three prominent merchants and directors of the West India Company, Samuel Godyn, Kiliaen

van Rensselaer, and Samuel Blommaert, dispatched two representatives to New Netherland with the mission of purchasing
from the Indians suitable lands for colonies. The two emissaries
were Gillis Hossitt, referred to as a sailor, and Jacob Jansz, a
cooper. Nothing is known of these two persons nor why they were
given the responsibility of such an important assignment. The
possibility that one or the other, or even both, may have been
members of the May or Verhulst expeditions must not be dis-
counted ; it would be logical for the merchants to employ men
who had been in America and were familiar with the terrain.

The dominant figure in planning the Swanendael colony was
Samuel Godyn, then the president of the Amsterdam Chamber.
He was well informed about the events in New Netherland ; he
had read the reports and correspondence from the beginning ;
he had been one of the policy makers for the Company's New
Netherland colony. He had been a co-author of the *articulbrieff*,
adopted March 28, 1628, by the Assembly of XIX, and issued
to May.[1] He had been one of the signers (as also had been van
Rensselaer) of the second set of instructions issued to Verhulst on
April 22, 1625, and also of the special instructions given to Cryn
Fredericksz.[2] Godyn was fully aware that the Company had
withdrawn its settlers from the island in the Delaware River ;
that it remained an area with unlimited commercial potential ;
that it was unoccupied and thus ideal for staking out a patroonship.

Godyn was also in possession of what at the time was very
important information ; it had been reported to him by Peter
Minuit, and by other Company representatives in New Netherland, that many whales had been sighted in the bay of the
Delaware River. He had been told that schools of whales entered
the bay at certain times of the year and came so close to the

---

[1] *Van Laer*, p. 255.
[2] *Ibid.*, p. 168.

shore that harpooners stationed on the beach could detect them and immediately take off in small boats for the kill. Whale oil was worth sixty guilders a hogshead in Holland, and Dutch and English interests were already contesting in the whale fishing in waters surrounding Spitsbergen. The Greenland Company was making regular whaling runs to the Arctic in an effort to meet the heavy demand for whale oil in European markets. The oil rendered from whale blubber, commonly called " train oil," proved to be an excellent lubricant for machinery, as well as a fuel for lamps. Many uses were also found for the baleen, or whalebone.

Godyn must have reasoned that whale oil could be obtained in the bay of the South River at considerably less expense than in Arctic waters, if the reports that reached his desk were accurate. He didn't need a fleet of fully equipped whaling vessels, whose support was a heavy drain on one's finances, to sail out in search of whales. In New Netherland the whales came in from the seven seas (for reasons that were not given) and, having reached coastal waters, they could be pursued and caught by men living at land stations provided with small whaling boats. These fishermen could be put to useful agricultural labor on the land at times of the year when the whales were in more distant waters.

The three patroons had evidently discussed their plans thoroughly before sending their emissaries to America, and had already decided on the lands they wanted to settle. This is made clear in a phrase by van Rensselaer to the effect that the emissaries were sent " to buy and pay for the places indicated to them."[3]

On June 1, 1629, Hossitt negotiated a purchase of land from the Indians along the west shore of Delaware Bay in the area known to the Dutch as the " South Hook." The land he bought was eight Dutch miles long and half a Dutch mile in width. He

---

[3] *VRB,* p. 238.

gave the Indians in payment cloth, axes, adzes, beads, and other European goods, with which he was well supplied before leaving Holland.[4] The Indian owners, whose villages were not far distant from the site purchased by Hossitt, were the Algonkian-speaking group called by him the *Ciconicins*, a name given in many forms in the early records, e.g., *Sickonesyns, Siconesius, Siconese,* etc.[5] These Indians were also known to the Dutch as the *Great Siconese*, in contrast with the linguistically related *Little Siconese* living along Oldman's Creek in New Jersey.[6]

The sachem of the *Great Siconese*, at the time of the purchase by Hossitt, was a boy whose mother, according to the Algonkian concept of matrilineal descent, was evidently of " royal " blood. In view of the chief's minority, the Indian council appointed two adults, Quesquakous and Eesanques, to go to Manhattan, as requested by Hossitt, so that the sale could be officially confirmed by Director-General Minuit and registered as a patroonship in the records of the West India Company.

In the meantime, back in Holland, Samuel Godyn on June 19, 1629, notified the Amsterdam Chamber of his intent to become patroon of a colony on " the bay of the South River." He then sent a message to Minuit by a departing vessel requesting that he register the colony in the Company's books at Manhattan. By the time the message reached America, Minuit had independently taken the necessary action, for on July 11, 1630, Quesquakous and Eesanques appeared before him and his council to confirm the land sale to Hossitt, acting for the absent patroons. There are two documents covering the transaction, one dated July 11

---

[4] Not only was Hossitt well provided with sufficient merchandise to make land purchases, but he was given " further consent that he might exchange the remaining mechandise for furs " (*ibid.*).

[5] *Dunlap & Weslager, 1950,* p. 38.

[6] C. A. Weslager, " Robert Evelyn's Indian Tribes and Place-Names of New Albion, " *Bulletin 9*, Archaeological Society of New Jersey, November, 1954, p.11 ; *Dunlap & Weslager, 1958,* p. 10.

and the second, with slightly different phraseology, dated July 15, both of which are reprinted in Appendix A.

Having completed this assignment for his employers, Hossitt sailed up the Hudson and, acting principally in van Rensselaer's behalf, on July 27 bought land which was to become part of another patroon colony called Rensselaerswyck. This colony covered a much larger land area than Swanendael, parts of it having been bought from the Indians in May by Bastiaen Jansz Krol, the commis, and Dirk Cornelisz Duyster, his assistant, in van Rensselaer's behalf. Hossitt's purchase increased the size of the territory for van Rensselaer. An interesting aside to Hossitt's purchase occurs in a contract written in the Dutch language which the historian James Grant Wilson discovered in Amsterdam. An English translation quoted in the first volume of his *Memorial History of New York* contains the following pertinent passage :

That Gilles Hosset, on the twenty-seventh of July, 1630 in sailing up the river, arriving at the place where Jan Jansz Meyns was encamped with his men for the cutting of round timber for the new ship . . . . .

The " new ship " was the vessel *New Netherland*, built and launched during Minuit's administration. (Wilson states, without giving any authority, that it occurred to two Walloon shipbuilders to utilize American timber to construct a vessel instead of exporting it ; that Minuit was won over to the project, encouraged it, and pledged the Company's funds for its execution.) In Chapter 7 we will see that the Company was severely criticized for permitting this expenditure, which was deemed an extravagance.

Back in Holland another director of the Company, Albert Conraets Burgh, having been informed of Hossitt's purchase for Godyn, registered a third colony, November 1, 1629. This patroonship was to be located on the east side of the Delaware

Bay, in present-day New Jersey, opposite the proposed site of Godyn's Swanendael. Although no immediate action was authorized to extinguish the Indian ownership, Burgh indicated it was his intention to send out colonists at the first opportunity. This, too, was doubtless to have whale fishing as its principal objective.

The four patroons — Godyn, Blommaert, van Rensselaer, and Burgh — entered into a joint account on February 1, 1630, for their projected colonies. We are not told the reason for this merger, but several advantages seem obvious ; for example, they could have one capitalization for the whole venture, so that in the event of failure of one colony the principal patroon retained an interest in the other colonies to balance his losses ; there were shipping advantages in sending vessels to distribute supplies or reinforcements to several points ; one colony could assist a sister colony in time of need. Godyn and Burgh planned their colonies to be laid down on the South River, van Rensselaer upon the Hudson, and Blommaert decided to locate his on the Connecticut River. In this interlocking directorate, it was planned that the principal patroon should own a two-fifths share of his own colony, the others each participating to the extent of one-fifth ownership each. For example Godyn, as the managing patroon of Swanendael, owned a two-fifths interest, whereas Blommaert, van Rensselaer, and Burgh each had one-fifth of a share. This was later changed. (See Appendix A for further details.)

Before the first colonists were sent to the South River, Godyn made arrangements with his partners to admit a number of other men as co-patroons in the Swanendael project. By the time the colony was laid down there was a total of ten subscribers. Prominent among them were the adventurous mariner, David Pietersen de Vries, and the geographer-historian, Johan de Laet. The others were Mathys van Ceulen, Nicholaes van Sitterich, Johan van Harinckhouck, and Heynrick Hamel. De Vries stated that he and de Laet were the first to be taken in with the original patroons and then the four others named above were admitted as co-patroons ; he adds that " we made a contract with one other whereby we were all placed on the same footing."[7] Each of the ten co-patroons of the Swanendael venture had served the Company, at one time or another, as a director. Appendix A includes excerpts from two letters written by van Rensselaer complaining that there were too many persons in the directorate of Swanendael, which caused confusion and quarreling.

The objectives in establishing Swanendael were unmistakably set forth by de Vries, " to carry on the whale fishery in that region, as to plant a colony for the cultivation of all sorts of grain for which the country is well adapted, and tobacco."[8] There can be no question that whale fishing was the first consideration ; in another passage, de Vries refers to the whale oil which " they thought they might realize a good profit thereon, and at the same time cultivate that fine country." Note the absence of any reference to the fur trade. This was a very touchy subject — not only were the opponents of the patroon plan suspicious that the patroons were trying to divert the fur trade to themselves, but Article XV of the *Charter of Freedoms* stated :

It shall also be permitted the aforesaid patroons, all along the coast of New Netherland and places circumjacent to trade their goods, products of that country, for all sorts of merchandise that may be had there *except* beavers, otters, minks and all sorts of peltry, which trade alone the Company reserves to itself. But permission for even this trade is granted at places where the Company has no agent, on the condition that such traders must bring all the peltry

---

[7] *Narratives, Myers,* p. 7.

[8] *Ibid.,* p. 8. It is not generally known that the patroons also registered a colony for " the Sankikans on the South River, " but it was not settled, according to van Rensselaer, because of lack of co-operation from the Company (*VRB,* p. 248). Regrettably the registration for this colony is evidently missing.

to the island of Manhattan, if it is in any way practicable, and there deliver them to the director, to be by him sent hither with the ships and goods, etc.

This question of the fur trade became a serious issue when Gillis Hossitt and Jacob Jansz returned from New Netherland in 1630 to make a report to their employers. They had not only purchased lands from the Indians, but in the patroons' interests had traded their excess merchandise for peltries, which some of the members felt should not have been allowed. Hossitt's return to Holland, incidentally, has been overlooked by a number of historians, who assumed he remained in America and joined the settlers when they arrived at Swanendael from Holland. His return home is described, as well as the criticism advanced by other members of the Company regarding his engaging in the fur trade, in a memorial presented by van Rensselaer to the Assembly of XIX on November 25, 1633. Therein is found the following account :

These persons on returning home reported with joy that, to the great satisfaction of the inhabitants, though in spite of the opponents, they had purchased, paid for and obtained title to the land ; that, furthermore, they had exchanged the remaining merchandise for furs and sent these with bill of lading and with knowledge of the director [Peter Minuit] to their patroon [Samuel Godyn]. The returns of the sale of these furs, amounting to about f5,600 (from which must be deducted the merchandise given in exchange, the interest, the insurance, the expenses, the freight, and the duty to the Company), were so magnified by the contrary-minded, who had their supporters as well among the directors as among the chief participants, that [it seemed that] two individuals with but a small quantity of merchandise had purchased a large quantity of land and had besides obtained immense returns, from which these opponents took occasion to proclaim that the patroons were not contemplating colonization at all, but only the securing to themselves of the fur trade and depriving the Company of the same, which would be total ruin to the Company, etc.[9]

Hossitt made a map of the South River when he was in America, as ordered by Godyn. (See fn. 1 of the document dated June 1, 1629, in Appendix A.) The whereabouts of the original state of this map is not known, nor is it certain that it is still in existence, but it must have influenced other seventeenth-century Dutch cartographers.

Article III of the *Charter of Freedoms* obligated the patroon to send a minimum of fifty settlers to his colony, one quarter within one year and the remainder before the end of three years. Colonists were to be transported in the Company's ships, unless permission was given to the patroons to use private vessels. Since the Company's ships were often overcrowded and their departures and returns irregular, Godyn and his associates obtained special permission to outfit their own vessel, an 18-gun ship of one-hundred-and-fifty lasts appropriately called the *Walvis* (*Whale*). They engaged as her master Captain Peter Heyes of Edam, a navigator who had experience sailing Dutch whaling vessels in the waters off Greenland. Gillis Hossitt, perhaps as a reward for his services to the patroons, was employed as the agent or *commis* in charge of the colony. The *Walvis* left Holland on December 12, 1630, with eighty persons aboard, and a cargo of lime, bricks, tiles, four horses, twelve cows, ammunition, provisions, merchandise, tools, and several small whaling boats. The account of her cargo and her sailing is given in the aforementioned memorial by van Rensselaer, reprinted in Appendix A.

The *Walvis* sailed first to the West Indies to discharge a number of her passengers for another colony in the making, and then proceeded with the others to New Netherland. Hossitt, an experienced seaman, probably guided Heyes through the shoals in Delaware Bay to the land which he had purchased the previous

---

[9] *VRB*, p. 239.

year from the Indians ; perhaps he used as reference a copy of the map he had made for Godyn. There on the stream named Blommaert's Kill (later to be known as the Hoerenkil and much later as Lewes Creek) a total of twenty-eight men were placed. There were no women or children in the colony ; presumably they would be sent later at the discretion of the patroons. Godyn's name became attached to the bay and it would be so known for many years to follow in Dutch journals and maps. In his colony on the Hudson, van Rensselaer honored his associates by assigning their names to certain physical features, i.e., *de Laets Kill, de Laets Island, Godyns Kill, Godyns Island, Godynsburch, Blommaerts Kill, Blommaerts Island, Blommaertsburch,* etc. Apparently Godyn did not return the favor ; at least, no record has yet been found of local place-names preserving the names of any of the other eight co-patroons of Swanendael..[10]

The time of the arrival of the *Walvis* in Delaware Bay is usually given as the spring of 1631, and although the date is unknown, it must have been prior to May 5. On that day, Captain Heyes and Hossitt bought an additional fourteen square (Dutch) miles of land from the Indians on the east side of the bay. The purchase was confirmed June 3, 1631, at Manhattan by ten of the Indian owners in the presence of Director-General Minuit, Heyes, Hossitt, and the members of Minuit's council, some of whom were the Dutch skippers then present (see Appendix A). This purchase was intended to pave the way for seating the second South Bay colony, of which Albert Conraets Burgh was the principal patroon. Following this transaction, Hossitt returned to Swanendael to complete the house and the fortifications, clear and plow the land for cultivation, and prepare for the whaling season.

---

[10] Conratz Bay (Sandy Hook Bay) was named for Albert Conraets Burgh (see *Buchelius Chart,* frontispiece, *Narratives, Jameson,* see also p. 102). Hamels-Hoofden may have been named for the patroon Heynrick Hamel (*ibid.,* p. 102).

When the construction at Swanendael was finished, there was a large dwelling house of yellow bricks brought from Holland ; the house was surrounded with palisades. There was also a cookhouse made of brick, probably outfitted with vats for boiling whale blubber. Although the place has been referred to as Fort Oplandt, this name appears to be a corruption of a descriptive phrase used by de Vries which has been mistranslated.[11] Evidently no individual houses were built, nor were individual plots of land laid out for the men. They occupied the main brick structure as a sort of barracks ; there was a loft in it where merchandise used in the Indian trade was stored, and a pair of stairs leading to the loft. Hossitt's quarters were also in this main house. Unfortunately no record exists of the names and occupations of the original settlers. There must have been a bricklayer or carpenter among them, as well as farmers and harpooners experienced in catching whales, cutting up the blubber, and removing the valuable whalebone. All the " charts, maps and papers " concerning the colony were turned over to the West India Company by the patroons in 1635 and are among the missing records.

Leaving Hossitt after the land purchase from the Indians, Captain Heyes turned the prow of the *Walvis* homeward, arriving in Amsterdam in September with a complete report for the patroons. He did not bring them any whale oil from the South Bay, nor any merchandise from the West Indies, which they had hoped he would carry home to pay for the voyage. The trip had been an unprofitable one — Heyes brought back only " a sample of oil from a dead whale found on the shore."[12] Heyes reported that he had arrived in the South Bay too late for the whaling season, which the patroons learned was from December to March. Some of the patroons objected to investing additional money in the venture, which seemed to hold little prospects for commercial

[11] *Dunlap, 1956*, p. 29.
[12] *Narratives, Myers*, p. 8.

success. Godyn retaliated by telling them that the Greenland Company, chartered in 1614 with a monopoly in the waters between Davis Straits and Nova Zemlya, had suffered two bad voyages before enjoying any profits.[13] As a result of his insistence and encouragement, the patroons agreed to equip a ship and a small yacht and sail again to Swanendael with the aim of arriving at the beginning of the whaling season. The principal aim of this voyage was " to conduct the whale fishing during the winter, as the whales come in winter and remain till March." The vessels, incidentally, would also carry supplies to Hossitt and the colonists. De Vries was named leader of this expedition, which was made ready early in 1632. Only thirty-seven years of age, he was a capable and experienced commander, having made his first voyage in 1618 to the Mediterranean, followed by other voyages to different parts of the world. He had recently returned from the East Indies, where he had gone in 1627 while in the service of France as captain of a fleet of seven vessels. De Vries said of his voyage to America that he was the first patroon actually to visit the New World, a statement which cannot be disputed. Very little information is known about his crew, but there must have been included sailors experienced in whale fishing.

The *Charter of Freedoms* required the patroon to replace the agent of his colony every two years, and Hendrick de Forest was selected to accompany de Vries as Hossitt's successor.[14] Before de Vries sailed, news reached Holland that the Swanendael colony had been destroyed by the Indians and all the men massacred![15] De Vries stated later that it was proposed that the Company

---

[13] *Ibid.*

[14] *VRB*, p. 75, fn. 24.

[15] Minuit probably brought the news of Swanendael's destruction ; he arrived at Plymouth April 3, 1632, en route to Holland "with quite a number of people, their wives and children on board." Although detained by the English, Minuit had ample opportunity to send messages to Holland (*NYCD*, 1 :45, 46).

avenge this murder by making war against the Indians, the patroons reminding the directors that Article XXV of the *Charter of Freedoms* obligated the Company to protect the colonies laid down by the patroons. However, punitive action, which was strongly recommended by Godyn, was not taken, and de Vries wrote, " The Company would not permit it and replied we must keep at peace with the Indians."

On May 24, de Vries sailed from the Texel in the *Walvis* with fifty men aboard, accompanied by a yacht of ten lasts named *Teencoorntgen (Little Squirrel)*. The account of the voyage, the story of the arrival at Swanendael, and the incidents that followed are related by de Vries in his journal, a remarkable story of personal experiences in the New Netherland.[16]

In his journal de Vries relates that when he arrived at Swanendael he found the house destroyed and the palisades burned. Scattered over the property were the skulls and bones of thirty-two men[17] and the skulls of the horses and cows they had brought from Holland and the calves that had been born since the landing. An Indian informant told de Vries what had happened, and since there were evidently no survivors, the native's version is the only account of the massacre.

It seems that Hossitt had set up a post to which was fastened a piece of metal painted with the arms of Holland. One of the Indians, intrigued with the metal, took it to make tobacco pipes

---

[16] Published at Alkmaar, Holland, in 1655, it bears a lengthy title but is usually referred to as the *Korte Historiael*. Sections relating to New Netherland were translated by Henry C. Murphy and published in 1853 by James Lenox, and again in 1857 by the New York Historical Society in its *Collections,* 2nd Series, 3 : 1-129. A Dutch edition was published in 1911, *Korte Historiael ende Journaels Aeteyckeninge,* ed. H. T. Colenbrander, 's-Gravenhage. Excerpts from the journal were revised by van Laer and English versions published in *Narratives, Myers, pp.* 7-29.

[17] There were twenty-eight men in the original colony, but de Vries himself states that thirty-two were killed (*Colls. N.Y. Hist. Soc.,* 2nd Series, 1 : 268). This indicates that reinforcements, probably from Manhattan, joined the original group prior to the massacre.

not realizing that the Dutch would consider it a serious affront to their government. The Dutch became incensed over the misdeed and the Indians wanted to make amends. They slew their guilty comrade and brought his head to the Dutch as a token of their remorse. Instead of showing forgiveness, this act of extreme rashness further displeased the Dutch, and Hossitt evidently reproved the Indians for committing what he considered a terrible crime. The Indians then left, angered and confused at the unreasonable attitude shown by the Dutch. The friends of the slain Indian planned vengeance against the white men. They waited until an opportune time when the Dutchmen were working in the field. Three Indians approached Hossitt, who was standing near the house, under pretense of wanting to trade beaver skins for Dutch goods. Hossitt invited them into the house and he ascended the stairs to the loft where the stores were kept. As he descended the stairs, Hossitt was attacked, one of the Indians cleft his skull with an axe, and he fell dead. The Indians then killed a sick man who lay abed in the house. Then they turned on a dog, chained to a post, and shot twenty-five arrows into his body before he died. Other Indians then joined the first three and together they went into the field where the men were working, and going among them " with pretensions of friendship struck them down."

The Swanendael massacre is often attributed to Hossitt's bad judgment, but only one side of the story has been told. The full facts leading to the bloodiest massacre that ever took place along the Delaware will never be known. In Appendix A are reprinted seventeenth-century references to the massacre.

The directors of the Company held fast to their refusal to move against the Indians, deferring to the articulate group of stockholders who had strongly opposed the patroon movement from the beginning. The Company had been extremely uncooperative in Godyn's Swanendael venture, as de Vries wrote,

" constraining him to dismiss the people whom he had undertaken to convey thither and surrender them [the colony] to the Company."[18]

Due to pressure from the anti-patroon faction, de Vries was not permitted by the Company to take more than three-hundred guilders worth of merchandise for the Indian trade " for which they obtained about two-hundred beaver and otter skins while they would have obtained much more from nations who had never traded with the Company if they had more merchandise . . . ."[19] The small quantity of trade goods permitted de Vries was largely used as presents in negotiating a treaty and restoring friendly relations with the Indians at Swanendael ; he gave them " duffels, bullets, hatchets and various Nuremberg trinkets. They promised to make a present to us, as they had been out a-hunting."[20] Evidently some of the two-hundred peltries de Vries carried back to Holland were obtained from these natives.

De Vries was very disappointed in the whale fishing ; he saw a number of whales in Delaware Bay, and his men actually killed seven of them and set up a kettle in which to render the blubber. However, these seven whales produced only " 32 cartels " of oil. En route to Holland he stopped at Manhattan, and when queried by Governor van Twiller about whale fishing in the South River, he replied,

I answered him that we had a sample ; but that they were foolish who undertook the whale-fishery here at such great expense, when they could have readily ascertained with one, two or three sloops in New Netherland, whether it was good fishing or not. Godyn had been a manager of the Company as long as the Company had been

---

[18] *VRB,* p. 239.

[19] *VRB,* pp. 241-242.

[20] *Narratives, Myers,* p. 17. It was probably the trouble-making secretary, Johan van Remund, successor to de Rasière, who complained about de Vries' trading for furs. He tried to confiscate some of the beaver skins from de Vries (*ibid.,* p. 190).

in existence, and also of the Greenland Company at Amsterdam and ought to have known how it at first ought to have been undertaken with little expense.[21]

Upon his return to Amsterdam on July 24, 1633, de Vries found his merchant partners engaged in heated dispute with the anti-patroon faction in the Company, who had gotten wind of his having obtained furs from the Indians, even though the quantity involved was insignificant. The belief persisted that the patroons were trying to take the fur trade away from the Company. Impatient with this internal bickering, grieved over the failure of the Swanendael venture, disgusted with the contention among the co-patroons, de Vries withdrew from the syndicate and set out independently as a patroon in his own right. This effort also proved to be a failure.

As a result of the massacre of the colonists at Swanendael, lack of success in whale fishing, and friction within the Company, no settlers were ever placed on Burgh's land on the east side of Delaware Bay. Godyn and his associates also gave up further colonization at Swanendael. In 1635, having allowed their land rights to lapse, under the provisions of the *Charter of Freedoms,* the patroons transferred the two " South Bay tracts " to the Company for 16,500 guilders. They had suffered a substantial financial loss in this venture. The document effecting the transfer to the Company is included in Appendix A.

The English had also been disappointed in the quality of the whales found in American waters ; in 1614 Captain John Smith arrived in New England, and he wrote, " our plot was there to take Whales and make tryalls of a Myne of Gold and Copper."[22] After some experience, Smith concluded the whales were " a kinde of Iubartes, and not the Whale that Yeeldes Finnes [whale bone]

---

[21] *Narratives, Jameson,* p. 187.
[22] *Smith's Travels,* Arber-Bradley, 1910 edition, 1 : 187.

and Oyle as we expected." [23] Undoubtedly porpoises, grampus, and similar fish were confused with whales, but it would be incorrect to conclude that whaling in American waters was entirely unprofitable. In 1683, William Penn wrote that two companies of whalers would soon begin their work in Delaware Bay, and two years later he said, " Mighty Whales roll upon the coast, near the Mouth of the Bay of Delaware. Eleven caught and workt into Oyl one season. We justly hope a considerable profit by a Whalery ; they being so numerous and the shore so suitable." [24] The same type of coastal whale fishing was carried on in waters off the south of Long Island, Denton stating that " in the Winter lie store of Whales and Crampasses which the inhabitants begin with small boats to make a trade Catching to their no small benefit." [25]

The West India Company made no attempt to reopen the whale fishery after taking over Swanendael. Evidently Dutch traders continued to visit the bay area from time to time to barter for furs with the Indians, but the Company did not re-populate the settlement. The name Swanendael eventually fell into disuse, and the indelicate name, Hoerenkil (" Harlot's Creek "), became widely used as the area name. Under a number of variants, including the anglicized " Whore Kill," the place was so identified on maps and journals. As time went on, this place-name came to be used broadly to refer to a large district of land lying in what is now Kent and Sussex Counties, Delaware. The question

---

[23] *Ibid.*

[24] *Narratives, Myers,* pp. 241, 229, 265. James Claypoole in 1684 wrote that several Companies were engaged in whaling one-hundred-and-fifty miles off the Delaware shore and a whale producing " several hundred Barrels of Yole " had been reported caught (*ibid.,* p. 293, fn. 1), Gabriael Thomas wrote, " The Commodities of Capmay County [present-day New Jersey] are oyl and Whale-Bone, of which they make prodigious nay vast quantities every year, having mightily advanced that great Fishery, taking great numbers of Whales yearly " (*ibid.,* p. 352).

[25] Daniel Denton, *A Brief Description of New York* (1670), Gowan's " Bibliotheca Americana, " New York, 1845, p. 6.

of the derivation of the name has provoked a friendly disagreement between two authors, each of whom has expressed his opinion relative to its origin in separately written papers.[26]

In 1657, two boatloads of Englishmen were shipwrecked at the Hoerenkil, and the members of the party were captured by the Indians.[27] The Dutch later ransomed fourteen of these Englishmen, and the very fact that this rival nation was again trespassing on their territory called for action by the Dutch. The officials decided that the Hoerenkil should again be fortified to exclude the English and with the expectation that trade with the Indians could be improved and perhaps colonists could be encouraged to settle there.

There was the matter of paying the Siconese Indians to be considered ; they were growing less friendly, although thirty-nine years before Hossitt had bought land on the creek from them for the Dutch. William Beekman, Alexander d'Hinoyossa, and twenty soldiers, well supplied with trade goods, went south under orders to seek the native owners. They " sent out a savage for the chiefs of that country there that they should come down to make an agreement with them." Subsequently, on June 7, 1659, an agreement and bill of sale was drawn up and signed by sixteen chiefs and great men. The Indians deeded to the Dutch a strip of land lying between Cape Henlopen and present-day Bombay Hook on the west side of the Delaware, extending westward about thirty miles. A contemporary English translation of the document was published by one of the present authors in 1949,[28] and is reprinted in Appendix A.

Following the purchase, Stuyvesant ordered the Hoerenkil

---

[26] The latest opinions may be found in *Dunlap, 1956*, p. 34, and C. A. Weslager, " An Early American Name Puzzle, " *Names*, 2, No. 4 (Dec., 1954), pp. 255-262.

[27] *NYCD*, 12 : 201.

[28] C. A. Weslager, " The Indians of Lewes, Delaware, and an unpublished Indian deed dated June 7, 1659," *BASD*, 4, No. 5, (January, 1949), 6-14.

fortified to keep off intruders, and in 1659 a fort was built, usually referred to as "the Company's fort."[29] A sailboat ferry was in operation in 1660 to facilitate movement back and forth to the New Jersey shore. A " garrison " is also mentioned the same year, but its size is not given.[30]

Because of losses and drains on its resources, the West India Company could not maintain its position on the Delaware, and in 1656 sold Fort Casimir and the lands between the Christina River and Bombay Hook to the city of Amsterdam. In 1663, the city bought the whole river (including " the company's fort " at the Hoerenkil) and the bordering lands from the Company. During the period of the city's ownership, the director was responsible to the burgomasters of the city. With the permission and encouragement of the burgomasters, another Dutch colony was started at the Hoerenkil under the leadership of one Peter Cornelis Plockhoy, a Mennonite. Plockhoy envisioned an ideal, semi-socialistic community based on the equality of man and held together by Christian principles. Reprinted in Appendix A is his contract with the burgomasters and magistrates of Amsterdam, executed on June 9, 1662 — the final Dutch attempt to organize a colony on the Delaware.

A year after the contract was signed — July of 1663 — Plockhoy settled " 41 souls with their baggage and farm-utensils at the Horekil,"[31] but the colony had short life. In 1664, when Sir Robert Carr seized the Delaware territory for the Duke of York, he either confiscated or destroyed the property of Plockhoy and his followers. Gerrit van Sweringen, one of the Dutch officials on the Delaware at the time of the attack, wrote :

There was likewise a boate dispatched to the Whorekill and there

---

[29] *NYCD,* 12 : 273.
[30] *Ibid.,* p. 321.
[31] *NYCD,* 12 : 436 ; see also Leland Harder, " Plockhoy and His Settlement at Zwanendael," *Del. History,* 3, No. 3 (March, 1949), 138-154.

plundred and tooke possession of all effects belonging to the Citty of Amsterdam, as alsoe what belonged to the Quaking Society of Plockhoy to a very naile, according to letter written by one of that company to the Citty of Amsterdam, in which letter complaint was made that the Indians at the Whorekill had declared they never sold the Dutch any land to inhabitt.[32]

Plockhoy remained at the Hoerenkil for several years following the English attack, and then moved to Germantown in Philadelphia, where he died. Perhaps some of his followers continued to live at the Hoerenkil—persons with such names as Wiltbanck, Wolgast, Klasen, Kipshaven, Gronedick, and Droochstraeder (just to mention certain of the non-English surnames in a list of 1671) lived there under the English government.[33] Some of the events that took place during the early days of English control have been recorded,[34] but one incident, which is not well known, brought disaster to both Dutch and English occupants. During the period of Dutch reoccupation—starting August 8, 1673, with the seizure of New Castle from the English and continuing until February 19, 1674—the Hoerenkil again fell under Dutch authority. To prevent the Dutch from taking the houses there, Charles Calvert, Lord Baltimore, sent forty horsemen under command of Captain Thomas Howell to sack the settlement. On the cold Christmas Eve of 1673, they burned down all of the dwellings, after taking away all the boats and weapons of the occupants. A deposition by Philemon Lloyd giving an account of this assault, which has not previously appeared in print, is included in Appendix A.[35]

As time passed, the animosity was forgotten, and the Hoerenkil

---

[32] *NYCD,* 3:346.

[33] *Ibid,* 12:522.

[34] C. H. B. Turner, *Some Records of Sussex County, Delaware,* Philadelphia, 1909.

[35] Leon de Valinger, Jr. published five other contemporary depositions narrating this tragic story ("The Burning of the Whorekill, 1673," *Penna. Magazine,* 74, No. 4 [October, 1950], 473-487).

was developed as a port for ships, under English control. In September, 1680, the justices of the court there asked Governor Andros " to give the whorekill some other name,"[36] a request that does not seem unreasonable. He evidently complied, for a reference the following June indicates the court was being held at " Deale for the Towne and County of Deale." The new name had little opportunity to become established before William Penn, in 1682, again changed the name of the county to Sussex — and on January 9, 1682, court was held at " Lewis for the County of Sussex."[37] Lewis became Lewes, the present name, and the indelicate " Hoerenkil," and its English equivalent, eventually fell into disuse.

[36] *NYCD*, 12:659.

[37] Turner, *op. cit.*, p. 85. Penn personally paid a visit to the Whorekill in 1682 (*Maryland Archives*, 24:374).

V

Indians—and the Building of Fort Nassau

The Indians with whom the Dutch explorers and colonists were thrown into contact belonged to two different language groups. Among those speaking the Iroquoian tongue were the members of the strong, aggressive League of the Five Nations— the Mohawk, Oneida, Onondaga, Cayuga, and Seneca, living in upper New York state—and the so-called Minquas, occupying the Susquehanna River and its tributaries in eastern Pennsylvania. The second linguistic group, those speaking the Algonkian language, comprised the tribes on Long Island, Manhattan Island, and in the territory drained by the Hudson River and its tributaries. Also included among the Algonkian-speaking Indians were the natives of New England, as well as the Lenni Lenape, whose principal villages were in the area of the Delaware River system.

The Algonkian and Iroquois peoples differed in cultural traits as well as language, an important consideration in understanding Dutch relations with the Indians. The Dutch minister, Johannes Megapolensis, recognized the linguistic difference when he wrote of the Mohican (Algonkian) and Mohawk (Iroquois) that " These two nations have different languages, which have no affinity with each other, like Dutch and Latin."[1]

When the Dutch arrived in America, the Five-Nations Iroquois had conquered and were exercising an overlordship over some of the neighboring Algonkians and were intimidating others. The Minquas had also been attacking villages of the Algonkians,

---

[1] *Narratives, Jameson,* p. 172.

particularly those situated on the west side of the Delaware River. To further complicate a situation which was difficult for the newly-arrived Dutch to understand, the Five Nations had been sending war parties to raid the Minquas villages in Pennsylvania.

This inter-tribal warfare was characterized by many native practices unfamiliar and strange to the Dutch : the paying of wampum tribute by a subjugated tribe to their conquerors ; the feminization of certain of the defeated Lenni Lenape by the Five Nations, symbolically depriving them of male accoutrements; the Mohawk acquisition of lands on the upper Hudson through conquest of the Mohican ; the Minquas proprietorship, also by right of conquest, over the homeland of the Lenni Lenape ; the loss, some years later, by the Minquas of their own territory to the conquering Five Nations, who settled thereon other tributary nations ; the influence of matrons in the Five Nations councils ; the functions of war chiefs in Indian society. Not only were the Dutch and other Europeans ignorant about these and other native customs and beliefs, but they evidently had little interest in enlightening themselves.

Misunderstandings, such as occurred at Swanendael, were often at the root of Indian troubles. Yet, with few exceptions, the officers of the West India Company and its employees had no desire to devote serious study to Indian customs, nor did other Europeans during the period of exploration and settlement. The Indian way of life seemed primitive, in some phases barbaric, when measured against European standards of living, and the whites saw no reason to study a patently inferior, unchristian race. As we reread the journals of the early explorers we find only brief notes, based on superficial observation, about the Indians. When they referred to the Indians as " heathens," for example, Dutch scribes reflected the naïve attitude of most Europeans toward Indian religion. They obviously did not know that there existed among the natives a well-developed pattern of religious beliefs, practices, and ceremonies based on a pantheism as sacred to the Indians as Christianity was to the whites. De Laet illustrated this lack of understanding when he wrote : " They have no sense of religion, no worship of God ; they indeed pay homage to the devil."[2]

The regulations for the colonists who accompanied May in 1624 enjoined them " by their Christian life and conduct seek to draw the Indians and other blind people to the knowledge of God and his word. . . ."[3] Verhulst was also instructed that " by the example of godliness and outward discipline on the part of the Christians the heathen may the sooner be brought to a knowledge of the same."[4] Jonas Michaëlius, the first Dutch minister in the New Netherland, wrote in 1628, soon after his arrival at Manhattan, that he hoped " to keep a watchful eye over these people [the Indians] and to learn as much as possible of their language, and to seek better opportunities for their instruction than hitherto it has been possible to find."[5] However, he found the Indians difficult to teach and later described them as being " stupid as garden poles, who serve nobody but the Devil." Moreover, he was so occupied with the problems of his Dutch and Walloon communicants at Manhattan, and in writing letters complaining about Director-General Minuit, that time did not permit him to conduct missions among the Indians.

Megapolensis, who arrived at Rensselaerswyck in 1642, patiently learned the language of the Mohawk in order to preach to them, but he was not very successful in winning native converts to the Reformed Church.[6] He spent two years teaching one Indian novitiate to read and write the Dutch language and instructing him in the Bible. The young fellow " took to drinking

---

[2] *Ibid,* p. 57.
[3] *Van Laer,* p. 2.
[4] *Ibid.,* p. 36.
[5] *Narratives, Jameson,* p. 129.
[6] *Ibid.,* p. 172.

brandy, he pawned the Bible, and turned into a regular beast, doing more harm than good among the Indians."[7] Unlike the Jesuit priests, certain of the Swedish Lutheran preachers, and the later Moravian missionaries, the ministers of the Dutch Reformed Church were not successful in spreading the Christian gospel among the Indians. So far as the West India Company was concerned, their commercial interests in the New World took precedence over spiritual redemption.

The Dutch ministers — as well as their countrymen — disparaged what, according to their moral standards, appeared to be loose marital relations and censurable conduct on the part of the Indian women. They also belittled the Indian husband who left the chores of the field and other menial tasks to his seemingly overburdened wife while he hunted and fished. In so doing, they showed further misunderstanding of the basic relations between the sexes in Indian society, the necessary division of labor, and the place held by women in the family.

The Dutch also failed to understand the tragedy of introducing the Indian to strong drink. They did not know the resultant sensations would be new to the Indian, who had never tasted alcohol ; they did not realize that the Indian had been disciplined from childhood never to display his emotions in interpersonal relations ; they did not realize that these inhibitions would suddenly be released, and with unpredictable results, by a cup of spirits. When a drunken Indian went beserk he was berated for not being able to hold his liquor and behaving like a beast. Social drinking in moderation or raising of a glass to seal a bargain or to cement the bonds of friendship were European customs which were never properly taught the Indian. He drank to become intoxicated. " They are great lovers of strong drink," Denton wrote, " yet do not care for drinking unless they have enough to make themselves drunk; and if there be so many in their Company, that

---

[7] *Ibid.*, p. 399.

there is not sufficient to make them all drunk, they usually select so many out of their Company, proportionable to the quantity of drink, and the rest must be spectators."[8]

Differences in the concept of land tenure between Indians and whites also caused mutual misunderstanding. The Algonkians, for example, did not grasp the Dutch institution of land ownership and sale. Land to them, like air, was everywhere and freely accessible to those who wanted to make use of it ; like the ocean waters, it could not be disposed of by sale. If Dutchmen were generous enough to want to enrich the Indians with articles of value to acquire " use " rights to the hunting territory or other lands occupied by Indians, that was evidence of the white man's good faith expressed in the best aboriginal manner. In transferring these " use " rights in exchange for the gifts, the Indians never intended permanently to dispose of land and exclude themselves from its use. This would have been suicidal to a people whose subsistence came from the forests and streams. Yet, when the Dutch " purchased " property from the Indians, they expected to possess it exclusively, as they did in Europe, and to deny the Indians further access if it so suited their purpose.

Like most Europeans, the Dutch were basically selfish in their relations with the Indians ; traders sought furs which the native trappers and hunters could supply ; employees of the West India Company wanted land or food ; military men were after allies ; preachers wanted converts ; others had different interests and aims. When they got what they wanted, the whites were inclined to regard the Indian as an intelligent and cooperative friend. When they did not get what they wanted, the tendency was to call the Indian a savage, a heathen, and refer to him in other uncomplimentary terms.

The Indians, who also had selfish interests, were not blameless

---

[8] Daniel Denton, *A Brief Description of New York* (1670), Gowan's " Bibliotheca Americana, " New York, 1845, p. 7.

in their conduct with the Dutch, and frequently they were guilty of starting trouble. They usually took the law into their own hands, failing to understand the peaceful, legal process for a redress of wrongs. They often misinterpreted actions taken by the whites and turned against those who were trying to befriend them. They made promises they did not keep, and were known to lie, cheat, and steal. Nevertheless, as we look into the past from the perspective that the years have afforded, certain facts must be recognized. It was the Indian whose homeland was being invaded, and the invaders brought such unwelcome evils as whiskey, guns, powder, and diseases to which the Indian had no immunity.

A trait in the culture of the eastern Indians was that of extending hospitality to visitors. Wassenaer wrote, "They are extremely hospitable, and one lodges with the other without thought of compensation." Denton added that if a white man chanced upon an Indian town, " they shall give you the best entertainment they have."[9] Not only would a visitor be given a comfortable place at the fireside, but he would receive food and other presents, and under certain circumstances he would be invited to share the wigwam and the favors of one of his host's daughters, or even of his wife.[10] The Dutch did not always recognize such warm hospitality as being offered in good faith ; to them it seemed to conceal treachery. Not to be taken by surprise, the Dutch visitor kept his gun loaded and within reach, and the Indian naturally assumed that the visitor intended harm. Thus, what was meant as a gesture of genuine friendship on the Indian's part became a cause of mistrust.

When Henry Hudson sailed into the river which now bears

---

[9] *Narratives, Jameson,* p. 70 ; Denton, *op. cit.,* p. 11.
[10] " The men are not jealous, " de Vries wrote, " and even lend their wives to a friend " (*Narratives, Jameson,* p. 218).

his name, Juet wrote, " . . . wee found very loving people, and very old men : where wee were well used."[11] But when the Indians came to visit Hudson on the vessel, Juet said they " came aboord of us making show of love, and gave us Tobacco and Indian Wheat . . . *but we durst not trust them.*"[12] The words italicized typify the suspicious attitude characteristic of the Europeans in their relations with the Indians.

Even on the initial contact between the crew of the *Half Moon* and the natives, there was serious trouble. John Colman was killed and two other of Hudson's seamen wounded ; a number of Indians were wounded or slain by the sailors during their explorations. The facts behind these assaults are not fully known, but an account of Hudson's voyage appearing in a Dutch history in 1648 stated candidly that Hudson's crew " lived on bad terms with the natives of the land, taking their things by violence."[13] Hudson himself acquainted the Indians of New Netherland with their first taste of Dutch liquor when he invited them into his cabin on the *Half Moon* "and gave them so much wine and Aqua vitae that they were all merrie."

When Hendrick Christiaensen (Corstiaenssen), who made a total of ten voyages to America, and Adriaen Block explored the Hudson River several years later, they persuaded two sons of one of the Indian sachems to return to Holland with them for a visit. Many of the Dutch merchants, as well as government officials, had not previously seen American Indians and the two natives were no doubt the center of attention. After returning to New Netherland, one of the lads, named Orson by the Dutch, killed

---

[11] *Ibid.,* p. 21.
[12] *Ibid.,* p. 20.
[13] *Verhael van de Eerste Schip-vaert der Hollandsche, etc.* trans. Brodhead, *Colls. N.Y. Hist. Soc.,* Second Series, 2 : Part 1 (1848), 369. Van Meteren also wrote of Hudson's crew that they " behaved badly toward the people of the country, taking their property by force . . . " (*Narratives, Jameson,* p. 7).

Christiaensen, according to Wassenaer, but he " was paid in like coin ; he got a bullet as his recompense."[14]

Wassenaer did not give any further details, but in the notarial records at Amsterdam there is reference to this incident that promoted suspicion and mistrust between the Dutch and Indians. It appears that Christiaensen (in the Dutch records he was also called " Hendrick Carstiens ") was in 1618 in command of a vessel, *de Swarte Beer* (*The Black Bear*), owned by two private merchants on a trading mission in the Hudson River. While bartering in the Hudson, the vessel was attacked by Indians (the native named Orson may have had something to do with the attack), with the result that the " said skipper and majority of the crew had been murdered in the said ship by the Indians." Only five members of the crew were left unharmed, including Jacob Janss Wit, the ship's carpenter, and Jacob Mayer, the cook, who told the story of the attack when they returned to Holland. Luckily, Adriaen Jorissen Thienpoint was trading in the Hudson River at the same time, in command of a small vessel from Vlissingen. He put several members of his crew aboard the crippled *de Swarte Beer,* repaired her, made the former carpenter the first mate, and brought her back to Holland safely.[15]

Two years after Christiaensen's death another of his fellow explorers, Cornelis Hendricksen, made the report to the States General mentioned in Chapter 2. The report included this passage :

that he also traded with the inhabitants of Minquaus and ransomed from them three persons belonging to the people of this Company, which three persons had suffered themselves to be

---

[14] *Narratives, Jameson,* pp. 78, 81. In 1614 Christiaensen was named a skipper (*NYCD,* 1 : 11) ; he was one of the first Dutch sailors to enter the Hudson (*Narratives, Jameson,* p. 78).

[15] *Iconography,* 6 : 5. A lesser-known skipper, Pieter Fransz, and two of his crew were killed by Indians in 1614 while attempting to trade in the Hudson in the vessel *De Vos* (*ibid.,* 4 : 41).

employed by the Maquas and Machicans giving for them kettles, corals, and merchandise.[16]

On the " Figurative Map " accompanying his report, the following legend appears :

Regarding what Kleytjen and his companion have told me of the situation of the River and the places occupied by the tribes, which they had found when going inland away from the Maquaas and along the New river down to the Ogehage namely the enemy of the aforesaid northern nations I cannot at present find anything but two sketches of small maps partly finished.

And when I think how best to make the one correspond with the rough notes to the best of my knowledge I find that the dwelling-places of the Sennecas, Gachoos, Capitannasses and Jottecas ought to have been indicated rather more to the West.

What these legends seem to mean is that a Dutchman named Kleytjen (sometimes spelled Klienties) and two companions, who had all evidently been stationed at Fort Nassau on the Hudson, made their way inland for reasons that are not clear. Hendricksen did not say what was the nature of their employment with the Mohawk and Mohican Indians, but in the course of their travels they made at least two sketch maps of undiscovered lands. When they reached the headwaters of the Delaware or Susquehanna Rivers they were taken prisoner by the Minquas Indians. In the meantime Hendricksen had sailed up the Delaware River on an exploring mission, and in the process of trading with the Indians he learned of his countrymen being held as prisoners. He effected their release by paying the Minquas a ransom in European goods. The Dutchmen then gave Hendricksen their sketches and notes, which he incorporated on his " Figurative Map." Apart from the relevance of this incident to the entries

---

[16] This translation, and the legend, are Stokes' version (*Iconography*, 2 : 73). A slightly different translation appears in *NYCD*, 1 : 14, where the map is reproduced.

on the map, it further shows that long before the Dutch sent colonists to New Netherland their representatives were in trouble with the Indians.

Reference has already been made to Kriekenbeeck's indiscretion at Fort Orange when he violated the neutrality the Company tried to maintain by siding with the Mohican Indians in their war with the Mohawk. Krieckenbeeck and three of his men were killed, many Indians were slain, and Dutch-Mohawk relations were badly strained.[17]

As the Dutch population increased, clashes with the natives became more and more frequent, culminating in the Indian war. During Kieft's administration atrocities were committed by both whites and Indians.[18] Following a truce in May of 1643 there was a temporary cessation of hostilities, but within a few months the Indians were on the warpath again, attacking farms and committing acts of terror against the colonists on the Hudson. The Dutch sought allies from the English in New England, and the war culminated in an attack by joint English and Dutch forces against the Indians, resulting in the death of more than five hundred men, women, and children.[19] Bad relations with the Indians continued through the Stuyvesant administration when the natives arose again and attacked the Dutch settlements.[20]

To the credit of the West India Company it must be said that the directors, desirous of keeping on good terms with the Indians, realized the importance of the Company's employees treating the natives with honesty and kindness. The *articulbrieff* dated March 28, 1624, instructed the colonists sent out on the *Nieu Nederlandt* that :

---

[17] *Narratives, Jameson,* p. 84 ; *Van Laer,* p. 212.

[18] De Vries gives details of this warfare (*Narratives, Jameson,* pp. 213-216, 225-234). Father Jogues (*ibid.,* p. 263) says sixteen-hundred men, women, and children were slain in 1643-1644, " which obliged the rest of the Indians to make peace."

[19] *Narratives, Jameson,* pp. 282-284.

[20] *Ibid.*

They shall take especial care whether in trading or in other matters faithfully to fulfill their promises to the Indians or other neighbors and not give them any offense without cause . . .[21]

The instructions to Willem Verhulst contained a number of rules to govern his conduct with the Indians. He was directed to " see that no one do the Indians any harm or violence, deceive, mock or condemn them in any way, but that in addition to good treatment they be shown honesty, faithfulness, and sincerity in all contracts, dealings, and intercourse, without being deceived by shortage of measure, weight or number, and that throughout friendly relations with them be maintained."[22]

The second set of instructions cautioned Verhulst to maintain good Indian relations " without however forcing them thereto in the least or taking possession by craft or fraud lest we call down the wrath of God upon our uprighteous beginnings, the Company intending in no wise to make war or hostile attack upon anyone, except the Spaniards, and their allies and others who are our declared enemies."[23]

Despite these injunctions, the officials and other employees of the Company failed to keep on good terms with the Indians. There were many factors contributing to this unsatisfactory situation, which had its inception in the days of exploration, worsened as settlements were established, then became critical as they grew larger. Some of the major cultural differences basic to the misunderstandings have already been cited, and to these must be added grievances and specific acts of aggression on record. The cattle of the Dutch farmers roamed the woods and trampled down the Indian cornfields, which were unfenced ; the Indians retaliated by killing the cattle, and the whites then punished the Indians ; traders persisted in selling rum and brandy to the

---

[21] *Van Laer*, p. 17.
[22] *Ibid.*, p. 39.
[23] *Ibid.*, p. 106.

Indians despite efforts by the authorities to prevent or control the liquor traffic ; Dutch traders bartered guns and ammunition, putting a new and terrible weapon in the Indians' possession ; Indians employed as domestics stole from the households where they worked ; whites stole corn and furs from the Indians ; unprincipled traders and soldiers took advantage of the Indian women ; traders cheated the Indians ; the Indians broke their solemn word to trade exclusively with the Dutch by taking their furs to others when the Dutch were temporarily out of goods to trade.[24]

Against these clouds that darkened Dutch-Indian relations on the Hudson and immediate vicinity, let us now see what happened on the Delaware River when the two peoples were thrown together.

The Lenni Lenape, who were later to become known as the Delaware Indians, were divided into a number of small groups, or bands, known to the whites by local names. These names were often transferred to the streams on which the Indians lived. In the seventeenth century, European writers and cartographers made references to the following Indians living on the east bank of the Delaware : *Sanhickans, Kechemeches, Manteses, Little Siconese (or Sikonesses), Asomoches, Eriwonek* (also given as *Armeomeks, Armewamese,* and so on) *Ramcock, Axion, Mosilian, Sewapois, Narraticons,* and others.[25] On the western side of the Delaware such names as *Passayunk, Okanickon, Minguannan* Indians, *Brandywine* Indians, and the like were used by whites to refer to particular Indian bands. In the Swanendael area dwelt the *Great Siconese,* to whom previous reference has been made.[26]

---

[24] See *Narratives, Jameson,* pp. 273, 274, 277, 303. An Indian name for the Dutch was *Swaneckes,* or *Swannekus (NYCD,* 13 :47, 85). The form *Swannekens* was also used. The meaning of the word is uncertain.

[25] C. A. Weslager, " Robert Evelyn's Indian Tribes and Place-Names of New Albion, " *Bulletin 9,* Archeological Society of New Jersey, Nov., 1954.

[26] Cf, Chapter 4.

Although these scattered groups were affiliated culturally and spoke dialects of the Algonkian language, they maintained a certain autonomy, having their own villages and chiefs. It was perhaps this loose organization that made them easy prey when the Minquas war parties invaded the Delaware Valley. There were two major groups of Minquas, the Minquas proper (also known as *Andastes* and sometimes as *White Minquas*) and the *Black Minquas,* so called because they wore gorgets of black stone. The Minquas were not only aggressive warriors, but they were skilled hunters and trappers, as indicated in the following passage from a Dutch contemporary account :

Thousands of Beavers can be bought here [on the Delaware] and around the Schuylkill . . . . brought down in great abundance by the Southern Indians, called Minquas, and by the Black Indians.[27]

The term " Southern Indians " was an inexact one, applied to the Minquas proper, probably because they lived in the territory south of Manhattan Island. The Algonkian word for southerners, *suwanoo, sauwanoo, sauna,* is shown on a number of seventeenth-century Dutch maps.[28]

The war between the Minquas and the Lenape was in progress when the Walloons first settled on the Delaware River, as was pointed out in Chapter 2. Some of the Indians living in villages on the west bank had deserted their homes and moved to the opposite side of the river to escape their enemies. Not only did the Minquas loot the Lenape towns and burn their cornfields, but they also stole their women.

When the Dutch began to trade with the Indians the Minquas apparently intensified their pressures on the Delaware River Indians. The cause of this war has never been satisfactorily explained, but it seems clear that it was prolonged because the

---

[27] *NYCD,* 1 : 588.
[28] A. R. Dunlap and E. J. Moyne, " The Finnish Language on the Delaware, " *American Speech,* 27, No. 2 (May, 1952), 87.

Minquas were deliberately trying to eliminate the Lenape as competitors in this profitable commerce so they would have it to themselves. This is what prompted de Rasière to say of the local Indians living along the Delaware that they were " afraid to hunt in winter being constantly harassed by war with the Minquas." [29] Unless they hunted in winter, when the best pelts were obtained they had nothing to trade with the Dutch.

The consuming desire on the part of the Dutch for furs, particularly beaver pelts (principally used in the manufacture of men's hats), was no less than that of the American Indians to possess what to them seemed priceless merchandise offered by the white merchants. Beads, hatchets, clay smoking-pipes, inexpensive jewelry, combs, mirrors, iron pots, jews'-harps, and household utensils were greatly in demand by the natives. One of the European products sought after by all the Indian peoples was the coarsely woven wool cloth known as " duffel cloth " or simply " duffels," named for the town of Duffel near Antwerp. Lindeström wrote that the Indians held this cloth " in as high esteem as the finest scarlet." [30] Prior to white contact the natives wore " a deer skin or mantle, a fathom square, of woven Turkey feathers or peltries sewed together. They now make great use of duffel cloths, blue or red, in consequence of the frequent visits of the Christians." [31]

Denton explained how the duffel cloth was worn, the Indians taking about a yard and a half " which they hang upon their shoulders ; and half a yard of the same cloth, which being put betwixt their legs and brought up before and behinde, and tied with a Girdle about their middle, hangs with a flap on either side." [32] Duffel cloth was also used at night as a bed covering in

---

[29] *Van Laer*, p. 211.
[30] *Lindeström*, p. 226.
[31] *Narratives, Jameson*, p. 270.
[32] Denton, *op. cit.*, p. 13.

lieu of blankets. Some white traders, according to Lindeström, cheated the Indians when measuring duffels, " the savage taking hold of a corner of the frieze and the Christian on the edge, whereupon they pull the hardest they are able, stretching thus the ell [about two yards] for the savage, so that he for three ells barely gets more than two ; which the savage thinks should be thus, and does not understand himself cheated in this." [33]

The aboriginal medium of exchange was bead " money," known as *sewan* or *sewant* to the Dutch. In New England it was called *wampumpeake* and abbreviated to *wampum* or *peake*. Among the Indians this *sewant* actually meant more than money meant to the Europeans, for it was used ceremonially as well as for personal adornment. When engaged in barter with the Indians for pelts, the white trader had to have a supply of *sewan*. For a time, the bead money was used by the inhabitants of New Netherland as a medium of exchange instead of Dutch money. Four beads of *sewan* on a string was valued at one stiver, about two cents. Six loose beads were of equivalent value. [34] The manufacture of these shell beads required much patience, labor, and a marked degree of skill, since the Indians, having no metal tools, worked with implements of bone and stone. The beads were wrought mostly by women and were of two colors, purple and white; the purple or dark-colored beads were considered more valuable than the white. The beads were strung singly on strands of sinew or were fabricated into belts in which symbolic figures were often neatly and deftly wrought.

With the intention of cheating the Indians, the Dutch were accused of manufacturing *sewan* in Holland and bringing a large quantity to New Netherland. The Indians saw that it was counterfeit and refused to accept it. [35] In the fur trade a beaver pelt was

---

[33] *Lindeström,* p. 226.
[34] *NYCD,* 1 : 344, 425.
[35] *Lindeström,* p. 232.

worth seven to eight florins in *sewan*, a florin being equivalent to twenty stivers, or approximately eighty cents per skin.[36]

Perhaps it was the competition to supply the white man with beaver pelts that was the cause of hostility between the Black Minquas and the Minquas proper. War broke out between them about 1653, at which time Governor Johan Printz wrote that the fur trade had been seriously affected because, as he said, " the Arrigahaga [Black Minquas] and the Susquahannoer [Minquas proper, or White Minquas] from whom the beavers come begin to fight one another."[37]

Arrigahaga seems to be a Swedish rendition of the Iroquoian word *Eriga*, with its variants *Rigué, Rike-haka*, and so on. These terms refer to the Indians who were known as the Cat (panther) Nation and were also called the *Erie*.[38] A legend on Augustine Herrman's map of 1670 states in part ". . . formerly those Black Mincquas came over as far as Delaware to trade but the *Sassquahana* and *Sinnicus* went over and destroyed that very great Nation." Since the Susquehanna Minquas and the Seneca were enemies, and not allies, Herrman's note can be taken to mean that they independently warred against the Black Minquas.

Owing to the loss of the West India Company's records, there is no account of Indian relations on the Delaware during the May–Thienpoint and Verhulst administrations. It is quite likely that land, doubtless including Burlington or High Island, was purchased from the Indians on behalf of the Company. Verhulst's instructions were clear that if any Indians " be living on the aforesaid Island or make any claim upon it . . . they must not be

---

[36] *Ibid.,* p. 224.

[37] *Inst. for Printz,* p. 188.

[38] *Bulletin 30,* Bureau of American Ethnology, Washington, D.C., 1907, 1 : 431 ; see also C. A. Weslager, " The Minquas and Their Early Relations with the Delaware Indians, " *BASD,* 4, No. 1 (May, 1943), 14-23. Johnson (*Swedish Settlements,* 1 : 190) errs in saying the Black Minquas could not be the Eries.

driven away by force . . . but by good words be persuaded to leave, or be given something therefore to their satisfaction . . . a contract being made thereof and signed by them in their manner." [39]

Since the West India Company's objective in the New World was to promote commerce — and since the Walloon settlers had been withdrawn from the Delaware — there was no reason for the Dutch to make extensive land purchases there from the Indians ; at least, this seems to have been the reasoning of the directors. The Company wanted animal pelts, and it did not require real estate on the Delaware River for the promulgation of this trade. From the time Hendricksen, May, and others had started to trade in the river, the Dutch enjoyed what amounted to a monopoly in the fur business there. All that was needed was a storehouse as the base of trading operations and, as de Rasière wrote, " having a fort there, one could control all the trade in the river," and it was for this reason that Nassau, a fortified storehouse, was built in the first place.

Many historians have stated that Cornelis Jacobsen May was the builder of Fort Nassau. Apparently the documentary evidence on which this assumption is founded occurs in a report drawn up in 1644 containing the following passage :

In the years 1622 and 1623, the West India Company took possession, by virtue of their charter, of the said country, and conveyed thither, in their ship, the New Netherland, divers colonists, under the direction of Cornelis Jacobsz Mey and Adriaen Jorissz. Thienpoint, which Directors, in the year 1624, built Fort Orange on the North River, and Fort Nassau on the South River, and after that, in 1626, Fort Amsterdam on the Manhattes. [40]

The date 1624 given above is incorrect for the building of

---

[39] *Van Laer,* pp. 51-52. These instructions may have also applied to Manhattan Island, which is relevant to the question as to whether it was purchased by Minuit or Verhulst.

[40] *NYCD,* 1 : 149.

Fort Nassau ; it was erected in 1626 after May had returned to Holland. The writer doubtless confused it with the trading post on Burlington Island, which was probably built in 1624 and whose builder was undoubtedly May. We now know from an unpublished Bontemantel document that this trading house was " provided with palisades and battlements though afterwards abandoned." [41] There are other factual errors in the above 1644 report which make it inadmissible as valid historic evidence.

After Fort Nassau was built, the Dutch found that it was needed only at certain times of the year. In the winter season (when the best animal pelts were to be had) the Indians roamed the forests trapping beaver and otter and hunting other game. Instead of maintaining permanent employees there, it was less expensive for the Company to send sloops from Manhattan at designated times to meet the Indians when they returned from hunting and were ready to barter their winter haul. Wassenaer wrote in 1628 that the Company was then retaining only one vessel in the Delaware for trading purposes.

In describing his visit to Fort Nassau in 1631 (see Chapter 2), Peter Lourenson mentioned a " trading house " and the presence of ten or twelve Company employees ; this was one of the occasions it was occupied. Following the Swanendael massacre, Fort Nassau remained the only Dutch post on the Delaware, and although it was occupied intermittently, the Company considered it the stronghold of their southern frontier. The boast made in an official report that it was " maintained with a constant garrison until the year 1650 " is, of course, an exaggeration. [42] On the other

---

[41] *New Netherland Papers,* Manuscript Division, New York Public Library, being the papers of Hans Bontemantel, sometimes known as the *Bontemantel papers,* which Victor H. Paltsits was in process of translating at the time of his death in 1951. The above is quoted from the document entitled " Extract from the general letter from New Netherland dated Oct. 30, 1655. "

[42] *NYCD,* 2 : 137.

hand, it was never actually vacated in a permanent sense, as some writers have surmised.

This post on the Delaware should not be confused with an earlier trading post, also called Fort Nassau, built on Castle Island near present Albany, and the predecessor of Fort Orange. The first Fort Nassau was destroyed by floods,[43] and its first commander, and probable builder, was the aforementioned Hendrick Christiaensen who lost his life in his vessel on the Hudson during an Indian attack. The use of the name Nassau for two forts commemorates the family of a Dutch hero, William the Silent, Prince of Orange, Stadholder of Holland and Zealand, and champion of the provinces in their revolt against Spain, who was from Nassau. Assassinated by an agent of the Spanish king in 1584, William was considered a martyr to the cause of freedom. One of his sons, Maurice of Nassau, became almost as popular as the father by gaining victory after victory over the Spanish until the twelve-year truce was signed in 1609. Maurice's younger half brother, Frederick Henry, was also popular with the people, and the latter's son, William, fell heir to the title of Prince of Orange.

Maurice, who died in 1625, was at the height of his popularity during the period of Dutch exploration of New Netherland ; his name was given to the Hudson River, usually Latinized as *Mauritius*. Fort Nassau on the Delaware was probably named in his honor, as the first Fort Nassau, built before his birth, had honored his illustrious father. Although it is difficult to relate the name of the specific individual intended, many of the geographical names in New Netherland, as well as names of vessels and forts, honored members of the family, e.g., *Nassau, Orange, William, Willems, Wilhelmus, Hendricx,* and so on. Sometimes the person's title appeared in the name, e.g., *Prince*

---

[43] *Brodhead*, p. 35.

William, Prins Maurits, Prince Hendricx, and the like.

No contemporary description of the southern Fort Nassau is on record, but it was probably constructed along the lines of other forts built by the Company or the patroons. Usually a central building of wood or brick was erected within a palisaded enclosure to serve as office for the Company's agent, or commis ; it was also used as a storehouse for pelts and for merchandise used in the Indian trade, and as a barracks for the soldiers. The palisades were logs sharpened at the tops and set closely together to form an enclosure, usually with bastions at the corners where cannon could be positioned. A site was customarily selected along a natural stream. The traders and soldiers lived within the palisaded area ; colonists could reside outside the palisades and fall back to the fort in the event of attack. At Fort Nassau there were no colonists to consider during the early years of its existence — they were to come later when competition with the Swedes for possession of the river grew keen.

Historians have long held divergent views about the site of Fort Nassau, and a joint effort by committees of the New Jersey Historical Society and the Pennsylvania Historical Society in 1852 did not settle the question. Their investigation was occasioned by the finding of an unidentified log structure at the confluence of Big Timber and Little Timber Creeks in Gloucester County, New Jersey. There was general agreement from a study of maps and documents that the fort belonged somewhere in this general area. After examining the log structures, the committees did not feel " warranted in expressing a belief that the ruins in question are a part and mark the site of Fort Nassau."[44]

Edward Armstrong, a member of the committee representing the Pennsylvania Society, prepared a paper outlining his observations during the search for the fort site. As an addendum he presented testimony of an elderly informant who stated the fort

---

[44] *Proceedings,* New Jersey Historical Society, 6, No. 4 (1853), 160.

had been situated on the south side of Big Timber Creek and " that the remains are still to be seen in a bank of earth of horse-shoe form, which have been pointed out as those of Fort Nassau. And further, that a number of Indian relics, and Dutch bricks, with letters upon them, were found at different times on the spot."[45] Armstrong agreed that this location deserved more thorough examination, but there is no record of such investigation ever having been made. Armstrong also suggested that information would probably come to light at some future date permitting the site of the fort to be placed with exactness.

Such data have, indeed, become available, and it is now possible to fix the location of Fort Nassau. The most convincing piece of evidence is a map made in 1643 entitled *Kaert vande Suyd Rivier in Niew Sweden* (facsimile in F. C. Wieder, *Monumenta Cartographica,* plate 79) on which the fort is indicated. It is shown on the east bank of the Delaware south of a stream called *Timmer Kill* and north of the *Verkeerde Kill* near the latter's point of junction with the Delaware.

Another contemporary map, c. 1630 (C.Pl.39, in *Iconography,* vol. 2) shows Fort Nassau immediately south of the *Timmer Kill.*

When these seventeenth-century maps are compared with modern maps it becomes clearly evident that the *Timmer Kill* is the stream now called Newton Creek. The stream now called Big Timber Creek is none other than the one shown on the old maps as *Verkeerde Kill* which means " wrong creek " or " turned about creek," probably from its course."[46] In terms of modern geography, Fort Nassau was situated on the east bank of the Delaware River on a point between Newton Creek and Big Timber Creek ; the site is probably covered by the present city of Gloucester. If one rereads that section of de Vries' journal describing his visit to

---

[45] Edward Armstrong, " The History and Location of Fort Nassau upon the Delaware, " *ibid.,* pp. 187-207.
[46] It is identified in Weslager, "Robert Evelyn's Indian Tribes," p. 8.

Fort Nassau in 1633, the relation of *Timmer Kill* to the fort becomes immediately apparent. He went past the fort on his way upstream to enter the *Timmer Kill.*[47] The *Timmer Kill,* however, was not present Big Timber Creek, as Myers would have us believe, nor was the fort, as he said, " near the south side of the mouth of the present Big Timber Creek."[48] Armstrong's informant also erroneously placed it here, a consideration which may have influenced Myers. The confusion between old *Timmer Kill* and the modern Big Timber Creek has caused this mistaken identification of the fort site.

Although Fort Nassau stood on a point of land close enough to the Delaware to challenge vessels coming up the east side of the river, it could by no means command the river. Its location, as the next chapter will reveal, proved to be both a commercial and military blunder.

De Vries' journal gives us a clear picture of the way the Indian trade was conducted at Fort Nassau. The Indians were accustomed to meeting Dutch trading vessels from Manhattan, and when they saw de Vries' yacht, *The Squirrel,* at anchor, some forty-two or forty-three Indians paddled out in their canoes and climbed aboard with quantities of beaver pelts. The fort was a sort of market place where Indians from both sides of the Delaware, as well as more distant places, came with their furs to await the coming of the Dutch. For the first ten years of their commerce in the Delaware, Dutch traders had practically no competitors ; they held the upper hand, and the Indians came to them. When the Swedes and English decided they ought to share in this profitable trade, the story was a different one ! Of course, the Dutch did not anticipate this rivalry, which was a serious mistake in judgment, and equally serious was their misunder-

---

[47] *Narratives, Myers,* pp.18-22. Hudde is authority for the information that the fort was on a " point " (*NYCD,* 12 : 370).

[48] *Narratives, Myers,* p. 18, fn. 3, and p. 19, fn. 2.

standing of two factors in Indian affairs. By overlooking these two things, the officials of the West India Company permitted Fort Nassau to become almost valueless as a trading post when other nationalities began to compete for the beaver trade.

First, the Minquas' war with the Lenape had a disruptive effect on the bands living on the Delaware, particularly those forced to flee from the west to the east bank. Displaced from their hunting territories, unsettled, and living in fear of their enemies, these local Indians were unable to produce the large quantities of pelts sought by the Dutch. What good was a trading post set in a land of defeated and impoverished people?

Secondly, the source of the highest quality beaver pelts was in the Minquas' homeland, ninety to one hundred miles west of the Delaware. When they came from their country bringing pelts to trade, the Minquas followed canoe routes and ancient land trails or portages, one of which led from the present-day Bohemia River to Appoquinimink Creek ; another brought them to the Christina River ; still another — and of especial importance to Fort Nassau — terminated on the southside of the Schuylkill River. The terminal points of these trails were on the *western* side of the Delaware River ; to make contact with the Dutch traders at Fort Nassau, the Minquas had to cross the river to the opposite shore. They could be expected to tolerate this inconvenience only until such a time as trading posts more accessible to them were erected on the western side of the river or somewhere nearer their homes.

Although Dutch vessels from Nassau sometimes crossed the river and sailed into the Schuylkill to meet the Minquas at designated points, the Company failed to see the importance, until it was almost too late, of protecting the Minquas trade routes by erecting strong posts on both the Christina and Schuylkill.

VI

Intruders, Forts, and Beaver Trade

In the summer of 1633, Arent Corssen, an employee of the West India Company, was sent from Manhattan to Fort Nassau. He crossed the Delaware River, sailed up the Schuylkill, and there purchased a small plot of land from the Passayunk Indians. The place was called *Armenveruis,* presumably an Indian word, but what it means is unknown ; however, it was one of the places where a Minquas trail touched the river. There he erected a small, crudely built trading post — not a permanent station, but a shelter to occupy when trade with the Indians was in process.[1] This was the first gesture indicating awareness by the Company that the western side of the Delaware could be potentially important in the fur trade. Now the Dutch sloops sent from Manhattan could make two profitable stops, first at Fort Nassau and next at the hut Corssen built — and they still had the beaver trade practically to themselves. Unknown to them, other nationals were preparing to challenge that monopoly.

In the fall of 1634 the two Englishmen previously mentioned, Thomas Yong and his nephew and lieutenant Robert Evelyn, came into the Delaware River, but neither in his writings made

---

[1] *NYCD,* 1 : 588. A list of Dutch grants indicates that land on the Schuylkill was patented June 8, 1633 (E. B. O'Callaghan, *History of New Netherland,* vol. 2, Appendix, p. 581). The Swedes later pulled down the structure and erected their own Fort Nya Korsholm on the site. Hudde was referring to the house Corssen built when he wrote in 1648 that " . . . the Swedes had destroyed the house heretofore which the Honorable Company had formerly in front of the Schuylkill, and built a fort there " (*Inst. for Printz.,* p. 274).

reference to Fort Nassau or the Dutch trading post on the Schuyl-kill. They did, however, encounter Dutch trading vessels, and Yong said they " came to trade as formerly they had done." In his " Relation " he deliberately avoided reference to prior Dutch occupation on the Delaware. In the letter he addressed to Sir Francis Windebanke accompanying the Relation, he indicated he intended to build a fortification on the Delaware ; see the complete letter in Appendix B. Yong may not have known about Swanendael and the settlement on Burlington Island, both of which were vacated at the time of his visit, but he certainly knew about Fort Nassau. There was a good reason why he did not mention the Dutch in terms of their having fortified or settled on the Delaware. The special commission issued to him by the king, " to search, discover and find out what parts are not yet inhabited in Virginia and other parts thereunto adjoining," contained the following qualification :

and in our Name and for our use to take possession of all such Countries, Lands and Territories, as are yet undiscovered or not actually in the possession of any Christian Prince, Country or State, and therein to erect our Banners . . . .[2]

Obviously, any admission by Yong of Dutch possession would have invalidated his right to claim that territory for his sovereign and his own personal gain. His expedition was at his own expense, and his commission empowered him to seize unsettled territory and to prohibit others from trading or settling there without getting a license from him. If he found gold, silver, or precious stones he was permitted to retain four-fifths, rendering one-fifth to the Crown. Furthermore — and this was overlooked by Myers and others — Yong was given authority " to make and set up Factories [i.e., trading houses where factors, or agents, could be

---

[2] The commission appears in Thomas Rymer's *Foedora,* 19 : 472-474 ; Yong's Relation is in *Narratives, Myers,* pp. 37-49.

stationed] in any places he shall discover, and there to fortify with Fortresses and Ordnance, and leave as many of our Subjects with Arms, Munition and other Provision at the discretion of the said Thomas Yong, as to himself shall seem needfull, thereby to resist those Nations and Countries that shall attempt by force to expell them from thence. . . ."

Yong's " Relation " says nothing about stationing men on the Delaware, but the accompanying letter to Windebanke indicates his intention of building a fort, which would obviously require a garrison. James Waye, in a deposition made in 1684 (see Appendix B) states that such a settlement was " made by one Peter Holmes an Englishman near fifty years since [i.e., 1634] brought thither by one Captain Young at a place called *Arrowamex.*" Waye's phraseology is confusing — it is not clear whether he meant that Yong placed Holmes and others at *Arrowamex* to establish an English base (after he had written his letter to Windebanke) or whether Holmes was one of a party landed by Yong in Virginia, who later came up the Delaware to take possession. The only other evidence that can be found to clarify the incident is in Governor Berkeley's letter of protest to the Swedes, written in 1642. The following passage suggests that Yong brought settlers, including Holmes, and placed them on the Delaware :

> and the same river and Bay possessed, planted and traded nyne years since [1634] by Captain Young, Lieft Euelin, Mr. Holmes and others . . . .[3]

---

[3] Swedish Settlements, 1 : 179, fn. 60. In a thesis entitled " Sir Edmund Plowden's New Albion Charter 1632-1785 " submitted in partial fulfillment of the requirements for the M.A. degree, University of Pennsylvania, Edward C. Carter II discusses this letter (p. 129). He points out that Sir Edmund Plowden had petitioned Charles I asking relief for unauthorised settlements being made in New Albion. Charles I reaffirmed Plowden's ownership ; in 1642 Plowden petitioned Parliament reciting his grievances, and Parliament wrote the governor and council of Virginia asking that assistance be given Sir Edmund. The above letter from Governor Berkeley to Printz, protesting the Swedish colony, was the result.

As he agreed to do before departing from England, Yong sent Lieutenant Evelyn as his courier back to England, via Virginia, with a relation of his travels and the letter to Windebanke, dated October 20, 1634. Both communications were written while he was still lying in the Delaware River ; since neither missive refers to a settlement having been made, he must have placed Holmes and his party at *Arrowamex* sometime after they were written.

Yong had another objective on this voyage, and there was only veiled reference to it in his commission. He was seeking that elusive goal that Henry Hudson and dozens of earlier adventurers had failed to find ; namely, the all-water passage to the Orient. Thus, after taking possession of the Delaware for England, and assuring himself that he could not pass through it to the western ocean, he evidently left a party of men and departed to seek the passage through the waters of New England. In leaving the men on the Delaware he was implementing his commission, which authorized him to " leave as many of our Subjects with Arms, Munition and other Provision . . . thereby to resist those Nations and Countries that shall attempt by force to expel them from thence and to keep and defend for Us the said Countries, Ports and Places."

There is no problem in identifying the place *Arrowamex* where these Englishmen were seated. The word is an English rendition of the form *Arwamus,* which Peter Lourenson stated was the name of the place where Fort Nassau was located. In a letter written to Sir Edmund Plowden's wife, Robert Evelyn refers to the place as *Eriwoneck,* stating it was " where we sate down." The name, an Algonkian word of unknown meaning, occurs in many variants, depending upon the ear conditioning of the scribe recording it. In its various forms it was also used to describe the Indians in the neighborhood, e.g. *Armeomeks, Armewanninge, Ermemormhai, Armewamese,* and so on. These Indians were not friendly to the whites — they were among a larger group who attempted to murder de Vries and his men when he visited Fort Nassau in 1633, and they attacked some of the Dutch settlers during Hudde's administration.

If credence can be given to James Waye's deposition, it was a threatened Indian attack that caused Holmes and his party to leave *Arrowamex*, aided by the Dutch. The Dutch had a different version of this incident, and their account provides a very interesting item of information : the English party had indeed " sate down " at *Arrowamex*, but the place of their seating was in the Dutch-built Fort Nassau ! Furthermore, as soon as Yong had left the river, either the Dutch ousted the Englishmen or the latter decided to leave due to a threatened Indian attack. On September 1, 1635, the English party was in Manhattan, and de Vries relates in his *Journal* what happened :

> While I was taking my leave of the governor [van Twiller] the bark of the Company arrived bringing 14 or 15 English with them, who had taken Fort Nassau from our people, as our people had no one in it, and intended to guard it with sloops, but they found they must take possession of it again, or else it would be lost to the English. This arrival of the Englishmen delayed me six days longer, as Governor Wouter van Twiller desired that I should take them to the English Virginias, where the English were expected to assist them. They therefore took their leave of Wouter van Twiller, who was governor, and came, bag and baggage on board my vessel.

De Vries said the English commander was " named Mr. Joris Hooms," probably the same person as the aforementioned Peter Holmes.[4] This passage from de Vries has been generally interpreted to mean that the Dutch captured the English intruders at

---

[4] This account is in *Narratives, Jameson,* p. 195. One of the English party was Thomas Hall, an indentured servant, who ran away from his master and became a prominent citizen at Manhattan. " He came to the South River in 1635, in the employ of an Englishman named Mr. Homs, being the same who intended to take Fort Nassau at that time and rob us of the South River," (*ibid.,* pp. 375–376).

Fort Nassau, taking them to Manhattan as prisoners. De Vries' words, however, do not make this a certainty, and viewed in light of the James Waye deposition it can be argued that the Englishmen asked the Dutch to take them away. De Vries carried the English party to Point Comfort in Virginia, as directed, arriving there September 10, 1635. There he found another vessel with twenty Englishmen preparing to sail to the Delaware to reinforce their countrymen. De Vries' arrival resulted in cancellation of the operation — thus the Dutch had successfully blocked the first English attempt to seat the Delaware.

The West India Company now began to have fears about the security of its position on the Delaware. The various directors and their councils at Manhattan had taken the Delaware for granted, but now the growing English colonies in New England and Virginia seemed to be closing in on New Netherland from the north and south. If the Walloons had not been withdrawn a decade earlier, or if Swanendael had been reoccupied when the company bought the lands from the patroons, the colony on the Delaware might have grown strong enough to deter intruders — but the Company had not been so inclined. It would seem to have been an error of judgment, for now the directors found it necessary to consolidate a poorly held position, at a late date when their enemies were strong, and at a cost that the Company could not well afford. Already the expense of developing commerce in New Netherland was cutting deep into the Company's profits — and now Fort Nassau must be strengthened and properly garrisoned to deter further English encroachment.

In 1636 or 1637 a group of soldiers was sent from Manhattan to Fort Nassau, with Jan Jansen of Ilpendam appointed commis and Peter Mey his assistant. About this time Gillis Pietersen van der Gouw, a master house carpenter, was sent to build " a large house " to replace the former house then in disrepair.[5] In 1638

---

[5] *NYCD*, 12 : 20 ; 14 : 9.

the Company sent Jan Pietersen of Essenfeldt as surgeon at a salary of ten florins a month.[6] Nothing was done to improve, strengthen, or expand the position on the Schuylkill—the officials stubbornly clung to the notion that a stronger Fort Nassau was the key to the Indian trade on the Delaware.

In the spring of 1638 a new threat challenged the Dutch position: Peter Minuit, the former director-general of New Netherland, but now out of favor, had found employment with another company formed in Sweden, and into the Delaware he sailed with two vessels under Swedish colors! It was only Minuit's former high position with the West India Company that made his new situation appear an unusual one ; actually, many Dutch soldiers served in Swedish armies, and Dutch skippers commanded Swedish vessels. Dutch brains and finances developed some of the Swedish industries and there was considerable intercourse between the two nations.

Before starting to build the stronghold called Fort Christina (at the mouth of the Christina River, thus controlling access to a major route to the Minquas country on the west bank) Minuit sent a sloop up the Delaware to investigate the status of Fort Nassau. Not having been in America for six years, he did not know whether or not Nassau was occupied, or what changes might have taken place there under the administration of his successors. His doubts were soon ended—as the sloop passed the fort, the sailors could see the new building and the activity on the shore. After reporting back to Minuit, the sloop undertook a second trip up the river, and this time Peter Mey sailed out from the fort to challenge the intruders. At this moment Jan Jansen, Mey's superior, was on a trip to Manhattan ; later he returned to issue a formal protest to Minuit from the newly arrived Governor Kieft. Kieft's letter was blunt and uncompromising. He warned Minuit that he was trespassing on Dutch property ; that

---

[6] *NYCD*, 12 : 19.

he objected to Minuit's building a fort on the Company's lands ; that the Dutch would hold him responsible for all " damages, expenses and losses, together with all mishaps, bloodsheds and disturbances, which may arise in future time therefrom and that we shall maintain our jurisdiction in such manner, as we shall deem most expedient."[7]

Minuit ignored Kieft's threats. They didn't come as a surprise to him, for he had expected the Dutch would object once they got wind of what he was doing ; he had a good idea how they would react, because he had previously held the position Kieft now occupied. Minuit had also correctly anticipated that if there were a garrison at Fort Nassau, it would not be strong enough to prevent the execution of his plans, and that the Company's officers at Manhattan would not be disposed to send ships and soldiers to drive him away.

After buying land on the western shore of the river from the Indians, Minuit built the stronghold he called Fort Christina in honor of the Swedish queen. The members of his company promptly started to barter with the Indians for beaver pelts, underselling the Dutch agents. When the full realization of what was happening dawned on Kieft, he was prompted to make an eloquent understatement : " to behold this contentedly, to be thus hectored, deprived of the trade and robbed of our land is a vast annoyance."[8]

With the Swedes consolidating their position at Fort Christina, the English from New Haven beginning to send traders to the Delaware, and the English of Virginia eager to share in the Minquas trade, Fort Nassau was at the most critical period in its history. Its support became a heavier drain than ever on the Company when measured against the decline in the receipt of furs — now the Swedes and English were getting part of the

---

[7] *NYCD*, 12 : 19.
[8] *NYCD*, 1 : 592.

business that had heretofore belonged exclusively to the Dutch. Fort Nassau was too weak, its garrison in 1640 consisting of only twenty men ; and it was not placed strategically to prevent Swedish activity on the opposite side of the river. Kieft wrote in 1640 that he was attempting to treat the Swedes with all civility, but they were " forcibly sailing up past our fort, trading, threatening to run off with our sloop, and so forth."[9]

On one occasion Jan Jansen attempted a display of strength by firing three cannon shot and a musket ball at a Swedish sloop passing the fort, but he did no damage.[10] The Swedes at this time, although few in number, were probably strong enough to have seized the Dutch fort, but it was of no use militarily or commercially, and, moreover, they preferred to pursue their own ends peacefully and without open conflict with the Dutch. Swedish and Dutch interests coincided on one important issue ; neither wanted the English in the Delaware Valley. Nevertheless, the English came, and it was primarily the quest for furs that brought them.

In 1642 a party of New Haven English under the leadership of Nathaniel Turner and George Lamberton settled on the Schuylkill. Both Lamberton and Turner had previously traded with the Indians in the Delaware area, and James Waye (see his deposition in Appendix B) stated that these same English had settled in 1641 at " Wattseson " (Watcessit), a place on the Salem River, then called Varckens Kill. After establishing their little colony on the east side of the Delaware and south of Fort Nassau they sent a party of men to build on the Schuylkill where they could make ready contact with the Minquas. The Dutch could not tolerate this threat to their commerce ; they reinforced Jansen with two sloops, the *Real* and the *St. Martin,* with orders to drive the English away.[11] He then " destroyed Lamberton's

---

[9] *NYCD,* 1 : 593.

[10] *Swedish Settlements,* 1 : 207.

[11] *NYCD,* 12 : 23, 24 ; *Swedish Settlements,* 1 : 214-215.

house there in the Schuylkill " and carried the English occupants off to Manhattan as prisoners for trespassing on Dutch land.[12] Yet the English could produce Indian deeds to prove they had *bought* the land, for both Lamberton and Turner had rounded up the Indian chiefs and native owners and paid them handsomely for land rights. James Waye was present when the negotiations were made, and goods equal to forty pounds sterling were given the Indians for land along the western bank of the Delaware from the Schuylkill all the way down to the sea! An English version of the incident provides additional details regarding Jansen's actions :

they had duly purchased of the Indian Sachems and theire Companies several tracts or parcells of land on both sids of Delawarr bay or River to which neither the Dutch nor Swedes had any just title yet without any legall protest or warning Monsere Kieft the then Dutch Governor sent armed men [in] 1642 and by force in a hostile way burnt theire trading house seized and for som time detained the goods in it not suffering their servants soe much as to take a just Inventory of them ; hee there allsoe seized theire boate and for a while kept theire men Prisoners for which to this day they can get no satisfaction.

2 secondly That the said Dutch Governor [in] 1642 compeled Mr. Lamberton theire Agent by force or threatenings to give in at the Manhattoes an account of what beavers he had traded within Newhaven limits at Delaware and to pay recognition for the same.[13]

Although the settlers from New Haven had been ousted, the Delaware would soon have English visitors from the more northerly Massachusetts Bay Colony. There had been formed in Boston a syndicate of merchants who were given a trade

---

[12] *Inst. for Printz*, p. 234.

[13] Edward Hopkins' letter to Stuyvesant, Sept. 16, 1650, in *Colls. N.Y. Hist. Soc.*, 1 : 224 (1811). In 1651, a company of fifty men from New Haven again started for Delaware Bay with a commission from Governor Eaton, but Stuyvesant prevented their going further than Manhattan (Edward E. Atwater, *History of the Colony of New Haven*, New Haven, 1881, p. 195).

monopoly for twenty-one years to seek out a great lake supposed to lie in the northwest part of the territory from whence the profitable beaver trade was supposed to originate. Access to this region was believed to be southerly via the Delaware River system, and the merchants outfitted a pinnace with provisions and trading stuff in 1644. William Aspinwall, a resident of Boston, was in charge of the party of fourteen men. In his journal, Governor Winthrop gave the English view of what happened to the expedition :

The Dutch promised to let them pass, but for maintaining their own interest he must protest against them. When they came to the Swedes, the fort shot at them, ere they came up : whereupon they cast forth anchor, and the next morning, being the Lord's day, the lieutenant came aboard them, and forced them to fall down lower ; when Mr. Aspenwall came to the governor [Printz] and complained of the lieutenant's ill dealing, both in shooting at them before he had hailed them, and in forcing them to weigh anchor on the Lord's day. The governor acknowledged he did ill in both, and promised all favor, but the Dutch agent [Jansen], being come down to the Swedes' fort, showed express orders from the Dutch governor not to let him pass, whereupon they returned. But before they came out of the river, the Swedish lieutenant made them pay 40 shillings for that shot which he had unduly made.[14]

What really happened was this :

Neither the Swedes nor Dutch wanted Aspinwall's party (or any other English) in the Delaware, but neither wanted openly to obstruct the Puritans. Governor Printz and Governor Kieft had agreed that these English really intended, in Printz's words, to " erect a fort above our post at Zanchikan [Sankikans] and equip and garrison it with people and cannon and then to strengthen

---

[14] *Winthrop's Journal*, 1630-1649, ed. J. K. Hosmer, New York, 1908, 2 : 180-181 ; *ibid.*, p. 190. For additional details, see *Inst. for Printz*, pp. 222-223 ; *Swedish Settlements*, 1 :396.

their position there, so as to draw to themselves the entire profit of the River here."

Although Kieft allowed Aspinwall to sail past Manhattan en route to the Delaware, he promptly sent orders to Jansen to prevent his going above Fort Nassau. Printz agreed with Kieft secretly that he, too, would pretend to be friendly to the English, but would do everything possible to prevent them from executing their plans. As a result of this conniving, Aspinwall was forced to turn back without achieving his objective. His situation was made worse because the captain of his little vessel was a drunkard and " when they should have left the vessel to have gone up to the lake in a small boat, he would in his drunkenness have betrayed their goods, etc. to the Dutch, whereupon they gave over and returned home ; and bringing their action against the master both for his drunkenness and denial to proceed as they required, and as by charter party he was bound, they recovered two hundred pounds from him, which was too much, though he did deal badly with them, for it was very probable they could not have proceeded."

Johan Printz, long experienced in Swedish military strategy, now began to move aggressively in the direction of blocking the Dutch. At this moment, so far as the Swedes were concerned, the Dutch were a more formidable competitor than the English. When Printz arrived in 1643 in the area Minuit had first named " New Sweden," he quickly sized up the situation. Evidently he saw the untenability of the Dutch position at Fort Nassau ; he recognized the importance of the western side of the Delaware and the Schuylkill and Christina systems in pursuing the beaver trade with Minquas. While pretending friendship with Kieft (witness his cooperation in preventing Aspinwall from seating his people), he proceeded to strengthen the Swedish position against the Dutch. He did what the Dutch could have done years before ; lower down the river on the east shore he built Fort Elfsborgh, by means of which, according to a Dutch report, " he closes the entrance of the River so that all vessels, either those arriving from here [Manhattan] or other places, are compelled to cast anchor . . . to obtain his consent . . . no matter whether they are Englishmen or Hollanders and regardless of their commissions."[15]

Among the buildings erected by Printz, three in the Schuylkill area were intended to further Swedish beaver trade with the Minquas before they reached the banks of the Delaware. The first post, called Fort Nya Korsholm, was described as being " on a very convenient spot on an island near the edge of the Kill, which is from the west side secured by another kill and from the south-south-east and east sides with underwood and valley lands."[16] This was the place where Corssen had built his little trading house, which the Swedes removed before building their post.

The description of the place where the second fort was built reads as follows : " at a little distance from this fort [Nya Korsholm] runs a Kill extending to the forest, which place is named *Kinsessing* by the Savages." The second fort was called by the Swedes, Fort Vasa or Wasa."[17]

---

[15] *Inst. for Printzz*, p. 255. Sir Edmund Plowden's attempt to found New Albion remains to be more fully told than in Keen's account (*Winsor*, 3 : 457-468). There were also English trading efforts which were blocked by the Dutch and Swedes, e.g. Scarburgh's sloop *Sea Horse* was seized by Hudde, taken to Fort Nassau, and her colors pulled down; see Susie M. Ames, *Studies of the Virginian Eastern Shore in the 17th Century*, Richmond, 1940, p. 48; cf. Eva L. Butler and C. A. Weslager, "Thomas Doxey's Letter from the Delaware, 1651," *Del. History*, 8, No. 1 (March, 1958), 51-53.

[16] *Inst. for Printz*, p. 257. Johnson says it was on Province Island (*Swedish Settlements*, p. 331, fn. 101). Another name for this place was Kievit's Hook (*NYCD*, 1 : 588). (There was also a Kievit's Hook in Connecticut [*ibid.*, p. 287 ; *Colls. N.Y. Hist. Soc.*, 2nd Series, 2 : Part 1, 277, fn. ; cf. Chapter 9 under " Kievit "].) Nya Korsholm was later torn down by the Indians (*Lindeström*, p. 126).

[17] *Inst. for Printz*, p. 258. George P. Donehoo, *Indian Villages and Place-Names*, Harrisburg, 1928, p. 80, says Kinsessing was the name of the area between Cobbs Creek and the Schuylkill.

The third fort, " built on the same Minquas road," was named Molndall, and here Printz erected a water-powered grist mill, as well as a log blockhouse.[18] The Indian name of this place was *Kakarikonk*.[19]

A Dutchman looking this situation over wrote, " Thus no access to the Minquas is left open and he, too, controls nearly all the trade of the Savages on the [Delaware] River, as the greatest part of them go a hunting in that neighborhood [the area drained by the Schuylkill, especially its upper branches] which they are not able to do without passing this place [*Kakarikonk*]."[20]

Printz could confidently report early in 1647 that " when the great traders the Minquas wish to travel to the Dutch trading place or their house, Nassau," they were now obliged to pass his posts, where he could negotiate for their furs.[21] Not only did Printz control the territory and trade routes, but he made commerce with the Swedes more attractive to the Indians by allowing the " wild people to obtain the necessary things they need for somewhat more moderate price than they are getting them of the Hollanders from Fort Nassau or the adjacent English."[22]

Jan Jansen must have tried to meet Swedish competition, for he was accused of wronging the Company by " giving more to the Indians than the ordinary rate." The complaint against him

---

[18] *Inst. for Printz,* p. 131.

[19] *Inst. for Printz,* p. 258. Donehoo, *op. cit.,* p. 19, says that *Kakarikonk* was the name of Carkoens Creek, also known as Amesland Creek or Cobbs Creek. He gives " place of wild geese " as the meaning in Algonkian. *Dunlap, 1956,* points out that *calcoen* is a Dutch word for " turkey " and the Swedish cognate is *kalkon*. The place became known to the Swedes as *Karraconks Hook* and the Molndall mill came to be known as *Karraconks Mill* (*New Castle County Land Surveys* [1760-1769], Memorial Library, University of Delaware, Microfilm No. 86, p. 31).

[20] *Inst. for Printz,* p. 258.

[21] *Ibid.,* p. 132.

[22] *Ibid.,* p. 80. In 1647, " Mr. Thomas Pell of Newhauen afforesd traded in Delaware " (*Colls. N.Y. Hist. Soc.,* 1 : 5 [1869]). The quotation above, however, refers more specifically to the English of Virginia, characterized by Printz in one of his letters as " evil neighbors " (*Inst. for Printz,* p. 150).

included other instances of alleged misfeasance, and on October 12, 1645, his case was tried in Manhattan. Andries Hudde was sent to Fort Nassau provisionally to examine the books, take physical inventory of the goods and " to excercise command there as commissary until further orders."[23] Hudde was capable, intelligent, aggressive ; he was well educated, experienced as a surveyor, and had been in the Company's employ at Manhattan as a " commis of stores " as early as 1634.[24] Upon his arrival at Fort Nassau, he lost no time in making a complete survey of the situation. He not only saw the pitiful condition of the small supply of merchandise, but he quickly recognized that the fort was ineffective to compete in the beaver trade with the Swedes, who held superior geographical positions.

Hudde was not to be frightened by the bravado of Governor Printz, and he told him confidently that " the place, which we possess, we possess in right ownership and have had a just title to them, perhaps before the South River was heard of in Sweden."[25] Hudde received his answer while he and his wife were dining with the Swedish governor. " The Devil," said Printz, in a response that has been recorded, " was the oldest proprietor of Hell, but that he might even admit a younger one !"[26]

Among the members of Hudde's garrison were Sander Boyer, who was both quartermaster and interpreter to the Indians, and David Davitsen and Jacob Hendricksen, soldiers.[27] Two of the freemen then at the fort were Philip Gerraert and Juriaen Planck. The latter was supercargo of a private sloop sent with merchandise to trade with the Indians. These names were taken from one of Hudde's reports — there were others, but he did not name them at this time.

---

[23] *NYCD,* 12 : 25-26. On March 23, 1647, Kieft granted Jansen a plantation on Long Island (*NYCD,* 14 : 137, 152).

[24] *VRB,* p. 304. Hudde is also mentioned in 1632 (*ibid.,* p. 228).

[25] *NYCD,* 12 : 34.

[26] *Ibid.,* p. 35.

[27] *Ibid,* 12 : 30, 33.

Dutch strategy now, at long last, was to try again to place permanent residents on the Delaware, and in 1646 Kieft granted one hundred morgens of land [a morgen was about 2,900 square yards] to Abraham Planck, Symon Root, Jan Andriesen, and Pieter Harmensen.[28] The land was on the west side of the river " opposite to a little island called *'t Vogele Sant [the Birds Sand]"* and the intention of the grantees was to establish " four bouweries or plantations and to cultivate them within a year from date, or earlier, if possible."

Hudde was also instructed to buy a certain specified plot from the Indians, which he did on September 25, 1646 ; this is one of the earliest purchases from the Indians which relates to specific land now included within the limits of the present city of Philadelphia. See Appendix B for the complete document, herein published for the first time.

In 1647, the militant Peter Stuyvesant replaced Kieft as Director-General of New Netherland, bringing considerable experience as a soldier. Kieft's vessel was lost at sea on the return voyage and he was never heard of again. Through the Bontemantel documents we learn that he had taken with him many of the New Netherland records, including documents pertaining to the South River, and all of these went down with the vessel.[29]

---

[28] *Ibid.,* p. 27. On April 16, 1649, Alexander Boyer, Simon Root, Peter Harmansen, David Davitsen, and Cornelisen Mouritsen bought a tract on the east side of the Delaware north of Rancocas Creek from the Indians. Witnesses were Thomas Broen, Jan Andriesen, Antony Petersen, Johannes Marckusen, Harmen Jansen, Jems Boecker, and Jan Duten (*NYCD,* 12 : 49). One of the reasons the Company permitted this purchase by individuals was to prevent the Swedes buying the land (*ibid,* 2 : 53).

[29] The unpublished *New Netherland (or Bontemantel) Papers,* New York Public Library, translated by Paltsits. The document telling of the loss of the South River records appears under the title " Extract from the general letter from New Netherland dated October 30, 1655. " The same document states that records were recently sent by the vessels *Valconier* and *Waeterhont,* but they were badly written due to " the drunkard Johannes Dyckmans. "

Printz had maintained very friendly relations with Kieft, but he would soon learn that the new Dutch commander was too much like himself, and not of a mind to tolerate threats or insults to his employers or his government. Shortly after his arrival, Stuyvesant ordered Hudde to erect a new house at Fort Nassau and put everything there in repair. He sent boards, building materials, and a house carpenter named Pieter Cornelissen to do the work.[30] He authorized Hudde to discharge and give a former Company employee, Jan't Dyrsen, and a companion, a place to build a house near Fort Nassau if he thought it advisable.[31] Stuyvesant was also aware of the importance of placing permanent residences in an area under dispute, something his predecessors had not foreseen.

Starting with Stuyvesant's appointment and continuing until 1651, a series of " incidents " characterized Dutch - Swedish affairs, and the friendly relations of the Kieft and Printz administrations no longer existed ; things became progressively worse as each moved to block the other. The turning point came when Hudde, who now recognized that Fort Nassau could not control the Delaware regardless of how well it was built or how its garrison was strengthened, urged Stuyvesant to permit him to build a stronghouse on the Schuylkill. Hudde painted the crisis with such clarity that Stuyvesant immediately saw there was no alternative.

Hudde knew that with three Swedish posts flourishing at key locations there remained only one place in the Schuylkill open to Dutch traders as an anchorage for convenient barter with the Minquas. Then, when he received intelligence that the Swedes were laying up hemlock logs near that very place, he feared they

---

[30] *NYCD,* 12 : 56,57. The *Bontemantel papers* contain an entry as of 1650 of the salaries paid to the Company's executives in New Netherland, which includes this line : " Foreman of the Laborers at Fort Nassau 10 gl./80 gl. board money. "

[31] *NYCD,* 12 : 56.

would erect a fourth fort which would completely exclude the Dutch. He wrote as follows :

With the exception of this place there is no access to the great forest to trade with the Minquase, whereby their trade is snatched from our people, and this River would be of very little consideration, therefore, not daring to neglect it, I wrote to the Governor [Printz] as I had no orders to undertake anything for its preservation. Thereupon I received orders, that in case the Swede should come to build and settle on any new, unoccupied places, I should with all civility settle down beside him in the name of the Company.[32]

To carry out his orders, Hudde met on April 24, 1648, with the principal Passayunk chiefs, who consented to his building a trading post at the site in question ; in fact, they *gave* him the plot of land on which to build ! He reported further that Mattahorn and Wissemenetto, two of the principal chiefs, " themselves took and planted there the Prince's flag and ordered me to fire three shots as a sign of possession."[33]

On April 27 he started to erect the post called Fort Beversreede, evidently a small structure, but he does not describe it except to state it was surrounded by palisades.[34] The exact location of this fort is not known, but it was on the east bank of the river in the present district known as Passayunk.[35] The name is derived from two Dutch words meaning " beaver road," i.e., " the road of the beaver." Needless to say, the Swedes strongly opposed this project, but if we can believe Hudde, the Indians supported him and turned to several of the Swedes and asked :

---

[32] *Inst. for Printz,* p. 272.

[33] *Ibid.,* p. 273.

[34] *Ibid.,* p. 273.

[35] John P. Nicholson, " Fort Beversreede," *Penna. Magazine,* 15 (1891), 252-253. Henry D. Paxson, *Where Penna History Began, etc.,* Philadelphia, 1926, p. 65, says that Fort Beversreede stood between present Penrose Ferry Bridge and Passayunk Bank ; see also p. 83 for his location of Fort Nya Korsholm.

By what authority did they (the Swedes) build on the land, or whether it was not enough that they had already taken possession of *Matinnekonck,* the Schuylkill, *Kinsessingh, Kakarikon,* Upland and the other places occupied by the Swedes, all [of] which they had stolen from them? That Minwit, now about eleven years ago had purchased no more than a small piece of land at *Paghahacking* [Fort Christina] to plant some tobacco on it, the half of which they, the natives, should receive as an acknowledgement. Could they (pointing to the Swedes) by purchasing a piece of land on their arrival, take, in addition, all that lay on the main [river] as they (the Swedes) had done and still do here on the River? That it excited their wonder, that they (the Swedes) should prescribe laws to them, the native proprietors, that they should not do with their own, what they pleased.[36]

In receipt of these exciting reports from Hudde, Stuyvesant, ever eager for action, decided it was time to make a personal inspection of Fort Nassau and Fort Beversreede ; he reasoned that a commander should make his own appraisal of a critical situation whenever possible. He made two attempts to leave in the vessel *Prince William,* but each time adverse weather forced him back to port.[37] When the weather cleared he was forced to cancel the trip due to pressing business, sending in his place Lubberthus van Dincklage (also given as Lubbert van Dinklagen), his vice-director, and Dr. Jean de la Montagne, a physician and councillor. The two officials arrived at Fort Nassau on June 7, 1648.[38] Hudde arranged for them to confer three days later with the principal Passayunk chiefs at Beversreede who owned the district *Armenveruis,* namely, *Amattehooren* (Mattahorn), *Alibakinne,* and *Sinquees.* There they reconfirmed the land purchase

---

[36] *Inst. for Printz,* p. 274.

[37] *NYCD,* 12-58. Stuyvesant had with him one Cornelis Jansen, a colonist intending to settle at Fort Nassau. Whether he came on a later vessel is not known.

[38] *Ibid.,* p. 37.

made in 1633 by Arent Corssen ; the new document they drew up for the records was worded to indicate that Corssen had bought more than the district called *Armenveruis,* for there is reference to " adjoining lands." The officials from Manhattan then gave the chiefs the balance owed them by Corssen, who had not paid in full for the lands.[39] It is possible that retroactively they were making Corssen's purchase seem more important than it was, because it was now necessary for the Dutch to be able to prove to the Swedes that they occupied the lands by right of *bona fide* purchase from the Indians! Witnesses to the instrument, in the spelling given, were " Augustyn Heermans,[40] Govert Loockermans,[41] Jeuriaen Planck, Cornelis Jansen Coele, Sander Leendertsen."[42]

The two emissaries also authorized certain Dutch colonists to take up land and build houses. Next they paid a visit to Governor Printz's log mansion on Tinicum Island to register official protest against his actions. They were not graciously received, and Huygen and Papegaya " kept their Honors standing in the open air in the rain for about half an hour."[43]

Stuyvesant continued to encourage colonists and traders to leave Manhattan and settle on the Delaware, particularly in the

---

[39] *NYCD,* 1 : 593.

[40] Augustine Herrman, a Bohemian by birth, was an early member of the Dutch colony and later became a large landholder in Maryland of "Bohemia Manor." Mention of his map was made in Chapter 5; see also Chapter 11.

[41] Govert Loockerman came to New Netherland at the age of seventeen as cook's mate on the yacht *St. Martyn ;* was taken into the Company's service by Wouter van Twiller ; later became a freeman, taking charge of the trade of Gillis Verbruggen & Company (*NYCD,* 1 : 432). His son Jacob settled on a plantation near Easton, Maryland, and Jacob's son Nicholas moved to Dover, Delaware ; see Annie Jump Cannon, " The Lockerman Mansion House Near Dover, Del., " *Del. History,* 3, No. 2 (Sept., 1948), 97-104.

[42] *NYCD.,* 1 : 593. Leendersteen in 1649 had delivered wheat from Stuyvesant to Hudde at Fort Nassau (*NYCD,* 12 : 62).

[43] *Ibid,* 12 : 37.

Schuylkill region, something that his predecessors might have done years before. The Swedes did everything in their power to thwart his design by interfering with the house building and trading. Thomas Broen started to build a house at a place called *New Hooven* (New Farm) and it was promptly pulled down by the Swedes.[44] Symon Root, an Englishman in Dutch service, attempted to build a house at *Wigquakoing* (one of the variants of *Wicacoa*, Indian name for the section of present-day Philadelphia purchased by Hudde from the Indians), but the Swedes interfered.[45] A house under construction by Hans Jacobsen on the Schuylkill was torn down and burnt, and Jacobsen was threatened with bodily injury if he tried to rebuild.[46] Jan Geraet came to trade in the vessel *Siraen*, and Printz confiscated some of his arms and powder.[47] Stuyvesant granted land on the " Mastemaecker's Hook " jointly to Symon Root, Peter Harmensen, and Cornelis Mauritsen ; but the Swedes promptly destroyed a second house there that Root had started to build.[48] Johannes Marcus and Harman Jansen witnessed this incident in company with Adriaen van Tienhoven. Jacob Claesen and Antony Pietersen also complained of Swedish interference with their plans to build on the same island.[49] Juriaen Planck came to trade in the sloop *Zeepaert*, and he ran into Swedish opposition.[50]

Among the " Swedes " mentioned by name in the Dutch complaints were Gustaf Printz, son of the governor ; Henry Huygen, the commissary ; Gregory van Dyck, sergeant ; Mans Kling, a lieutenant, then stationed at Fort Nya Korsholm ; Sven Skute, another lieutenant ; Carell Jenssen, a bookkeeper ; and

---

[44] *Ibid.*
[45] *Ibid.*, 1 : 594. Root was an Indian trader (*ibid.*, 12 : 57).
[46] *Ibid.*, 12 : 37 ; *Inst. for Printz*, p. 276.
[47] *NYCD.*, 1 : 595.
[48] *Ibid.*, 1 : 594 ; 12 : 44-45.
[49] *Ibid.*, 12 : 45-49.
[50] *Ibid.*, 1 : 595. ; 12 : 30.

Johan Papegaya, Printz's son-in-law. Huygen, a relative of Peter Minuit, and van Dyck were Dutchmen in Swedish employ, and Jenssen was a Finn. Not only were the Swedish forces made up of non-Swedish nationals, but some of the " Dutch " were of English and Scandinavian origin. A settler on the Delaware during this period would have benefited from knowledge of the Iroquoian tongue (spoken by the Minquas), the Algonkian (spoken by the Passayunks and other Delaware River Indians), as well as Dutch, Swedish, Finnish, and English, spoken by his associates or competitors.

On September 20, 1647, Hudde was reappointed commis on the Delaware, but in the fall of 1648 he was summoned to Manhattan to answer charges brought against him by van Dincklage of " Unfaithfulness toward the Company."[51] During his absence, Alexander (Sander) Boyer, serving as " deputy commissary," dispatched a letter complaining of Swedish encroachment and also of the need for more merchandise for use in the Indian trade. The Swedes, he related, had erected, on September 19, a building " right in front of our Fort Bevers reede."[52] He said that the Swedish building was thirty to thirty-five feet in length, twenty-five feet wide, and that the rear gable " comes within about 12 feet of the gate of the fort." This meant that Dutch sloops coming up the Schuylkill to trade with the Indians found a Swedish post at the anchoring place, blocking access to their own building.[53] To meet this emergency, Boyer stated he had only " six able-bodied men " in the two forts, Nassau and Beversreede, evidently referring to himself, David Davitsen,

---

[51] *Ibid.,* 12 : 41-42.

[52] *Ibid.,* 12 : 43, letter dated September 25, 1648.

[53] Boyer said that a Minquas chief with four of his followers had recently visited Beversreede to learn whether any Dutch vessels had arrived with goods. The Swedes were also awaiting goods from Europe for the Indian trade. The Minquas chief was dissatisfied " that this River is not steadily provided with cargoes by our people " (*ibid.*).

Adriaen van Tienhoven, Pieter Harmansen, Symon Root, and Andries Luycassen.

Hudde returned to Fort Nassau October 18, 1648, bringing with him several freemen, " to whom letter patents were issued to settle and build on the Schuylkill."[54] He had been cleared of the charges brought against him and resumed his position with Stuyvesant's full endorsement. He needed every ounce of moral and physical support that he could get to cope with the bold actions of the audacious warrior, Printz. Some of the Swedes cut down fruit trees on the Beversreede property—another one, Peter Jochim by name, broke down some of the palisades, " hacking with great violence the woodwork to pieces."[55] A garden behind Beversreede, planted by Cornelis Mourissen, Symon Root, and Philip Jansen, was destroyed and the fence around it burnt by Printz's soldiers.

Peter Cornelissen and Reynier Dominicus (both were house carpenters) prepared to build a dwelling on an island in the Schuylkill called *Harommuny* (or *Aharommuny*), but the Swedes destroyed the timbers. Sander Leendertsen, Abraham Stats, and Gerrit Hendricksen were granted land on the same island, and were also prevented from building by armed Swedes.[56]

Thomas Broen was given permission by Stuyvesant to live at Mantas Hook (on the east side of the Delaware south of Fort Nassau), but Printz bought the identical land from the Indians and set up the Swedish coat of arms to block the Dutch.[57] Printz also tried to buy lands from the Indians immediately above Fort Nassau. This activity on the eastern side of the river added insult to the injuries already inflicted by the Swedes.

The incidents herein cited—as well as others—were enumer-

---

[54] *Inst. for Printz,* p. 276.
[55] *Ibid.,* p. 277.
[56] Leendersten was a Dutch skipper. He and Jan Jansen were members of Printz's court that tried Lamberton in 1643 (*Inst. for Printz.,* p. 230).
[57] *NYCD,* 12 : 370.

ated in a formal letter of protest addressed to Stuyvesant by the principal residents and traders then in the Fort Beversreede environs. The signatories were " Symon Root, Cornelis Mourisen bont, Pieter Cornelissen, Juriaen Planck, Philip Jansen, Jan Gerardy[58] and Sander Govertsen." Witnesses to the letter were " Marten Cryger, A. Hudde, L. Jansen, Abraham Staets."[59] The letter makes reference to " our families," indicating the presence of women and children.

Stuyvesant now realized that Printz had effectively outflanked Fort Nassau with his three fortified posts on the Schuylkill; that the Swedes' Fort Elfsborgh could keep Nassau or Beversreede from being supplied or reinforced by water ; that the Swedes now had the upper hand in the Indian trade on the Delaware ; that it was much too late to expect to correct the situation by placing a handful of Dutch settlers on the Schuylkill. It had now become a military problem of major proportions, and after poring over his maps and charts, the old soldier Stuyvesant prepared for action. After secret, but thorough, preparation, he marched overland from Manhattan to Fort Nassau with a force of one-hundred-and-twenty armed men. There he had a prearranged rendezvous with eleven Dutch vessels that had sailed down the coast, into Delaware Bay, and up the river to meet him. This was the most powerful attacking force that had ever been seen in the Delaware. The Swedes were not able to repel this pincer movement applied by land and sea ; in fact, they offered no resistance.

Stuyvesant then proceeded to try to win the support and cooperation of the Indian owners of the lands on the Delaware

---

[58] Also called Johannes Gerardy, a merchant who went to the Delaware in 1649 in the yacht *Swan* (*NYCD*, 12 : 54).

[59] *Ibid.*, 1 : 595. Abraham Staets, whose name is given as Staes, Staas, Staats, etc., came to New Netherland in 1642 at the age of twenty-four to practice surgery. He had a nineteen-year-old wife and a servant boy (*VRB*, pp. 609, 678, 828). On August 30, 1655, he chartered his yacht to Stuyvesant for 6 guilders per day for use in recapturing Fort Amstel (*NYCD*, 12 : 96).

by paying them off in return for clear title. The irony of the situation is apparent — almost thirty years earlier, when the Dutch were the only Europeans in the Delaware Valley, they could have negotiated with the Indians for right to occupy any place or places they desired, and at their own price. Now the Swedes claimed that the Dutch had defaulted in this obligation, and *they* had bought the western side of the Delaware from the rightful owners, the Indians. The territory belonged to *them,* not the Dutch! Printz stated categorically that the land the Swedes had purchased from the Indians included the whole west side of the Delaware River " from Cape Henlopen up to Sanchikans in which the adjacent Schuylkill was included."[60]

Meeting with the three principal Lenape chiefs, Mattahorn, Pemenetta, and Sinques, at Fort Nassau, Stuyvesant asked them through Sander Boyer, his interpreter, " what and how much land the Swedes had bought from the Sachems or Chiefs of this river."[61] Wise old Mattahorn, acting as spokesman, evaded the question ; all nations coming here were welcome. he said, and they had sold their land to the first who asked it ; the Dutch, as everyone knew, had been the earliest comers and discoverers.

Stuyvesant persisted ; he wanted a direct answer, because the plan of action he had designed depended upon it. After reflection, Mattahorn told the Dutchman exactly what he wanted to hear : the Indians had sold Minuit only a tiny plot of land on the Minquas Kill big enough to set " a house on, and a Plantation included between 6 trees." Mattahorn declared further that " neither the Swedes nor any other nation had bought lands of them as right owners, except the patch on which Fort Christina stood, and that all the other houses of the Swedes, built at *Tinnecongh* [Tinicum Island, where Printz had his mansion], *Hingeesingh* [Kinsessing], in the Schuylkill and at other places

---

[60] *Inst. for Printz,* p. 233.
[61] *NYCD,* 1 : 597.

were set up there against the will and consent of the Indians, and that neither they, nor any other natives had received anything therefor." [62]

But how about the plot on the Schuylkill sold to Arent Corssen and reconfirmed by Stuyvesant's emissaries three years before? Yes, Mattahorn admitted, that plot belonged to the Dutch. Then Stuyvesant came to the main issue, the key to his plan of retaliation against the Swedes, using their own legal weapon — Indian deeds of sale. How about the land south of the Minquas Kill to the mouth of the river? Had that area been sold to the Swedes? To this Mattahorn replied, " Why do you ask that question so often? We told you the lands are not sold to any person." Stuyvesant then asked the final and critical question — if this land was not sold, would the Indians now sell it to him?

The three sachems deliberated over this request, because they did not want to be maneuvered into a position which would antagonize their Swedish neighbors. At the same time they saw the importance of maintaining friendly relations with the Dutch, whose show of strength had made a big impression on them. The reply they gave to Stuyvesant was a diplomatic classic. One wishes it had been preserved in their own Algonkian idiom. As it comes down to us in an English version of a Dutch translation of the Lenape words, it reads as follows :

The Swede builds and plants, indeed, on our lands, without buying them or asking us. Wherefore should we refuse you, Great Sachem, the land? We will rather present than sell the Great Sachem the land, so that, should the Swedes again pull down the Dutch houses and drive away the people, you may not think ill of us, and we may not draw down your displeasure. [63]

Stuyvesant promptly had a document drawn up, signed and sealed, to indicate that the native owners " have this 9 July given

---

[62] *NYCD*, 1 : 598.
[63] *Ibid*, 1 : 599.

and voluntarily presented to Peter Stuyvesant" the land in question on the western side of the Delaware. It extended from the west point of the present Christina River, called *Suppeckongh* in the document (" at the muddy river "), south to *Boompjes hook (Bompties:* " little trees "), known to the Indians as *Canaresse* (" at the thickets," i.e., " little trees ").[64] Although the document stated the land was received by Stuyvesant as a gift, he slyly paid off the Indians with " twelve coats of duffels, twelve kettles, twelve axes, 12 adzes, 24 knives, 12 bars of lead, and four guns with some powder." The goods were itemized in a second document marked " secret " which Stuyvesant and the Indian chiefs signed on July 19.[65]

The European witnesses to the first paper give the following spellings of their names: " Wilhelmus Grasmeer, clergyman, Cornelis de Potter, Isacck Alderton,[66] Bryan Neuton,[67] George Baxter [an ensign in Stuyvesant's forces], A. Hudde, Alexander Boyer, as Interpreter, R. de Haes, the mark of Jan Andriessen[68] . . . Marten Cregier, Lieutenant of New Amsterdam burghess company, Abraham Staats, Surgeon and elder of Renslaers Wyck."

The second and secret document was witnessed by: " Cornelis de Potter, Abraham Staes, Martin Kriegier, Gysbert Opdyck, Abraham Verplanck, Adriaen Dircksen Coen, Adriaen van Thienhoven, Egbert van Borsum [a skipper], Peter Caspersen, Joost

---

[64] *Ibid.; Dunlap & Weslager, 1950.*

[65] *NYCD,* 1 : 599-600.

[66] Isaac Allerton came to America on the *Mayflower* and had been traveling to the Delaware as a trader as early as 1643 (*Inst. for Printz,* p. 206). See also Eva L. Butler and C. A. Weslager, " Thomas Doxey's Letter from the Delaware, 1651, " *Del. History* 8, No. 1 (March, 1958), 51-53.

[67] A captain-lieutenant in Stuyvesant's forces, of English birth, but conversant in Dutch (*NYCD,* 1 : 426).

[68] " Jan Andriesen of Beren-Bach " arrived in Manhattan on the *Falconier* in 1650 and Stuyvesant permitted him to go to the Delaware to settle (*Ibid.,* 12 : 67, 68).

Michielsen, Jacob Janssen huys [another skipper], Wilhelmus Grasmeer, clergyman, Daniel Michielssen."[69]

The above names, as well as those previously cited in this chapter, have been introduced to show exactly those individuals, either of Dutch birth or foreigners in the employ of the Company, who were present on the Delaware during this critical period. Some of them were residents — others were here as traders — still others were members of Stuyvesant's forces.

Stuyvesant dismantled Fort Nassau, salvaging the cannon and other military supplies ; Fort Beversreede was evidently abandoned also. Then he sailed down the Delaware with his fleet, taking with him certain individuals who had previously been sent for the purpose of building homes. As the legal owner of the land south of the Christina, Stuyvesant landed at an unoccupied place on the west bank of the river below Fort Christina known as the *santhoek* (" sand hook "). There was then a sandy spit extending into the river, affording a good landing place.[70] On this site the final stages of his plan materialized ; he built a strong fortress, larger than Nassau, having four bastions. He named it Fort Casimir, probably in honor of Count Ernest Casimir of Nassau, one of the heroes of his native Friesland. He installed the cannon from Fort Nassau and other ordnance at the new fort and appointed Gerrit Bicker as commander, with the faithful Andries Hudde as the commis.[71]

The whole movement — from the rendezvous of his fleet with the ground forces at Fort Nassau, the acquisition of land from the Indians, the building of the new fort — had been a master stroke. It was accomplished without the shedding of a drop of blood ; it

---

[69] *Ibid.,* 1 : 600.

[70] *Lindeström,* p. 173 ; *Dunlap, 1956,* p. 50.

[71] Stuyvesant independently planned and executed the movement in the Delaware, without a Company directive and without giving the directors advance notice. They later questioned whether the demolition of Fort Nassau was " a very prudent act " (*NYCD.,* 12 : 72).

again brought the Dutch into full control of the Delaware. Fort Casimir could be of far greater logistic value than Fort Christina or any other Swedish post on the river. No ship could pass up the Delaware without being challenged by the Dutch. The Swedish colonists could be cut off from incoming vessels and their import and export trade with the Old World strangled if the Dutch so willed, provided they held and defended the new location. They were also in a position to dominate the profitable fur trade with the Minquas, now that they were established on the west side of the river. But, as history has revealed, the Dutch were not destined any more than the Swedes to remain masters of the Delaware. The period of their control at Fort Casimir would last only a few years until the English assumed authority. There were many factors contributing to the decline of the Dutch, not the least being the sharp differences of opinion among the merchant stockholders of the West India Company and the utter failure of the Company to give their Delaware settlements sufficient financial and moral support.

Some persons in Holland recognized the importance of furthering the colonization of the Delaware ; but, failing to get the Company's support, they arranged to settle under Swedish auspices. On November 2, 1642, a party of Dutch settlers from Utrecht arrived at Fort Christina under the leadership of Joost van Bogaert, who had been in New Netherland earlier and had been a member of Verhulst's council.[72] Evidently these Bogaert followers settled a short distance from Fort Christina, which made the Swedish authorities feel a little uncomfortable ; when Printz left Sweden to take charge of the colony, he was instructed to tell them " to leave that place and betake themselves further away from said fort."[73] It is not certain where these Dutch ultimately settled, but their community did not survive and the members

---

[72] *Van Laer,* p. 262, note 14.
[73] *Inst. for Printz,* pp. 76-78.

apparently scattered and settled among the Swedes and other Dutch.[74]

Ten years later Governor Printz, in a letter written to Chancellor Oxenstierna from the Delaware, made reference to the fact that " . . . although the Hollanders have settled strongly here and there between us, as now this year [1652] a man from Holland, called Barkhofen, has settled on the eastern side of our [Delaware] River with forty families, still others are coming. But if aid would arrive with a considerable number of people and [with] a good administration, the Hollanders would be obliged to get out of here, for all those who have settled here have nothing in reserve, a miserable and indebted people ; [they have] neither a cow nor any kind of cattle, and the West India Company cannot help them ; neither do they sow nor plow, but suppose [that they] will live from the trade of the Savages which they themselves have ruined."[75]

Like Bogaert's people, those of Barkhofen are not mentioned in subsequent records, which would indicate that their settlement in New Jersey was of a temporary nature. It failed, as had Dutch colonization effort at four other places prior to the building of Fort Casimir (in the order named : (a) Burlington Island, (b) Swanendael, (c) Fort Nassau, and (d) Fort Beversreede and environs), even though the Company's occupancy of the Delaware antedated that of their rivals.

---

[74] Johnson gives further details about this colonization effort in *Swedish Settlements* 1:136, 137, 200-203. See p. 203, fn. 21, to the effect that Bogaert was the individual called Bogot in Plantagenet's *Description of the Province of New Albion*.

[75] *Inst. for Printz*, p. 186.

VII

The Secret Instructions for Peter Minuit

In the previous chapter, the reader saw the Swedes coming into the Delaware River under the leadership of Peter Minuit, the ex-governor of New Netherland, to compete with the Dutch. In the shift of Minuit's loyalty from Holland to Sweden lies an interesting story which, because of the paucity of information, cannot be completely told ; nevertheless, sufficient data are available to give us a general understanding of what led up to his apparent double-dealing. Six years before, in the spring of 1632, while still in the employ of the West India Company, he had returned to Holland from Manhattan on the *Eendraght* (" Unity "). He and other members of his official family had been summoned to Amsterdam for questioning. Among these others were Jan Lampo, schout-fiscal ; Peter Bylvelt, councillor ; Gerrit Mattheusz de Reux, farm manager ; Johan van Remund, secretary ; and Jonas Michaëlius, New Netherland's first minister of the Reformed Church.[1] Coenraed Notelman, who replaced Jan Lampo as schout-fiscal, had brought the directive from Amsterdam ordering Minuit and the others to return home. In this shakeup, Bastian Jansz Krol, then commander at Fort Orange, was transferred to Manhattan to serve in Minuit's place until his return.[2] It should be emphasized that Minuit was not discharged, nor did he resign from the Company's service at the time of his recall.

---

[1] *Van Laer*, pp. 272–273, note 17; *VRB*, p. 291.
[2] *VRB*, pp. 31, 217, fn. 34. Krol served until March, 1633, when he was succeeded by Wouter van Twiller.

From 1626, when the council named him to succeed Willem Verhulst, until the arrival of Notelman on the *Eendraght* with the fateful orders, Minuit had been the Company's ranking officer in New Netherland. During this six-year tenure he had evidently served the Company to the satisfaction of a majority of the directors or they would have replaced him earlier. The limited data now available pertaining to his official acts consists of several Indian deeds bearing his signature ; a few letters written by him ; reports, journals, and both official and private correspondence in which his name is briefly mentioned. These allow but a fleeting glimpse of his administration, but nothing that can be seen suggests that he was not a capable and conscientious administrator, well regarded by his employers, at least until the terminal months of his American tenure.

Minuit must be given credit for recognizing the importance of concentrating the population on Manhattan Island, which one historian says extended into the sea " like a great natural pier ready to receive the commerce of the world."[3] Minuit must have seen the commercial possibilities of this location, and the record of pelts which passed through this port during his administration is proof of his business acumen. From 1626 to 1632, while he was in office, some 47,196 beaver skins and 5,388 otter skins were obtained from the Indians and shipped to Holland.[4] These pelts were of prime interest to the Company, representing the major source of income.

Not only had Minuit developed Manhattan Island as a port of trade and the capital of New Netherland, but he had also purchased Staten Island from the Indians in 1630, on behalf of the patroon Michiael Pauw, for " Duffles, Kittles, Axes, Hoes,

---

[3] Mrs. Schuyler van Rensselaer, *History of the City of New York,* 1909, 1 :49.
[4] *Colls. N.Y. Hist. Soc.,* 2nd Series, 1 (1841), 385.

Wampum, Drilling Awls, Jews Harps and diverse other small wares."[5]

Minuit successfully operated a farm, or bowerie, on Manhattan, which he leased from the Company, with the consent of the directors. To care for his livestock and crops he employed a foreman and farmers, including a runaway English lad who taught his employers to plant and cure tobacco using the methods practiced in Virginia. The tobacco plants were sown in the fall, covered with manure during the winter, and transplanted in the spring to mature.[6] Minuit's farm, incidentally, was granted by the Company to his successor, Wouter van Twiller, after his recall, although Minuit was permitted to sell his goods and livestock.

There has been preserved, in certain personal correspondence, information relating to the animosity that developed between Minuit and two of his immediate associates — Johan van Remund, the secretary, and Jonas Michaëlius, the minister. This friction immediately preceded and was a factor in Minuit's recall to Holland. Unfortunately, this information is neither complete nor unbiased, for it is taken from the personal letters of persons prejudiced either for or against Minuit. Van Remund and Minuit were, in the words of Sijmon Dircxz Pos (as his name is spelled in the records), one of the letter writers and a councillor at Manhattan, " very much embittered against one another." As a result of this clash, Pos remarked that " all is left to drift as it will ; they let trade slip away . . . but are very diligent in bringing exorbitant suits and charges against one another and in neglecting the interests and business of the directors."[7]

Pos also wrote to van Rensselaer in a letter dated at Manhattan, September 16, 1630, that "the minister Jonas Michielsz

---

[5] *Colls. N.Y. Hist. Soc.*, 46 (1913) 124 ; *NYCD*, 13 : 2.
[6] *VRB.*, p. 219, 233; see the inventory of goods on Minuit's farm (*ibid.*, pp. 223–224).
[7] *Ibid.*, p. 169.

[Michaëlius] is very energetic here stirring up the fire between them; he ought to be a mediator in God's church and community but he seems to me to be the contrary."[8] Michaëlius, on the other hand, had his own biased opinion of Minuit. In a letter dated at Manhattan September 13, 1630, he wrote to a correspondent in Holland that the governor "is most unworthy of his office; a slippery man, who under the treacherous mask of honesty is a compound of all iniquity and wickedness . . . cruel oppressor of the innocent. . . . he and his counsel cheating our Company."[9]

The cause of the estrangement between Minuit and van Remund is not given in the correspondence, but underlying it was the split in the Company officialdom over the patroon issue, which had become keener after new directors had replaced some of the old ones. Minuit was of the party favoring the system of manorial estates, whereas van Remund represented the opposite faction, which had grown to a majority. Thus, the division of opinion at home among the directors spread across the Atlantic to the American colony, bringing about an intolerable situation in the administration of the Company's business. Pos added to his letter to van Rensselaer that " the honorable directors hear nothing but idle complaints from their subjects ; one says this, the other that, so that in place of the Company's servants looking after the trading someone else in the meanwhile goes off with the skins."[10]

Van Rensselaer, who was in a position to hear and weigh the accusations on either side, blamed van Remund for fomenting the trouble, referring to him as " this false secretary, who has slandered many men behind their backs."[11] Of course, as a patroon, he strongly favored the manorial system and would be

---

[8] *Ibid.*

[9] A. Eekhof, *Jonas Michaëlius Founder of the Church in New Netherland,* A. W. Sijthoff's Publishing Co., Leyden, 1926, p. 68.

[10] *VRB,* pp. 169–170.

[11] *Ibid.,* p. 269.

expected to support Minuit against the opposition party. However, other evidence points to van Remund as a troublemaker who turned others against Minuit. For example, when Michaëlius arrived at Manhattan in 1628 he chose Minuit and Jan Huygen, the storekeeper and Minuit's brother-in-law, to serve as elders in the church there.[12] This suggests that initially the minister was friendly with Minuit until he fell under van Remund's influence. As the hatred between Minuit and van Remund worsened, Michaëlius said in a letter to a friend that he had " brought the whole business before the Directors of the Company," meaning that he had written letters describing the situation ; he complained in these letters that he was so unhappy that he wanted to be ordered home.[13] Van Remund wrote to friendly supporters in the Company's inner circle, upbraiding Minuit and criticizing his actions ; Marcus de Vogelaer, a director of the Amsterdam Chamber and commissioner for New Netherland affairs, was one of the executives of the anti-patroon party sympathetic to van Remund, who had come into a position of influence.[14] The net result of this wrangling was the recall not only of Minuit but of Remund, Michaëlius, and others to face a board of inquiry — a drastic course of action without parallel in the history of New Netherland.

En route, the *Eendraght,* " laden with peltries," was held in Plymouth in April of 1632, the English claiming that the Dutch had been illegally engaged in the fur trade in English territory, for they so considered New Netherland.[15] After wordy diplomatic exchanges and heated conversations, the vessel was finally released, and Minuit arrived in Holland in June to face the directors.

---

[12] *Narratives, Jameson,* p. 124.
[13] Eekhof, *op. cit.,* p. 68.
[14] *VRB,* p. 268.
[15] *NYCD,* 1 : 51.

No records have been found of the hearing, how it was conducted, the names of the testifiers, nor the nature of the testimony. Most historians hold to the idea, recently expressed by Ellis, that "the directors recalled Minuit in 1631 because they felt he was more interested in aiding the landholders than in guarding the company's monopoly of the fur trade."[16] On the other hand, another authority says that the States-General, having received complaints from the patroons that the Company was not fulfilling its obligations under the *Charter of Freedoms,* "set on foot an investigation of the Director, the patroons, and the West India Company itself, with the result that in 1632 Minuit was recalled and the power of the patroons was limited."[17]

The Company was under severe criticism, at the time of the recall of Minuit and his associates, for having incurred unnecessary expenses in the American venture. Doubtless Minuit bore the brunt of this criticism, and who is to say that some of it was not warranted? The Company was accused of bad management in allowing heavy expense for new construction in the colony instead of using its funds to increase the population by encouraging private persons to take up residence there. Among the unnecessary things was "building the ship New Netherland at excessive outlay, by erecting three expensive mills, by brick-making, by tar-burning, by ash-burning, by salt-making and like operations. . . ."[18]

Presumably these and other charges were aired during the hearing, and when everything was over, Johan van Remund was given a clean slate and returned to New Netherland to continue his official duties as secretary of the colony. As for Minuit, he was no longer in the Company's employ when the

---

[16] David M. Ellis, Chapter 1, *A Short History of New York State,* Cornell University Press, 1957, p. 23.

[17] Allen Johnson, ed., The Chronicles of America Series, vol. 7, *Dutch and English on the Hudson,* Yale University Press, 1921.

[18] *Narratives, Jameson,* p. 321 (1650).

hearing ended! Others beside him were involved in the judgment, for van Rensselaer wrote that Bylvelt and de Reux " were prevented from again returning thither," meaning they were banned from New Netherland, as Verhulst had been banned almost a decade earlier.[19] Perhaps Minuit was also forbidden from returning " thither," but this is not a certainty, since the full decision of the examiners is not known. Minuit had arrived in Amsterdam in late June ; on July 20, van Renssaeler wrote that Minuit's bowerie would be taken over by van Twiller, who was " going thither as director-general," as Minuit's replacement. This means that the hearing was held in the first part of July— and that it must have been concluded with deliberate speed.

Michaëlius, who had doubtless testified against Minuit, appeared before the Consistory at Amsterdam to make an independent report in which he related " different kinds of incidents which had happened, whereby his services and person have been subjected to many disturbances and troubles." Later he sought reappointment and an opportunity to return to his flock in New Netherland, but the directors of the Amsterdam Chamber rejected his application, and thus he was also prevented from returning " thither."[20]

So far as van Remund is concerned, chronically a troublemaker, he continued to undermine his superiors after his return to New Netherland. On April 23, 1634, van Rensselaer wrote to Director van Twiller, " The crown which the secretary [van Remund] had placed on the head of Minuict, rests now on yours ; the enemies of Minuict are now yours. This crafty knave has stirred up the present minister [Everhardus Bogardus] against

---

[19] *VRB,* p. 291.

[20] Eekhof, *op. cit.,* p. 73. Kapp says that Minuit sought reemployment by the Company, without success, but this author is not to be trusted. (Friedrich Kapp, " Peter Minuit aus Wesel," Sybel's *Historische Zeitschrift,* 1866, 15 : 225–250).

you, as he did the former against Minuict."[21] Before the van Twiller administration had ended, some of the directors may have wished that they had not recalled Minuit, because van Twiller's lavish spending brought the colony to the verge of ruin ; he was recalled in 1637 and replaced by Willem Kieft.

How Minuit, resentful over his treatment by the Company, left Holland and found employment with a Swedish company organized under Dutch influence has been told in detail elsewhere.[22] What has not been brought into sharp focus is the unique qualifications possessed by Minuit to command a Swedish expedition to the Delaware River where the Dutch had failed in their settlement efforts. There can be no question that Minuit, at the time he was engaged by Sweden, knew more about New Netherland than any other living person. He had been a member of the Verhulst expedition ; he was the Director-General when the Walloons abandoned their settlement on Burlington Island and returned to Manhattan ; he issued the patents to Hossitt for the patroons ; he was still in office when the Indians massacred the settlers at Swanendael. He had explored the Delaware River system for minerals, as Verhulst was instructed to have him do. He must have known that the two major tributaries, the Schuylkill and Minquas Kill, were vital arteries in the Minquas beaver trade. He was fully aware of the absence of fortifications to block the entrance to Delaware Bay and River, and he knew that Fort Nassau was too far upstream to deter his plans to found a settlement on the Minquas Kill. It was he who had informed Godyn about the opportunities for whale fishing in the Delaware. He

---

[21] *VRB,* p. 268.

[22] *Swedish Settlements,* vol. 1, Chap. 12. An authoritative biography of Minuit remains to be written. Kapp's account (*op. cit.*) is largely based on American sources and is not reliable. However, Kapp contributes an interesting note by stating that " Minnewit Island " was in Long Island Sound and was so called a century after Minuit's death. " Minnewits Island " was cited in 1673 by the captain of the frigate *Zee-hond* (*NYCD,* 2 : 655).

had long experience in the Indian trade and knew exactly what type of merchandise — duffels, axes, hatchets, mirrors, chains, finger rings, combs — was in greatest demand and would bring the maximum number of pelts. He realized the importance of bringing farmers who knew how to raise tobacco and grain. Above all, as an ex-governor, he knew the weaknesses and strengths of the West India Company, their procedures and philosophies of doing business, and he had access to many of their confidential reports not intended for the eyes of outsiders. In short, he was an ideal man for a competitor to hire!

Two vessels were rigged and outfitted for the long voyage across the Atlantic, a man o' war called the *Kalmar Nyckel* ("Key of Calmar "), usually referred to as the " ship," and a yacht, the *Vogel Grip* (" Bird Griffin "). A small sloop, to be used in the Indian trade, was carried by the *Kalmar Nyckel*. The crews of the two vessels were half Dutch, half Swedish. Jan Hindrickson van der Water was engaged as skipper of the *Kalmar Nyckel*, with Michel Symonssen, who was well acquainted with the North American coast, as first mate. Andrian Jöransen was skipper of the *Grip*. Both, of course, were subordinate to Minuit. In case of mishap, Symonssen was to take Minuit's place. Memorials and other papers were issued to the officers, according to custom, and a set of secret instructions was given to Minuit.

These secret instructions, written in Dutch, were intended only for Minuit's eyes. One reason for secrecy was the extreme importance of keeping the information away from the Dutch, because the Swedes feared strong opposition if news of the expedition leaked out to the West India Company. The instructions are anonymous, although Johnson suggested that Samuel Blommaert drafted and revised them.[23] Blommaert had left the West India Company and gone over to the Swedes, originally

---

[23] *Swedish Settlements*, 1 : 109, 114.

proposing a Swedish settlement on the Guinea coast to exploit the copper trade.

On the other hand, Minuit argued for developing the fur trade with the Indians and founding a colony in America to be known as *New Sweden* — a term that evidently was first used by him.[24] Minuit's idea was readily accepted by Blommaert (who invested 3,600 riksdalers in the project) and by the other Swedish and Dutch stockholders, who invested a total of 14,400 riksdalers, equivalent to 36,000 florins — approximately $15,000.[25]

Sprinchorn believed that the secret instructions may have been written by Minuit.[26] There is little question that the author of the instructions (or one of the authors) was familiar with the geography of the New Netherlands, and Minuit had been there, whereas Blommaert had not. Furthermore, Blommaert's letters are so different in style from the instructions that it is unlikely he was the composer, although he may have had a hand in them.

The secret instructions, which have not previously been translated into English, are preserved in manuscript in the Royal Archives in Stockholm. A microfilm copy may be consulted in the Memorial Library of the University of Delaware. There are also, in the Historical Society of Pennsylvania, two transcripts of the manuscript : one anonymous, the other by Sprinchorn. In the translation by Dunlap which follows, proper names are as they originally appeared ; punctuation is often supplied.

---

[24] The term was first used in his letter of June 15, 1636. An English translation appeared in *Penna. Magazine*, 6, No. 4 (1882), 458–459; for another English translation see *Winsor*, 4:445, fn 2 ; a facsimile of the original letter is in *Swedish Settlements*, 1: between pp. 96 and 97.

[25] *Swedish Settlements*, 1:106. It was Minuit's intention, after establishing a post on the Delaware, to convey peasants from the vicinity of Cleef as colonists (see Blommaert's letter, November 13, 1638, in G. W. Kernkamp, ed., *Zweedsche Archivalia*, 29:1–442 ; reprinted from *Bijdragen en Mededeelingen het Historisch Genootschap* [van Utrecht]).

[26] Carl K. S. Sprinchorn, "The History of the Colony of New Sweden," *Penna. Magazine*, 8, No. 3 (1884), 254, fn.

Instruction for the director, Peter Minuit, who as director shall sail to the coast of Florida with the ship named *Calmer Sleutel,* whose captain is Jan Hendrickse van de Waeter and the yacht named [blank],[27] whose captain is Erassmus Jeurianse.

So in the summer it shall be, as you shall depart out of Gottenborch, you shall fix your course to run around behind Schottland and to sail then in a suitable course of approximately 44 degrees, and, if it is feasible, to touch Ille de Sable, since we gladly would have proper inspection made there.

Concerning the same island, if it [the time] is in the middle of the summer, while it is smooth there, search everywhere with the boat, sounding the depths, to see if there is an entrance through which to bring ships, and note the condition that on the east side as well as on the northwest run reefs, and between them [we have] knowledge that a good haven exists.

You shall make a good sketch, for this island, of all havens, roads, steads, and other places.

You shall bring the sloop to land and there let the carpenter start operations, making sure that it [i.e., the work] is well done.

While the sloop is being put in shape, explore the island in order to become familiar with its possibilities.

You shall diligently undertake, since there are many black foxes there, to find out if any of these could be got hold of ; to that end you shall take with you a suitable hound as well as a brach.

You shall also diligently inquire concerning [other] animals, since for a long time animals have been thought to be very abundant there.

And as it would be convenient for us to have a few calves in the Seuyt Reviere [i.e., South, or Delaware River], if it shall be found advisable (since in the Minquaes kill[28] we intend to take possession)

---

[27] Left blank when the instructions were written, because it was thought that only one vessel (the *Kalmar Nyckel;* in Dutch, the *Calmer Sleutel*) would be sent. Later, the *Vogel Grip* joined the expedition.

[28] Note that the site of the Swedish settlement on the Minquas Kill (present Christina River) had been decided upon before Minuit sailed. Having been there before, he doubtless played a part in selecting it.

you shall [exercise] diligence to get a few and take them there.

In case you find this island suitable for populating and planting a colony, in order from there with yachts and sloops to have dealings with the mainland coast as well as to have tribute from the fishing which is carried on upon the great bank of Terra Nova, and any other consequent advantages, you shall take one of the coats of arms which are hewn in stone in Sweden, erecting it there solemnly and under proper jurisdiction, taking witness by all officers that you have gone there and, finding no people on the island, have taken possession of it for the crown of Sweden, naming the same Christina[29] [and] the best havens likewise naming after the great in Sweden.

You shall provide the sloop with food for a voyage of two or three months, placing thereon as captain a good person who is familiar with the whole coast, and giving him the title of captain of the sloop.

If you can get hold of a few cattle there, butcher them and salt them well in order to increase your food supply, the more [of it] on land to be able to leave and the better to provide for the sloop.

You shall likewise take plenty of fishing tackle in order to fish here, and in other places, to make the ship's food supply last longer.

However, if it happens that the wind comes from the west to such a degree that you are unable to sail directly but seek the principal route in order to sail through the Caribise islands, in such event sail and fix your course between Couba and Spaniolla and, if occasion dictates, place your sloop near Saona, and if any time is [left] over, you shall cruise with the sloop between Saona and Spaniola, where there is much movement of small ships which come from Sint Domingo and other places ; and meanwhile cruise with the ship between Mona and Saona, fixing a sure rendezvous where you shall find one another in order to proceed together to the South River, taking all care that not too much time be spent there [i.e., cruising]; and capturing some barques, you shall set the crews on land and

---

[29] The queen's name was to be given to Sable Island; nothing in the instructions told Minuit to apply her name to the Minquas Kill.

take the barques with you, first and above everything examining thoroughly the possibility of the area and the time when the greatest movement exists, without letting them know who you are or who has taken them.

Also if, in sailing, you do not go so far to the south and hold more to a middle course, you shall shun the very rocky island of Bermudes, which lies in twenty-three degrees of north latitude.

But it is our express wish that you shall do everything possible to reach the island of Sable ; you shall undertake this so that you can make a satisfactory report to us of its possibilities.

Sailing from the island of Sable, or Christina, you shall fix your course in order to be able to pass properly Cabo de Mallabare, seeing to it that the sloop does not stray from you.

However, if it turns out that through misfortune or in some other way you wander from one another, you shall fix a proper rendezvous where each may meet the other, which would seem to me to be best in the foremost place where sewant is made, which is named Cromegauege.[30]

And thus if it happens that the sloop at any time comes there before you, so shall you cause to be placed in the sloop some suitable cargoes so that meanwhile the one waiting there may barter for sewant ; consequently it would be wise to place someone in the sloop who has been there and has knowledge thereof, giving the same good instructions besides.

You shall sail forth along the coast and touch all places in which sewant is to be bartered; as much as it is convenient to do, you shall also have pelt-work (if it is to be had), as well as all the traffic in sewant.

You shall then sail away secretly to the South River without touching the North River, and run to the Minquaes Kill, doing all in your power, by means of gifts, to barter with the savages so

---

[30] The exact site of *Cromegauege* has not previously been named, although Johnson says it was on the New England coast (*Swedish Settlements,* 1 : 113, fn. 15). It was specifically in the Gardiners Bay sector of Long Island (*NYCD,* 1 : 360, 545, 565; 2 : 135). It is a Dutch word meaning " crooked country."

that everywhere in the land you make known that you have come there to trade with them in good fellowship.

You shall with the sloop run twenty miles up to the Sankikans Kill to do the like there, and show them every friendship, before everything taking care that good watch be kept and that no trouble be made for the people by the crew.

If you send the sloop elsewhere, give special instruction that no one is to trust them [i.e., the savages]; but good watch shall be kept, as well as good care taken, so that the pelt-work obtained by barter may be well preserved and not destroyed.

You shall, if you think it thoroughly advisable, place on the Minques kill, at a point which is naturally strong for defense, a lodge or house in which the people may dwell who remain there close to the sloop.

You shall raise there with ceremony a Swedish coat of arms, taking at the same time a testimonial signed by all officers that no European nation had been found there, [and] requesting of the natives that the land be made over to the crown of Sweden, everything in the presence of the officers; and let them, in the interest of trade, subscribe to the purchase of the land in possession of the savages.[31]

In the Sankikans kil you shall do likewise and raise a coat of arms with appropriate ceremonies, giving each a name.[32]

The land between the two erected coats of arms you shall cause to be named New Sweden; in case you discover land at the hook of Florida, you shall name that New Sweden and this [i.e., land on the South River] New Stockholm, the same also being named with ceremonies and firing of cannon, everything with the knowledge

---

[31] The " Affidavit of Four Men from the Key of Calmar," made December 29, 1638, indicates that Minuit carefully followed these instructions by settling on the Minquas Kill and there " building a fort on the bank of the river," after purchasing the land from the Indians. He erected the arms of " Her Illustrious Majesty of Sweden," accompanied by the firing of cannon and other ceremonies in the presence of " said sachems or princes and the country was called New Sweden " (*Narratives, Myers,* pp. 86–89).

[32] Minuit was instructed, as indicated, to give both the Minquas Kill and the Sankikans Kill European names, but was not told what names to use.

and attestation of officers, who alone the witnessing may attest.

Should you think it advisable to extend the limits higher and farther, let it be done and let the sloop go as far up the river as you can, in order to seek trade. In case you meet any French or English or Dutch or others alien to the Crown of Sweden, you shall reply to the same no more than serves full friendship.

However, if you come upon any Spaniard or Spanish ally attack them with courage and even try to prevail, but let neither ship nor yacht stand in peril, so that, in this way, the design mentioned by us above may not be concealed.

You shall also shun the limits of New Netherland in order not to become involved in any quarrel with the West India Company.

You shall then go everywhere with the sloop to seek trade, sailing in and out of all rivers to the south, and saying to any savages found [there] that the severe winter immobilizes the yacht, [but] that you will come again in the spring in order to trade with them.

You shall with the tribes named *Sinicus* [*Senecas*], *Minques*, *Maquaes* [*Mohawks*], *Astarogen*, *Sanckikans*, *Armewamecks*, *Sicanesen* [*Siconese*], and other strange tribes, make arrangements for trade.

And if any time remains in which to sail southwards, you shall do so with the ship along the coast of Florida, in order to discover good possibilities, and finding [opportunity] for trade outside the English territory, you shall raise there likewise a coat of arms; and if it should prove to be a sizeable land, it would be best to name it New Sweden, and to give the foregoing another name.

Of the new lands which you discover you shall make a suitable sketch, as well as keep a complete journal and daily record, so that in the event of death everything may come to our knowledge.

You shall in these quarters diligently undertake to find out if any ambergris is obtainable, as well as gold, silver, pearls, and other minerals.

And if the winter sets in early and the storms rise exceedingly in the beginning of September, do not remain there long but seek betimes suitable winter quarters, as the time may be too late to explore such a place in 1637.[33]

Accordingly you shall do the same about trade in the spring of 1638,[34] that is, about May, for then will be a suitable time to inspect all places.

Meanwhile allow the sloop to follow the trade, but if it turn out that the good Lord so blesses the trade that the greater part of the cargoes are sold, you shall, without any further exploration, return home, letting the sloop with some person and a youth remain there in order to hold possession and to keep the savages loyal so that we may continue to trade there, further exploration to be done on the next voyage.

However, if it happens that through domestic strife and other hindrances the trade proves to be so bad that the greater part of the cargoes are left over, you shall accordingly fortify a little the house that is erected on the land in the Minques Kill and may take from the ship two artillery pieces with ammunition to place therein. Remain there yourself with the sloop, and send the ship over with the captain (giving him [an] extract from these instructions concerning the conduct of the return journey), letting the ship sail with approximately twenty men. The rest of the crew [is] to remain with you in the house as well as on the sloop, and it would be suitable to let the people who remain on the land be officered by the petty mate—otherwise too great a burden [would fall on you].

You shall there [in] the winter do everything possible to get trade, and likewise journey everywhere in order to further trade.

You shall keep on land as much food as you can spare and [at the same time] conveniently send the ship home.

Also, having taken along for the people suitable seeds of rye, barley, oats, buckwheat, etc., you shall choose a good place and time for the winter sowing, in order that there may be no want thereof in the spring of the next year.

---

[33] The date should read 1638. When the instructions were written it was planned for Minuit to set out several months before the actual time of departure.

[34] In terms of historical events, this should read 1639.

In the spring you shall again prepare tools in order to bring the summer sowing into the earth, also green vegetables of that place.

You shall at a good opportunity sail with the sloop to the Manhates to see if you can buy there on credit, with the consent of the director, some horses, conies, sheep, goats, hogs, etc., and bring them to the Minques Kill.

In case you also have opportunity to sow more land, and seed is in short supply, endeavor there to buy the same.

And if, for this or that unanticipated inconvenience, it happens that it is impossible to make a profitable voyage, you shall exert every effort to make expenses; to that end consider tacking about with the ship and sloop to the Caribese islands and running there again to Saona in order there to entrap with the ship, between Mona and Saona, some cruising Spanish ships or barques, as before is related, letting the sloop run and haul close to the wind between Saona and the land of Spaniola.

Also consider crossing to the fast-land at Cape Caldero, between which cape and Crakes is much traffic in the months of March and April. In April and May many barques [likewise] pass by in the vicinity of Tortougas.

From there crossing to the Cabo de Tibron, which lies on the west side of Espaniola, keep watch at the little island of Navarra, where many ships pass; but you shall well look to it that you are not surprised by the fleet of Terre Firma, since it often takes this route.

In the early part of July until August do this on the northeast side of Couba, for whatever comes from Porto Rico, Sint Domingo, and the fast-land, also from Comma, Commenagotto, Sint Margeritta, comes past Monna, through between Porto Rico and Spaniola, and along the eastside of Spaniola and Cuba.

In July two ships coming from Spain for the governor of Havana pass there; in order to watch for these conveniently you must, by night or out of sight of land, sail past Baracoa. Lying on the northeast side of Couba are modestly fine bays as far as the sandbanks.

Among the wares to be found between Capo Crus and Ille de Pinnas is coral; from the bay[s] in the general area often 4,000 barges[35] are loaded yearly. Having been at Cartajenne, some small barques with three or four hundred barge[load]s[36] and other wares [may be found] sailing on the east side of Couba and running along the north side through the other channel near Havana, since none may run along the south side at Couba Corentes and Cabo Sint Antoon for fear of the king of Spain.

From Cartaiena to Porto Bello traffic is carried on during the whole year, and below Porto Bello, on the island of Sint Andries, one can conveniently keelhaul a ship, but there is very little fresh water or [opportunity for] unsalting any.

However, since the Spanish now sail there in strength with frigates and lately seized an English and a French ship, it is thus fitting to avoid this place.

When the fleet departs, for from four to twelve days many barques come out of Havana. To have much money and other wares, watch carefully with a sloop at the Caycas near Rio de Porcas. The ship must lie at the Cape Sint Antoni or elsewhere in order not to be seen.

This is something which can be taken into consideration if things turn out badly, in order to make good the expenses.

Some of these things demand cautious proceedings; thus in view of our small numbers it would be a mistake if these came into any difficulty, and so in my judgment it would be best to watch between Saona and Spaniola.

On the other hand [it would be best to watch] between Cabo Crus and Isle de Pinnas for the ships and barques with barge-[load]s[37] to pass.

However, we do not doubt but that the trade on the coast of Florida will turn out to be so good that nothing like this will prove necessary.

And since skippers and crews are often more inclined, and know [better] how to undertake to acquire good booty than to trade, you

---

[35] The Ms has *heuyden* (" hides ") which does not fit the context. A scribal error for *heuden* (" hoys," " lighters," " barges ") has been assumed.

[36] Cf. fn. 35.

[37] Cf. fn. 35.

shall communicate this instruction to no one, except the whole section related before about making good the adversities of trade or other inconveniences of the voyage.

You shall then fix your homeward course to sail to the Island of Sable in case this has not been possible in going there [to America], and do then all similarly, as was related before; it is our wish that you should undertake the exploration of this place in order to make us a thorough report thereof, keeping a complete record or draft of everything.

From there fix your course, if it is early enough, behind England, but if it should be late in the year, fix your course through the channel; and run into the river of Gottenborch, sending someone at once overland to Stockholm in order to let the honorable gentlemen of the government and company know of your arrival, requesting whether it were best to stay away, below, with the ship or to pass [through] the sound and come to Stockholm, since this is the first ship to have been out of Sweden on such a far journey.

You shall also, immediately upon your arrival above the sound, write to us here about the cargo of freight, and, in short, [inquire] whether to sail up this way at once or, below, to put cargoes aboard, to permit the ship to be sent on a second voyage before the winter.

And since, through the long-drawn-out war in Germany, otters are in small demand, which properly before used to sell for 8 or 10 guilders, but now for 3 [guilders] or thereabouts, few come asking for otter — most for beaver and bear and other skins.

You shall take care that in the ship as on land every morning and evening a prayer is read by someone appointed to do so, and a psalm sung, and on Sunday a chapter from the New Testament [read], being sure that everyone listens to it together, with attention.

This instruction thus far agrees with a copy found in Sweden.

And if the crown of Sweden favors this company with the loan of a yacht, so suit these changes to this instruction that you shall regulate it according to the prevailing circumstances.

In case you sail so early that you are able to be in the Caribische Islands about mid-July, fix your course for the Canarise islands in order to seek the principal route. Run straight for the Caribische Islands ; and ahead, near the island Espaniolla on the east-south-east side, lies an island named Saona, in eighteen degrees [of latitude]. If there is a suitable opportunity, put the sloop thereupon; and while the sloop is there, cruise with the yacht between the island and Spaniolla, between which there is much coming and going of small [blank — probably, " craft "] ; and with the ship you shall run to the island Angiles, which lies north of the island Sinte Marten, and there, upon seeing a suitable [blank], in all haste take in as much salt as may conveniently be loaded, wherewith those over yonder will be able to do much trading in the yacht; you shall also run with the ship to the island Seinte Cristoffer in order somewhere there to trade wine, brandy, stockings, shoes, etc. (whatever can be spared) for tobacco, seeing to it that the tobacco is not too highly valued, and getting as much for your merchandise as is possible.

You shall there, according to opportunity, diligently undertake [to learn] (however strong the Spaniards are upon Sinte Martin)—upon what islands salt is to be had, keeping good record of everything, so that in case of death everything may come to our knowledge.

The yacht shall meanwhile remain there until the ship returns (good rendezvous—in order to find one another—having been fixed); however, since [the island] of Cristoffel is on the southeast side below [blank], it would be best to put proper merchandise on the yacht for sale on Sint Cristoffel, letting the yacht carry on trade and running with the ship to Saona in order to place the sloop thereon.

And since the sloop will not require extensive restoration, you can provide it with crew and victuals, and let it cruise between Saona and Espaniola, where in some places there is not more than ten feet of water; the ship can meanwhile cruise between Mona and Saona until the yacht returns, and should there still be time enough the ship can run to Angille aforesaid in order to load salt and yet make rendezvous for the joint crossing to Virginia.

But could Monte Cristy, on the north side of Spaniola (about the middle of the island, in twenty degrees [of latitude]), be touched, determine if there is a salt-pan ; if you lack salt, you can try to get salt there.

Nearby also lies Rio de Sint Nicolaes ; you can run in there with the sloop and yacht. Along the west-hook of Spaniola there are skins, but you must take good heed that you are not surprised by Spaniards. Dwelling there, are about twenty or twenty-five Spaniards, who have with them a few blacks to do nothing but kill animals for the skins. Keep good watch, and above all things, under whatever protection possible, do not trust them but use all means to get into communication, offering that they may take away such goods as they desire in exchange for pelts; also you shall see if you can acquire a few calves there.

It remains to note that the months of March, April, May, June, and July are good for getting salt; then come the rainy months that dissolve the salt, although one year is more rainy than another.

In the month of April the frigates at Sint Jan de Lus depart to fetch what is in Compe[t]s[ch]y, since the frigates already laden with hides, cochineal, etc., sail there in order to meet them.

From Nova Spanien frigates and barques often come to Havana laden with meal, which will be very good merchandise to trade for tobacco at Sint Cristoffel and other places; so you shall gather this and other cargoes, all to be traded for tobacco.

Twenty-five miles westward from Competschy is a good river named Tabasco, where there are a great many hides, and cochineal.

En route, watch about the middle of August for a ship bringing pay for the soldiers to Margarita, Porta Dacaia, Cumana and other places of the mainland.

Many barques, tacking about from Cartajena for Marycaybo, Coro [blank], and other places on the mainland, pass Coba de La Vela with good merchandise.

However, since it is our intention to have dealings upon the coast of Florida, for which purpose the cargoes are prepared, you shall not spend too much time watching in an effort to bring prizes here, but cross betimes in order to come into the South River, making the

Indians everywhere aware of your coming, [and] also running in and out of all the rivers for the purpose of seeking trade.

So it seemed to me to be best that you run directly to Isle de Sable, as first related, in order to set up the sloop there, and with the yacht to run at once toward Caep de Mallabare, in order to pass it, giving the yacht good and suitable cargoes to exchange along the coast for good sewant, and losing no time while the sloop is being set up; and you shall fix [a] suitable rendezvous with one another.

The ship and sloop can then run directly to the south of the South River — and then as before related.

Thus the yacht to [all] appearances will be able to make more profit here this year when in the West Indies, even though the time for cruising there is supposed to be mostly over.

And you could then allow the yacht to tack about near the Caribise Islands earlier in the spring, in accord with the remarks in the instruction before related.

But in all things you shall govern yourself according to the opportunity of the times and discuss with one another what it is best to do.

And if it turns out that it is as late in the year as the latter part of August before you depart from Gottenborch, you shall do everything possible to be able to come upon the coast with speed in order to trade for sewant at the Crommegaue and wherever else you may do so, and then run past the North River to the South [River], remaining outside the limits of New Netherland [and] trading only southwards.

And when the month of December shall have passed, cross to the Caribise Islands with the ship and yacht and do there as before is related.

You shall let the ship remain there throughout the month of May and then cross over with the ship to the South River and there load all the skins acquired in trade, in order to return therewith to Gottenborch in time to prepare the ship and cargoes for the second voyage.

Since it well could happen that the ship might be long held up there, as soon as the trading in Virginia is concluded in May you shall order expressly what whoever goes with the ship is to remain lying in the West Indies no longer than May.

And if it should happen that the good Lord come to fetch you and that for that reason our affairs should be in arrears, Michiel Seymesse, mate of the *Calmer Sleutel*, shall succeed to your place and have the administration of everything, to whom we hereby give all authority as if you yourself were still alive.

And the boatswain of the ship, named Anderies Leuykasse,[38] shall concern himself with the trade along the coast, joining with him Jan Jansen or someone [else] who carries the quill.

And if your beloved self arrive with the ship, that sold the largest cargoes, you shall attend to all such persons there on land as you shall see fit, giving the same good information, telling them what to do if the yacht comes there, and doing everything which tends toward the interest of the company.

It is a matter of history that Minuit fulfilled his mission for the Swedes in an able manner, although circumstances may have necessitated certain departures from the secret instructions. For example, after leaving Sweden the two vessels were separated in the North Sea by heavy storms, and a month later Minuit was forced to visit the Texel to repair the leaking *Kalmar Nyckel* and replace her prow and mast. A week later the battered *Grip* also arrived in Holland for repairs. While Minuit was at the Texei, his patroon friend van Rensselaer asked him to carry goods to his colony and also to transport six persons, including a relative,

---

[38] Another form of " Andress Lucassen," a member of the expedition who had previously lived in New Netherland and who served as Minuit's Indian translator (*Narratives, Myers*, p. 86). In addition to Symonssen, van der Water, and Jöransen, also named in the instructions, other known members of the expedition were Peter Johanssen, upper boatswain from Beemster, Johan Joachinssen, the gunner, Hendrick Huyghen, commissioner, Mans Nilsson Kling, in charge of the Swedish soldiers, and Jacob Evertssen Sandelin from Scotland (*ibid.;* cf. *Swedish Settlements,* 1 : 112).

Arent van Curler, to New Netherland. Minuit continued to keep his destination a secret, and van Rensselaer wrote to Kieft, " I could only make out this much that he expected to go to Virginia, from which region I have asked him to try to find opportunity to send my goods and people to the Company's settlement." [39]

On December 31, 1637, the two vessels went to sea again, but nothing is known of the journey, because Minuit's journal, which contained this information, as well as a map, sketches of Fort Christina and two houses built there, and other papers, are now missing. From what is known of Minuit's activities after his arrival on the Delaware — the building of Fort Christina, setting up markers, buying land from the Indians, sending the *Grip* to Virginia, and sending other things — he evidently followed his instructions to the letter.

It was in the course of complying with his instructions that Minuit met his tragic and untimely end. He had left the *Grip* at Fort Christina and had gone to the island of St. Christopher on the *Kalmar Nyckel,* en route to Sweden, to exchange his cargo for tobacco.

What happened there is revealed in a letter written by Blommaert dated at Amsterdam January 20, 1640, from which the following passage was translated by Dunlap :

He had there exchanged his cargoes for tobacco and being ready to depart from there, went with his captain [van der Water] as a guest on board a ship from Rotterdam, named *de Vliegende Hart* [the " Flying Hart "] that lay there and traded. When they were about a half hour from shore, according to the explanation of the officers, the hurricane, an extraordinary storm-wind, which, so men say, comes only once in six or seven years, overtook them, where through all the ships, over twenty, were driven seawards from the road, some losing their masts and others perishing, including the

---

[39] *VRB,* p. 403.

ship the " Flying Hart," upon which were Minuit and his captain.[40]

Symonssen, as authorized by the instructions, took command of the *Kalmar Nyckel* and brought her back home, although he encountered storms again in the North Sea and was delayed by the Dutch at Mendemblik, where the pelts were unloaded. The *Grip* returned to Sweden in June of 1639, and her pelts were also sold in Holland.

For some years to come, Minuit's name was referred to disparagingly in Dutch communications dealing with the Swedish colony on the Delaware. The following is an example :

. . . a certain person named Pieter Minuyt, forgetful of the benefits conferred on him by the Company whose Director he had been in New Netherland, cast his eye upon it. But not knowing under what pretense to go there, he proceeded to Sweden and having as 'twas asserted, obtained a Commission from that Crown, transported himself thence to the South River, with one or two ships and some Swedes, the most of whom were bandetti . . . full twelve years after the Company had come there.[41]

There was, of course, always the danger that other officers employed by the Company would follow Minuit's example and sell out to a rival nation, and at least one made the threat. Alexander d'Hinoyossa, while tippling in a tavern in New Amstel, upbraided the Company's director and council for their actions toward him. He was reported as having said that he had a mind to " do as one Minnewit, the uncle of Henry Huygen, had done, who was badly treated by the Company and had introduced the Swedes here, saying, so I will go and fetch here the English or them from Portugal, the Swede or the Dane, what the devil do I care, whom I serve and repeating hereupon, etc."[42]

---

[40] Kernkamp, *op. cit.*, p. 177. Kapp (*op. cit.*) erred in stating that Minuit died in New Sweden in 1641 and was buried near Fort Christina. Kapp may have consulted Israel Acrelius, who, in 1759, said that Minuit died at Fort Christina (*A History of New Sweden*, 1874 edition, p. 28).

[41] *NYCD*, 1 : 588.

[42] *Ibid.*, 12 : 376.

VIII

Building Activities and Architecture

Gabriel Thomas did not describe in detail the " two or three houses " occupied by the Walloons on Burlington Island, which is unfortunate, because they were the earliest homes on the Delaware built by Europeans. Perhaps they were similar to the dwellings erected by their countrymen at Fort Orange, where, according to Catelina Trico, they built "hutts of bark"[1] (see Chapter 2). The rectangular bark hut or wigwam, with an arched roof, was a characteristic dwelling of the eastern Algonkian Indians. It was not uncommon for the first white settlers to copy the Indian style of shelter as temporary homes until they had materials to build houses similar to the ones to which they were accustomed in their homelands. The earliest Dutch homes at Manhattan, for example, were also huts made " of the bark of trees."[2] By 1628 the residents at Manhattan were constructing " a windmill to saw lumber," which enabled them to convert logs into planks and clapboards for use in house building.[3]

The palisaded " trading house " which Peter Lourenson saw

---

[1] As late as 1652 permission was granted to a resident at Fort Orange to " erect a small bark house on her lot " (Minutes of the Court of Fort Orange & Beverwyck, trans. van Laer, Albany, 1920, 1 : 22).

[2] *Narratives, Jameson,* p. 83. Father White said that the Yoacomaco Indians gave the first Maryland settlers their houses in which to live. One of these wigwams was used as a chapel where Mass was celebrated (*Narratives, Hall,* p. 42, 73).

[3] *Narratives, Jameson,* p. 131. An early illustration of this windmill occurs on the Cryn Fredericsz drawing made in 1628, reproduced in *View of Old New York, Valentine's Manual,* 1928.

on Burlington Island may also have been used by the Walloons
as a dwelling, and it, too, was probably crudely built. In any
event, these first settlers on the Delaware did not long occupy
their island homes, and after they had gone to Manhattan, the
structures on the island apparently fell apart.

One thing is certain : houses made of logs placed horizontally
and interlocked by corner notching were not built by either the
Dutch or Walloon settlers. They brought to America the architectural concepts of their homelands, and what is now known as
the " log cabin " was not characteristic of the dwellings in the
United Netherlands, France, or Belgium, as it was in the rural
parts of Scandinavia, Germany, and Switzerland. The Dutch
preferred brick and tile construction in their dwelling houses —
although some frame houses were built in Holland. When they
arrived in New Netherland, they were handicapped due to the
limited building materials accessible to them, but they did their
best, under adverse circumstances, to duplicate the houses with
which they were familiar.

Reference has already been made to the " great dwelling
house of Yellow holland brick " and the " kooke howse alsoo of
brick " that stood in Swanendael. Speaking of the former, de
Vries said that it had been " well beset with palisades in place of
breastworks," which seems to mean that it was surrounded by a
stockade of logs set vertically in the earth. The map entitled
De Zuid-Baai in Niew-Nederland (see Figure 1) shows an outline
of the palisades, with bastions, and a sketch of the house that
stood within. A second house is shown outside the palisades. Both
houses and the palisades were destroyed by the Indians after they
massacred the men working in the field.[4]

Reference has also been made to the " large house " at Fort
Nassau, where presumably the commis and the other officers of
the Company resided. Regrettably, this house is not described,

---

[4] *Narratives, Myers,* p. 17.

but the meager bits of information about it suggest that it was of frame construction. For example, a master carpenter built it originally ; later it was repaired with boards sent from Manhattan.[5]

When de Vries arrived in Delaware Bay in 1632, he examined the Swanendael ruins, and then set up a kettle on the beach to render the oil from the whales he expected his men to harpoon. He stated in his journal that he erected a " lodging-hut of boards " for them. This was probably a crude shelter, not more than a shanty, but necessary to protect the shore party from the wintry blasts that swept in from the bay. Of course, it was only a temporary dwelling, whereas the houses erected by the Company's employees and the traders and freemen in the vicinity of Fort Nassau and Fort Beversreede were intended as permanent homes. These dwellings cannot be described with accuracy because they, too, are mentioned only in general terms with vague allusions to " clapboards " and " ground timbers."

In a contemporary English account there is a brief reference to the dwellings at Fort Nassau, italicized in the passage below :

The afforesd yeare 1651; the sd Styvesant with what force he could possiblie raise marched ouer land to Deleware, & all the Interest the Dutch had then in the riuer was a small trading howse Called Fort Nassaw with *4: or 5: smaller houses adjacent,* and a small peece of barren land aboute 40 : leagues vp the riuer . . . .[6]

No references have been found to barns, stables, or other farm buildings which may have been associated with these houses on the Delaware. One must seek elsewhere in New Netherland for clues to the contemporary dwelling houses and associated buildings, and a 1638 Dutch account of farm property on Long Island contains a description which is probably applicable to

[5] *NYCD*, 12 : 56 ; 14 : 16.
[6] *Colls. N.Y. Hist. Soc.,* 2 (1869), 7.

some of the early homes built on the Delaware. In part the reference reads :

> One house surrounded by long round palisades; the house is 26 feet long, 22 feet wide and 40 feet deep with the roof covered above and allround with planks, two garrets one above the other and a small chamber on the side with an outlet on the side . . . .
> One barn 40 feet long, 18 wide and 24 high with the roof . . . .
> One Bergh with five posts, long 40 feet . . . .[7]

(A *bergh* was a shed for storing hay and grain, having open sides and a moveable roof which slid up and down.)

It is of interest that the above farmhouse was surrounded by long, round palisades. This terminology is undoubtedly descriptive of logs set vertically in the earth, not the conventional paled fence. De Vries described a house he occupied as having been constructed " with embrasures through which they could defend themselves " against Indian attack, and there are other references to palisaded houses in the seventeenth-century records of the Dutch occupation of Manhattan Island and Long Lsland. One would expect to find similar palisade fences built to protect the dwelling houses on the Delaware — and such evidence is at hand, as the reader will shortly see.

On Staten Island, in 1663, " within sight of Najeck " there was erected, to protect the settlers against possible Indian attack, " a small, slight wooden Block-house about 18 @ 20 feet square, in the center of their houses, which were slightly constructed of straw and clapboards."[8] Roofs of thatch were used on many of the early Dutch houses in New Netherland, although they proved to be a serious fire hazard. For example, attacking Indians destroyed four houses in the patroons' settlement of Pavonia, " by igniting the roofs which are all either of reed or straw."[9] De Vries

[7] *NYCD*, 14 : 10.
[8] *Ibid.*, 2 : 443.
[9] *Narratives, Jameson,* p. 279.

wrote about a colonist who was slain by Indians while he was " sitting on a barn and thatching it," which indicates that some of the farm buildings were also roofed with thatch.[10]

Regarding blockhouses, a Dutch description of this type of structure erected in New Netherland stated :

The blockhouses are built by putting beam upon beam, and for their better defense are each provided with two or three light pieces of ordnance of which one or two are pedereroes.[11]

In 1644, the houses at Rensselaerswyck were said to have been built " merely of boards and thatched. As yet there is no mason work except the chimneys. The forests furnishing many large pines, they make boards by means of their mills which they have for the purpose."[12] The patroon van Rensselaer shipped tiles from Holland to his agent at Rensselaerswyck, stating, " Use the tiles which I sent over for the roof of your house to protect it against [Indian] fire arrows."[13]

During its first decade, New Netherland had very few brick houses, although as early as 1628 bricks of a low grade were being manufactured at Manhattan.[14] In 1638, according to the master house carpenter, Gillis Petersen van der Gouw, there were

---

[10] *Ibid.*, p. 215 ; see also p. 198 wherein de Vries describes how a fire started when a spark ignited Cornelis van Horst's house, thatched with rushes.

[11] *NYCD*, 14:546. In 1656, it was planned " to build the blockhouse church " at Fort Orange (Minutes, Court Fort Orange, p. 263). For further references to Dutch blockhouses, see *NYCD*, 1:360; 2:402; 14:261. 449, 494. Blockhouses were constructed in most of the American colonies in the seventeenth century ; in Maine they were called " garrison houses " and in Virginia, " commaunders " (Harold R. Shurtleff, *The Log Cabin Myth*, Cambridge, 1939).

[12] *Doc. Hist. N.Y.*, 4:23. Between 1641 and 1646, three sawmills were erected (*NYCD*, 1:179).

[13] *VRB*, p. 551. On Jan. 18, 1656, to prevent fires, the Council of New Netherland ordered that no houses be roofed with straw or reeds and " no chimney be made of shingles or wood " (*The Records of New Amsterdam*, 1653–1674, ed. B. Fernow, 1:120, 1897).

[14] *Narratives, Jameson*, p. 131.

" five other brick houses " at Manhattan, in addition to the brick house within the palisades of the fort then occupied by Director-General Minuit.[15] Some of the bricks used in these dwellings were shipped from Holland, but the total supply of bricks, imported and domestic, was so limited that actually they could be spared only for chimneys, fireplaces, ovens, and foundations. The two aforementioned brick buildings at Swanendael were the only brick structures on the Delaware cited in Dutch records prior to the founding of New Amstel.

Lime for mortar was obtained from reducing oyster shells, which the Indians had left in large heaps, especially along the seacoast. There were, of course, many places where building stone could be quarried, with the result that foundations, fireplaces, some dwellings, and a church at Manhattan were built of stone.[16]

There is on record a copy of a contract dated May 30, 1649, made with a house carpenter to build two frame dwellings on the Delaware River. Each house is described as being "32 feet long, 18 do wide and 9 feet of a story ; breastwork 3 feet ; the wooden frame for a double chimney, with the 5 outside and inside doors, 3 window frames, 1 transom window-frame, 1 circular window frame, three partitions, according to circumstances, the roof thereon to be covered with planks."[17] The phrase relating to the chimney might be interpreted to mean that it was to be made partially or entirely of clay; presumably no wooden frame would be needed if bricks were to be used.

The carpenter agreed to cut and trim the pine timber in the woods two-hundred paces from the intended foundations, and the owner agreed to provide this timber at his own expense. The

[15] *Colls. N.Y. Hist. Soc.,* Second Series, 1 : 279 ; *Narratives, Jameson,* p. 259.

[16] *Ibid.,* pp. 259–260. De Vries rated the " good lime burnt of oyster shells much better than our lime in Holland " (*ibid.,* p. 212).

[17] *NYCD,* 12 : 50. The houses on Manhattan had " wooden and plastered chimneys " (*The Records of New Amsterdam,* 1 : 21).

owner further agreed that he would furnish the carpenter, his partner, and a servant food and drink gratis while the house was under construction. When the job was finished, he was obligated to pay the carpenter sixty winter-beaver pelts.

After the building of Fort Casimir in the summer of 1651, a number of Dutch families settled in and near the fort. A few of them had previously lived upriver in the vicinity of Fort Nassau and Fort Beversreede ; others had lived on the Hudson. Unlike immigrants newly arrived from Europe, most of them were seasoned in the house-building problems of the New Netherland.

The fort that dominated what was soon to become the new center of trade and government on the Delaware was 200 feet long and nearly 100 feet wide. It was surrounded by palisades, with an entrance gate on the eastern side facing the river. Between the palisades and the river bank stood an outer palisaded barricade mounted with cannon, a sort of first line of defense in the event of attack. Between this outer defense and the river, a long ramp or wharf crossed the beach and sloped down to the water's edge. The fort proper had four bastions mounted with cannon and their carriages.[18]

Within the palisaded area there was a dwelling house for the officers, a storehouse, a guardhouse, barracks, and other smaller structures. The troops of the garrison lived within the fort, some with their families. The Dutch settlers, among whom were several English families, built their homes and vegetable gardens south

---

[18] Johan Rising, the Swedish governor who succeeded Printz, seized Fort Casimir on Trinity Sunday, 1654, naming it Fort Trinity. The Swedes then held it for about a year, when the Dutch recaptured it. Lindeström stated that at the time Rising took the fort, " it had fallen into almost total decay," and Rising said that the Dutch cannons were useless, necessitating his borrowing " four fourteen-pounders from the ship and placed them in an entrenchment before the fort, the better to sweep the river straight across " (*Narratives, Myers,* p. 147). Lindeström rebuilt the fort and a reproduction of a drawing he made of it appears in *Lindeström,* opp. p. 172.

of the fort facing the river on what the Dutch called the " Strand." This line of little houses would later be called " the first row." Lindeström, writing in 1654, said that twenty-one houses had been built.[19]

From 1651 until the fall of 1664, when Sir Robert Carr seized the Delaware River territory for the Duke of York, the community that grew up around Fort Casimir was predominantly Dutch in social and political character. First under the jurisdiction of the West India Company, and later as a possession of the City of Amsterdam, when its name was changed to New Amstel, it was the capital of a sparsely populated river empire. (The Amstel was a river that ran through the City of Amsterdam.) The inhabitants included Swedes, Finns, a few English, and other nationalities, as well as Dutch, living along the Delaware and its tributaries. The acculturation that resulted left its imprint on the architecture, as it did on language and custom. The story of the town, its government, and its people, has already been told and needs no repetition.[20] The architecture and building activities are here of principal concern.

The unavailability of bricks, tiles, and pantiles necessitated the use of lumber, and no doubt the twenty-one houses reported by Lindeström were made of wood. Although a place called *Steenbackers Hoeck* (" Brickmaker's Corner "), a short distance below the fort, was referred to in 1656,[21] it was not until 1657 that there is record of a brickmaker, Sr. Cornelis Hogeboom, arriving on the Delaware. Evidently he came from Beverswyck and returned there after a short stay at New Amstel ; it is uncertain when, if ever, he started to manufacture bricks.[22] The ship *de Meulen*

---

[19] *Ibid.* Johan Rising in a 1654 report stated there were "22 houses built by the Hollanders " (*Narratives, Myers,* p. 143).

[20] See Jeannette Eckman, ed., *New Castle on the Delaware*, 3rd ed., New Castle Historical Society, 1950; and by the same author, *Crane Hook on the Delaware*, Delaware Swedish Colonial Society, Newark, Del., 1958.

[21] *NYCD*, 12 : 140, 177 ; *Dunlap, 1956*, p. 52.

[22] *History Bulletin 10*, vol. 3, N.Y. State Library, p. 266.

brought bricks from Holland to the Delaware colony in 1658, and both bricks and boards were shipped from Fort Orange, where there were brick kilns and sawmills.[23] These imported bricks were used principally for chimney making ; some seven or eight thousand of them were used to repair the masonry at Fort Altena.[24] (This was a name given by the Dutch to Fort Christina, which had been taken over from the Swedes, repaired, and was garrisoned by the Company.)

In 1659, Cornelis Herperts de Jager built a brick kiln at which he employed four persons, one of whom was a brickmaker who had previously resided at Fort Orange.[25] This artisan was soon accused of theft and was flogged in public, after which he persuaded his three fellow workers to run away from their master, de Jager, with whom they all lived. The production of bricks suffered as a result of this labor shortage.

When Jean Paul Jacquet, who had served the Company for many years in Brazil, took office on the Delaware as vice-director and chief magistrate on December 8, 1655, his instructions bade him clear a street four or five rods wide behind the first row of houses. The intent was to lay out a second street (present Fourth Street) running parallel to the Strand and separated from it by the Green. The houses built there became known as " the second row." Jacquet was further directed to build a bark hut outside the fort as lodging for any Indians who came to trade.[26] He was later criticized for tearing down David Wessel's house near the fort and using the wood to build a barn,[27] further indication that frame houses were built prior to his administration.

[23] *NYCD,* 12:201, 227.

[24] *Ibid.,* p. 225. The Bontemantel papers state that the Company, after the sale to the city, contemplated establishing "a village or city about Fort Altena" (" 1657 July, Papers from New Netherland arrived with the ship the *Bever,*" *New Netherland Papers,* New York Public Library).

[25] *Ibid.,* pp. 237–238.

[26] *NYCD,* 12:116.

[27] *Ibid.,* p. 170.

Jacquet was told to maintain the fort "in a becoming state of defense," and as a safety measure to grant no building or farm lots "between the Kil and the aforesaid Fort nor behind the Fort."[28] This small tributary to the Delaware lying north of the fort was later referred to as "ye Little or Towne Creeke," and the Dutch were the first to build a footbridge over it. The earliest reference to the bridge occurs in the minutes of Jacquet's council, November 8, 1656, when "It was further communicated to the community, that it was very necessary to make a bridge over the Kil, running by the fort, as the passage is impracticable and ought to be made practicable and as in some emergency occuring great difficulties would arise. They accepted to do this and the 12 inst, being Monday was set down for it."[29] There is no description of this bridge, but in 1661 at Manhattan there were "two firme timber bridges with railes on each side,"[30] and perhaps the one built at New Amstel was of similar design.

After the City of Amsterdam took over the town from the Company, Jacob Alricks was sent as the Director and Commissary General to replace Jacquet. He was a man of education, well informed on business matters, and keenly alive to the interests of his employers. Arriving on April 25, 1657, Alricks brought with him a number of new colonists and promptly granted each a sizable lot for a house and garden, "which was soon fenced or encircled with palisades."[31] The building of fences to exclude hogs, goats, and other domesticated animals and fowl had been governed by an earlier regulation which stipulated that "everyone shall have enclosed his plantation and lot under penalty of six guilders." On November 8, 1656, Herman Jansen and Jan Eeckhoft had been appointed "Overseers and Surveyors of

---

[28] *Ibid.*, p. 116.
[29] *Ibid.*, 12 : 155.
[30] *Narratives, Jameson*, p. 423.
[31] *NYCD*, 2 : 9–10.

Fences."[32] When pales were not available, logs were placed upright to form stockades around the houses and gardens ; the post and rail fence was also built by the Dutch.[33] In the construction of a paled fence, clapboards or slabs of wood were often used as pales.[34] The Dutch were strong advocates of fencing—not only to protect gardens and farms but, as we have seen, as a line of defense around their homes.

Alricks wrote that small houses were built on the lots he had granted the settlers ; " Though country fashion and make they require a quantity of nails especially double and single ones, a good many spikes and not a few wainscot nails inasmuch as a greater number of these are used for clapboarding or roofing the houses with wood."[35] He also asked for boards to caulk the older frame houses, built during Jacquet's administration.

Before long, Alricks was able to report that " this settlement is now pretty well looking and convenient, with 110 houses built."[36] (In addition to the Dutch houses he said there were some belonging to Swedish householders.) The new houses were necessary to accommodate the new population, because the homes built under the Company's administration were all fully occupied and the fort was in such poor condition that it was almost uninhabitable. The officers of Alricks' troops refused to live in the barracks, and the captain and lieutenant with their families had to " hire a proper house which they occupy and need." Both

[32] *Ibid.*, 12 : 140, 155.

[33] Lands on Long Island, " to be enclosed . . . with posts and rails " [1646] (*NYCD*, 14 : 73) ; " post and rail fence " [1647] (*ibid.*, p. 75) ; " half the land enclosed complete with posts and rails " [1651] (*ibid.*, p. 145).

[34] A lessee at Rensselaerswyck agreed to use boards furnished by the lessor to fence part of the property, and to enclose the remainder with " posts, slabs or palisades." *Albany Recs.*, 3 : 149. Arnoldus de Lagrange's land on the Christina River in 1683 was separated from his neighbors by a paled fence of clapboards (C. A. Weslager, *The Richardsons of Delaware*, Wilmington, Del., 1957, p. 22).

[35] *NYCD*, 2 : 16.

[36] *Ibid.*, pp. 69, 76.

officers had " already a somewhat large family and moveables." [37]

Alricks' letters to the commissioners of the " city's colony " in Amsterdam contain a wealth of architectural detail from which one can obtain a clear impression of the buildings in New Amstel. The fort was " nearly falling . . . especially in front of the beach," where a considerable part of it had washed away. The walls, inside buildings, gun carriages, and platforms were, Alricks wrote, " in a ruinous condition." [38] To make the needed repairs, he needed " palisades and other timber," as well as " cattle " to haul the materials and carpenters to do the work. [39] It was useless, he added, to try to repair the gun carriages because the wood would warp if it were not tarred ; therefore, he asked the commissioners to ship him five or six tons of tar from Amsterdam, which was done. [40] To show the Amsterdam burgomasters exactly what they had bought when they acquired the town, and what problems confronted him, he had a drawing made of Fort New Amstel, along with a map of the territory (on which an iron mine was indicated), and sent them back to Holland. [41] Perhaps somewhere in Amsterdam these drawings lie buried in bundles of musty records — unhappily they are not now available to us.

Within the fort there stood a gabled house which became Alricks' first home ; when he moved in, he found it was " covered with oak shingles which are so shrunk, drawn up and in part rotten that scarcely a dry spot can be found when it rains." [42] The Dutch were not partial to wood shingles, and avoided using them whenever possible. [43] As soon as a shipment of tiles arrived,

---

[37] *Ibid.*, p. 15.
[38] *Ibid.*, p. 10 ; 12 : 188.
[39] *Ibid.*, 2 : 10 ; 12 : 135.
[40] *Ibid.*, 2 : 16, 185.
[41] *Ibid.*, pp. 14–15.
[42] *Ibid.*, p. 10.
[43] In his 1626 instructions for laying out the fort on Manhattan Island, Cryn Fredericksz was told that he should use the most serviceable materials for the roof. " If no thatch, straw or anything else can be found, wooden

Alricks lost no time in putting them on the roof to replace the shingles. He also increased the height of the house one-third in order to add a chamber and garret, using some of the boards shipped from the sawmill at Fort Orange. Later, he built a large house on the Strand to which he moved ; it was later sold to Hendrick Jansen van Jevern.[44]

The old barracks within the fort was so decayed that Alricks was forced to pull it down and erect a new one, 16 to 17 feet wide, 190 feet long, 9 feet high and divided into "11 copartments." The roof, due to lack of tiles, was temporarily covered with reed.[45] He also built a new guardhouse within the fort, 16 feet wide, 20 feet long, roofed with boards. He erected a dwelling for the commissary made of squared timbers " 21 or 22 feet wide, 50 feet long the story about 9 feet high and garret, the roof covered with boards for want of tiles."[46] As a combination residence and storehouse for grain and bread, he built a " frame house . . . 30 feet wide and 36 feet long, the first story 10 feet, the 2d of 7 feet with a roof which requires some thousand tiles."[47]

He also erected a new bakery, 30 feet long by 20 feet wide, lower story 9 feet and second story $6\frac{1}{4}$ feet, with a garret. The roof was also covered with tiles.[48]

---

shingles will have to be taken at first " (*Van Laer,* p. 163). A church at Manhattan was roofed in 1642 by an English carpenter "with overlapping shingles cleft from oak," only because of the unavailability of tiles (*Narratives, Jameson,* p. 213). The English preferred shingles to tiles, and in 1681 Gov. Andros removed the Dutch tiles from " the great house " at Manhattan, replacing them with shingles. Previously the English had removed tiles from the church roof and substituted shingles (*NYCD,* 3 :311). The tiles had cracked as a result of the firing of guns, causing the roofs to leak (*ibid.*).

[44] *Ibid.,* 12 :204. Reference to the new house is in van Sweringen's letter (*Ibid.,* 2 :106). The house was situated " between ffop Johnsons and William Mauritts " (New Castle County, Del., *Deed Book* A–1, pp. 11 - 12).

[45] *NYCD,* 2 :69.

[46] *Ibid.*

[47] *Ibid.,* p. 49.

[48] *Ibid,* p. 50.

Under the influence of the Swedish and Finnish log house techniques, Alricks constructed a burgher watch house " built of logs ; it is about 20 feet square, the first story 9, the 2d 8 feet and covered with tiles."[49] The same type of log construction was probably used in the old *batstooft* (*badstu* : bath house) that stood behind the fort, possibly a vestige of the Swedish occupancy.[50]

There was no powder magazine when Alricks arrived, but he found eight or ten kegs of powder stacked in the house which was to be his residence. He didn't relish sharing his living space with powder kegs, and lost no time in digging a cellar " under the southeast bastion of the fort," where he could store as many as thirty-six to forty kegs.[51]

One of his most irritating problems was to find a safe, dry storage place for the meats, foodstuffs, clothing, liquors, tools, tar, pitch, and other supplies shipped from Holland. There was a storehouse in the fort, but it was small and much dilapidated. Therefore, he was at first " obliged to fix something tent fashion," which was later modified to a " sort of hut made of props and boards and covered with old sails."[52] As soon as possible he built, on one side of the fort, a storehouse of planks, with a loft under the roof. The structure served " for storage and delivery of goods and for the residence of the Commissary." Rations for the garrison were distributed from this building.[53]

Alricks complained frequently in his letters to the burgomasters of the shortage of building materials and skilled labor. In one of his early letters, he said he was " wholly deprived of materials such as stone, tiles and lime for the mason."[54] At another time he

---

[49] *Ibid.*, p. 69.

[50] *NYCD*, 12 : 134 ; *Dunlap, 1956,* p. 16.

[51] *NYCD,* 2 : 10. When Stuyvesant attacked the Swedes there in 1655 he found a guardhouse " about half a cannon shot from the fort . . . previously used as a magazine " (*Narratives, Jameson,* p. 384).

[52] *NYCD,* 2 : 9.

[53] *Ibid.*, pp. 50, 69 ; 12 : 208.

[54] *Ibid.*, 2 : 10.

wrote that he continued to be badly in need of a large supply of building materials, adding, "we have not a solitary brick in stock to repair an oven which is in ruin."[55] He explained that he had only one oven, whereas the needs of the colonists required two additional ones. He also requested carpenters' tools and nails for "clapboards which are used here instead of tiles for covering roofs."[56] He urged that carpenters and bricklayers be sent from Holland ; on October 10, 1658, he wrote that the brickmaker had died.[57] (This, however, was not the aforementioned Cornelis Herperts de Jager, who died in Manhattan in 1659.[58]) Alricks complained that the boards available locally were "badly sawed and not easily had."[59] His construction problems worsened because of trouble with the carpenters : "one of them is some-times sick or ailing ; the other will not work ; the third demands something better, and so forth." These would-be carpenters, who had come with the first contingent of colonists, were "bunglers or men of little capacity."[60] In a letter dated August 16, 1659, he said he had repaired, "according to the exigencies, the Clergy-man's house and that of the smith."[61] During the third year of his administration he built a "granary or barn and a new stable for the cattle."[62]

Prior to 1657, the Dutch had no separate church building on the Delaware, although religious services had been conducted within the several forts. Officials of the West India Company were adherents of the Dutch Reformed, the official church of Holland, and services in the Company's colonies were conducted

---

[55] *Ibid.,* p. 18.
[56] *Ibid.,* p. 11.
[57] *Ibid,* p. 52.
[58] *Ibid.,* p. 116.
[59] *Ibid.,* p. 10. The clapboards were obtained from Upland Kill (*ibid.,* 12:321).
[60] *Ibid.,* 12:218, 204.
[61] *Ibid.,* 2:69. See "Claes the Smith," *ibid.,* 12:134.
[62] *Ibid.,* 2:69.

according to its teachings. Before coming to Fort Casimir, Jacquet, for example, took an oath to maintain and advance the Reformed Church.[63] The Company pursued this policy with the patroons ; Article 27 of the *Freedoms & Exemptions* directed the patroons to find ways to support ministers in their colonies, and they were at least obligated to engage a comforter of the sick.

After capturing Fort Casimir in 1655, Stuyvesant wrote on September 12, " today we heard our first sermon."[64] In what building the services were conducted for his soldiers is not stated, but in order to continue with regular services, one of the freemen " was appointed to read to them on Sundays, from the Postilla. This is continued to this day [1657]."[65] In May of 1656, there still was no minister at Fort Casimir, and a couple who wanted to marry had to delay their nuptials.[66]

There is record on August 9, 1656, of " Mr. Laers, preacher and ecclesiastical deputy in matrimonial cases."[67] This was Laurentius Carolus Lokenius, a Swedish - educated Finn, a Lutheran minister — not a pastor of the Dutch Reformed Church. Lokenius preached at New Amstel on one occasion, with the result that Alricks was severely criticized by the commissioners. They wrote that " no other religion but the Reformed may be tolerated there so you must by proper means put an end to or prevent such presumption on the part of other sectaries. . . ."[68]

Upon his arrival, Alricks wrote that he had found neither church nor Dutch minister on the Delaware ; the City shortly sent Evert Pietersen as schoolmaster and comforter of the sick, fulfilling their agreement with the colonists to provide " a proper

[63] *Ibid.*, 12 : 117.
[64] *Ibid.*, 12 : 101.
[65] *Narratives, Jameson*, p. 395.
[66] *NYCD*, 12 : 145.
[67] *Ibid.*, p. 150.
[68] *Ibid.*, 2 : 61.

person for schoolmaster who shall also read the Holy Scriptures
and set the Psalms."[69] But the comforter of the sick possessed
only limited religious authority ; as the colony grew, the city sent
Dominie Everardus Welius, an ordained minister, to tend the
spiritual needs.

The church building at New Amstel in which Welius preached
was a dwelling house that had been remodeled in 1657. It had
formerly been owned and occupied by Andries Hudde, who had
held various positions under the Company and was employed as
clerk, sheriff, and surveyor under the City's administration.
Hudde, who had a wife and child, probably built the house soon
after he came to Fort Casimir, although the lot was not confirmed
to him until 1656. The house is not described, but on April 22,
1659, the commissioners wrote Alricks that " we are much pleased
to learn the improvement of the church and congregation and
approve the purchase of the house in which service was performed . . . ."[70] They added they would send him "the little
bell necessary for the church there." Evidently, the improvement
to which the letter refers was the further remodeling of the
Hudde house, for Alricks wrote, in the summer of 1659, that he
had " enlarged by one-half the church or place where service
was performed on Sundays."[71] In December of that year, the
church consisted of sixty members, " having been greatly
strengthened, formerly had only 19."[72]

This house-church stood in the Strand; a list of debts due
in the colony, listed December 12, 1659, included " 900 florins
due the creditors of Andries Hudde for the church."[73] The
structure was still in use June 6, 1662, the date of a letter from
Hudde to Stuyvesant claiming that he had only been partially

---

[69] *Ibid.,* 1 : 631.
[70] *Ibid.,* 2 : 61.
[71] *Ibid.,* p. 69.
[72] *Ecclesiastical Records, State of New York,* Albany, 1901, 1 : 457 - 459.
[73] *NYCD,* 2 : 111.

paid for the house. He stated he had previously " tried to get payment for the house sold to the Honble Director Jacob Alderick in the presence of scepens and municipality, to be used as a church for the benefit of the community as which it is still used." [74]

Judicial matters were decided in a courtroom " upstairs " in one of the buildings in the fort. The Dutch never built a separate courthouse at New Amstel, although the court met frequently in its upstairs quarters to sit in judgment on a variety of civil and criminal cases. [75]

The first tavern keeper mentioned by name at New Amstel was Fop Jansen Outhout, who had been commissary in the Stuyvesant expedition in 1655. His tavern was a residence on the Strand, modified to suit the needs of his customers, with tippling done in " the inner room of his house." [76]

In 1657, Alricks wrote that two soldiers from the garrison had run up " debts in the tavern." [77] In 1660, Jan Juriaen Becker was accused of illicitly selling strong drinks to both soldiers and Indians — but this was an extracurricular activity, for he had been engaged as secretary or clerk, not as a tavern keeper. [78] (Later he held the important position of notary in the colony at Albany, where he died in 1698.)

There were no retail shops in the town at this period, and the tavern was doubtless a hang-out for the men. Visitors stayed overnight here, and in 1659 Colonel Nathaniel Utie wrote that while in New Amstel he " put up at the public tavern." [79] The

---

[74] *Ibid.*, 12 : 374. Jeannette Eckman, " Dutch at New Castle," states that the site was that of present Nos. 26 and 28.
[75] *NYCD*, 12 : 353; H. Clay Reed, " The Early New Castle Court," *Del. History*, 4, No. 3 (June, 1951), 227 - 245.
[76] *NYCD* 12 : 378.
[77] *NYCD*, 12 : 193.
[78] *Ibid.*, p. 296.
[79] *Narratives, Hall*, p. 327.

tavern keeper obtained his beer and other beverages from Manhattan prior to the establishing of local manufacture. In 1663, d'Hinoyossa built a small brewery in one of the buildings in the fort. He was accused of stripping the citadel of palisades for wood to burn under the brew kettle![80]

Schoolmaster Evert Pietersen, who had twenty-five pupils, wrote that his school " is something of a novelty as it has not been done before." He neglected to say whether he held classes in a schoolhouse, whether the house-church was used as a school, or whether he taught the pupils in one of the homes.

New Amstel was at an economic disadvantage due to its lack of fast-flowing streams to turn grist and sawmills. Alricks complained of this handicap soon after he arrived, and the parts to construct a horse mill were shipped to him from Manhattan.[81] Almost fifty years before, the Dutch had built a horse mill on Manhattan Island (later replaced by a windmill), and over this mill had been erected " a spacious room sufficient to accommodate a large congregation . . . ."[82]

On August 5, 1658, the horse mill was under construction at New Amstel, but work was delayed " on account of Christian Barent's [the builder] death." Alricks complained that he was still " much embarrassed here for breadstuffs or flour."[83] The Swedes, during the Printz administration, had built a water-powered gristmill along Cobbs Creek, but it was too far for the New Amstel families to haul their grist conveniently. Later, water-powered mills would be erected on Shellpot Creek, Little Falls Creek, and elsewhere, but during Alricks' time the problem was critical. He urged Barent's widow to have the horse mill completed and to operate it and share the income. Who actually

[80] *NYCD*, 12:422, 442.
[81] *Ibid.*, p. 151.
[82] *Narratives, Jameson*, p. 83 (Nov., 1626).
[83] *NYCD*, 12:222.

completed it and who operated it is not known, but on December 3, 1662, a direct reference to the " horse mill at New Amstel " indicates it had been completed and was then serving the community.[84]

Obviously, a horse, or horses, constituted the source of energy, but how this natural " horsepower " was harnessed to the millstones is not stated. The device was apparently more complicated than a simple mill where a horse or mule walked in a circular path, a shaft extending from its neck to the millstone. Such a structure could have been fashioned without the services of a trained craftsman and in much less time than was required to complete the New Amstel mill. Its prototype at Manhattan, as indicated, was a sizable structure. (In the Albany records, there is cited on November 23, 1660, a contract for the building and leasing of a horse mill at Beverswyck, the owners agreeing to make available to the miller " two good draft horses to be used in the mill.)[85]

How long the New Amstel horse mill was in operation is unknown, but it probably accommodated the townsfolk for at least a decade. In 1681, Arnoldus de Lagrange, a Dutch merchant, who had formerly owned a store at Manhattan, was granted fastland at New Amstel, " towards ye north east end of town," and a small adjoining piece of vacant marsh. The land was granted with the express provision " that hee the sd De Lagrange according to his owne proffer shall build on ye sd Land a good windmill for the Common good of the Inhabitants and to haue for toul [toll] of grinding noe more than one Tenth part, and that hee draynes ye marsh : and all this to bee done within 12 months after date hereof, otherwayes & in deffect

---

[84] *Ibid.*, pp. 225, 369. See a later reference (*PA*, 5 : 620) to millstones, at the Hoerenkil, " fit for a Horse Mill."

[85] *Albany Recs.*, 3 : 46, 197, 198.

thereof hee to forfeit what is now granted." [86]

Although this agreement was executed after the Dutch had relinquished the colony to the English, it is cited because the windmill has close association with Dutch economic life, and the builder was a Hollander, son of Joost de Lagrange. The reader has seen that a windmill had been erected on Manhattan Island in 1628 for the purpose of sawing lumber, and it is quite likely that an earlier windmill had been built there for grinding grist. [87] De Lagrange evidently constructed the windmill at New Amstel and drained the marsh by ditching it in accordance with the agreement. Figure 2 is a facsimile of a surveyor's drawing of 1682 illustrating the windmill and showing the course of the ditch or moat. How long the windmill was in operation has not been ascertained, but the water-powered mills built later in the English period proved to be more efficient and practical.

Another important part of the Dutch building complex at New Amstel were the earthen dykes. The low, marshy terrain bordering the river was similar to the low farmland in Holland, which required draining, ditching, and dyking to make it arable and passable. The Dutch were long experienced in the techniques of land conservation, and they knew exactly how and where to build dykes and floodgates to rehabilitate the marshlands. Individual Dutch farmers threw up dykes on their properties, and one of the important private dykes, known as the " outer dyke," was built by Hans Block, gunner in the service of the colony. It came to be used as a pathway by the inhabitants of the town. In 1675, the authorities decided that Block's dyke needed to be repaired and strengthened and they ordered all male inhabitants to work on it. This dyke was " the Common and neerest footway from this Towne to *Swanewick* [a Dutch community about a

---

[86] *Records, Court of New Castle, 1676–1681,* Lancaster, Pennsylvania, 1904, p. 498.

[87] *Narratives, Jameson,* p. 131. In 1650, the windmill was leaky and rotted and had only two arms (*ibid.,* p. 326 ; see also p. 422).

mile northeast of New Amstel], Crane Hooke [*Trane Udden* in Swedish, a community of Swedes and Finns above *Swanwick*] and parts adjacent . . . ."[88]

At the same time, the authorities ordered the male inhabitants to build a new dyke across marshland, on the north side of the town, belonging to Captain John Carr. This dyke was " for the Concerns of the King & publique," whereas the former was "for Convenience of ye towne."[89]

These lines were written during the English administration, which explains the reference to the king. It meant that the dykes served not only as restraining walls but also as causeways, or highways, permitting traffic to move back and forth across otherwise impassable marshland. Hans Block's dyke was generally referred to as the " foot dyke," because it would accommodate pedestrians but not horse traffic. The dimensions of this dyke have not been recorded, but it was probably four or five feet high and wide enough at the top for a footpath.

The larger dyke built in 1675 was originally designed " ten feet wide at the bottom, five feet high and three feet wide on the top, providing it with well-made and strong floodgates. . . ." This dyke was variously known as the " broad dyke," " horse dyke," or " cart dyke," and was modified to accommodate horse carts. It constituted part of the principal highway from New Amstel to Crane Hook and thence to the ferry landing on the Christina River.

Figure 2 shows both dykes as of 1682, and illustrates that bridges were built at places where the dykes intersected streams of water. The bridge over " The Creek " permitted the traveler to

---

[88] *NYCD*, 12:535. It was known as the " Town Dyke " because it " leads in to ye Towne " (*Land Warrants*, 1671–1679 [Jan. 15, 1675]. Memorial Library, University of Delaware, Microfilm No. 64).

[89] *NYCD*, 12:532. Above information regarding the dykes also found in *ibid.*, pp. 531, 533, 534.

Surveyed for Mr. Amonius de Lagrange a certaine
peece of Draigned marsh, being that part of the Towne marsh
wch did belong to mr. John moll, Lying and being att the North
End of this Towne of New Castle, beginning att the corner
of the marsh wch by order of the Cort was laid out for yd.
De Lagrange the 23d of november 1681, att the beginning
of the broad Cart Dijke, and from thence Parrallell along
the sd. broad Dijke and the small mole or ditch, (: allowing
of some small breath of ground next to yd. broad dijke
sufficient for to use on occasions for the Constant Repair
of yd. broad Dijke :) N: b: E: something more Easterly
36 perches to y Creeke neare y Bridge, then downe
along y sd. Creeke following y Severiall Courses thereof
75 perches to y Creeke where itt Slopes against y foott
Dijke neare y Sluis, then W.S.W 26 perch: and West
18 perches along y small partition mole or ditch
to y first place of beginning att y Entrance of the
above sd. Broad Cart Dijke, Contayning & Laid out
for five acres and one quarter, — Surveyd the 15.
of november 1682. —

Pr mee Eph: Herman
Surr:

Figure 2. Surveyor's drawing of a marsh at New Castle (New Amstel) made in 1682 shows "The Broad Cartdyke," "The foott Dyke," "The Bridge" that crossed "The Creek," "a small ditch" that drained the marsh, and—of particular interest—a sketch of the windmill. From *New Castle County Land Surveys*, Memorial Library, University of Delaware, Microfilm No. 86, p. 126.

follow a continuous route from where the "broad dyke" left off on one side of the creek to where it resumed on the other side. Otherwise there would have been a break in the dyke road and travelers would have found it necessary to ford the stream or cross it by scow. Such bridge-crossing, incidentally, was frequently built in association with gates which could be opened and closed as needed to regulate the flow of water and so convert the marshy areas, or cripples, into grazing lands, or to make them suitable for raising corn and other crops. Of course, as explained, the principal objective of the dykes was to make passable highways, as clarified in the following words of the New Amstel magistrates : "No wagon or cart road could be made, unless the aforesaid dikes and floodgates had been constructed first to keep out the water."

Two items, broadly falling into the category of Dutch building activity as related to Delaware Bay and River, should also be mentioned here. The shoals in the river continued to menace the sailing vessels that moved back and forth from New Amstel, and after conferring with seafaring men, Alricks reported that "it was agreed that it would be best to lay five or six buoys there."[90] So far as is known, Alricks was the first to place buoys in the Delaware, a system that is still used to protect river vessels.

Alricks was also responsible for a suggestion that eventually materialized in dredging at a later period. He wrote that it was so shallow in places that "appropriations ought to be made to render it safer and better for incoming ships."[91] Incidentally, the system of engaging experienced pilots to bring vessels up the

---

[90] *Ibid.*, 2 : 11 ; see also p. 50 where it states, "The buoys will be laid down as soon as possible." In 1664, among the goods confiscated by Sir Robert Carr were "nine sea buyes with iron chains" (*Ibid.*, 3 : 346).

[91] *Ibid.*, 2 : 30. Alricks also recommended building a village on the New Jersey side of the Delaware, "in order to completely defend this river thereby" (*ibid.*, pp. 9, 15).

river, which is also still in use, was another improvement envisioned by Alricks. He recommended that pilots be employed " to look out at sea for arriving vessels and then to pilot or bring them in." [92]

In giving the reader a picture of New Amstel as of the 1660's, one must resist the temptation to use more romantic terms than the town plan and architecture actually warranted. In the years that have passed, the splendor of the town's historical background tends to color the image conjured up in the mind's eye. There can be no question of the beauty of the natural setting — words fail to portray it. In front of the fort stretched the sand beach, washed clean by the ebb and flow of the river tides and bleached by the sun. Downstream one could see the bend in the river as it gradually widened to form the great salt bay named first for May, then for Godyn, and lastly for de la Warre. Bordering the opposite shore as far as the eye could see was an expanse of timbered land, beyond which lay the Atlantic. Along the river shore were the marshes with their sabre-leafed grasses, reeds, pink and white mallows, and hummock-houses where muskrats lived and bred.

The important cities and towns of the Netherlands were situated on rivers and seaports, and many were crisscrossed by a system of canals, making the country what one author has described as a " waterland." [93] Topographically, New Amstel was reminiscent of the sites of such river-bank towns as Liège, Haarlem, Middleburg, or Utrecht. Yet like Antwerp, on the Scheldt, or Rotterdam, on the Meuse, it too was a seagoing port on a navigable river possessing the physical features necessary for the development of commerce.

As in the Netherland towns, the two rows of houses at New Amstel faced the river, and the second row was silhouetted against a backdrop unequalled in the homeland — dense woods

---

[92] *Ibid.,* p. 11.
[93] Sacheverell Sitwell, *The Netherlands,* B. T. Batsford Ltd., London,

of white oak, so esteemed for shipbuilding, walnut, yellow poplar, beech, maple, holly, sweet gum, and others. Into the heart of this woodland the Christina wandered in from the Delaware, its waters spreading beyond its banks and forming marshy skirts where great flocks of duck, geese, and heron came to nest and feed. One could go on and on describing the fish teeming in the streams, the large and small animals, the songbirds in the woods, and the other elements of the natural environment. But New Amstel's houses and buildings were not inspired with the same charm and beauty that characterized the natural setting.

The fortress dominating the town had yielded at different times to the tastes of several designers, builders, and repairers. The result was an architectural hodgepodge. The records state that Jacob Jansen Huys, a ship's master, and members of his crew had not only assisted in remodeling the fort, but had constructed other buildings in the town.[94] They were probably no better trained in carpentry than the inexpert workers that Alricks complained about to his superiors.

The dwelling houses were built of clapboards, of planks, and (a few) of squared or rounded logs, under Swedish-Finnish influence. They were of assorted shapes and sizes, their roofs a potpourri of tiles, boards, clapboards, straw, or reeds. In all probability these houses were unpainted, if we are to judge by the scarcity of house paint in New Netherland.[95] Pigments of various colors were found in America and were well known to the Indians as the basis of face paint, but as for the whites using these pigments for house paint, a Dutchman wrote that " the Christians are not skilled in them."[96] It would be incorrect, then, to think of New Amstel in terms of red barns or homes painted tastefully and fenced with white pales. If paint was used, it was

---

[94] *NYCD,* 2 : 115.
[95] *Ecclesiastical Records,* 1 : 461.
[96] *Colls. N.Y. Hist. Soc.,* 2nd Series, 2 : Part 1, p. 268.

crudely mixed, not durable, and it would not have given the homes the quality of the little Dutch houses which storybooks describe.

There was no steepled church, no courthouse or town hall, and probably no schoolhouse. The narrow, unpaved streets were dusty in dry weather and muddy after a rain. The records indicate that fowl, goats, and swine ran loose in the streets. Probably in the yards behind the houses there were coops, sheds, and henhouses of various dimensions and shapes.

These remarks are not intended as criticism of the spirit or the qualities of the Dutch. By training and disposition they were a diligent, home-loving folk whose dwellings in the Netherlands during the same period were models of neatness and cleanliness. If the houses they erected at New Amstel fell short of meeting the standards of perfection they had set for themselves in the Old World, it was for a very good reason. As we have seen, they were not provided with suitable building materials or trained workmen, and were, indeed, discouraged by their employers or sponsors from bothering about such things. It is now clear that neither the West India Company (whose famed office buildings and warehouses in Holland were designed by the leading architects of the day) nor the City of Amsterdam (which could boast of fine public buildings and residences) were much concerned with the architectural seemliness of the New Amstel colony. The common interest of prime concern to both the Company and the City was — profits! Other things were of secondary consideration, as evidenced by the letters and reports carried back and forth between Holland and America. In early chapters, comment has already been made about the reticence of the Company to assume the expenses of building houses and sending colonists to the Delaware. That the burgomasters of Amsterdam were no more idealistic than the directors of the Company is evident in the following paragraph taken from one of the letters that the commissioners wrote to Director Alricks :

We approve of the purchase of the lots and plantations; also of preparing and building a store, barracks for the soldiers, bakery, guard house, watch-house for the burgher corps, etc., but as the expense incurred by such buildings and public works must be met by the City, so, indeed, circumspection ought to be used herein and economy studied as much as possible; for it is yet too premature to attend to the ornamenting of such and other public works and to neglect what is most essential such as the pushing forward the cultivation of the soil which is the principal, yea, the sole object wherefore this City hath established this Colonie.[97]

Some twenty years after this letter was written (New Amstel was then under English control and had been renamed New Castle), two Dutchmen, visiting the town founded by their countrymen, were not much impressed by the architecture. This is what they wrote :

What remains of it consists of about fifty houses, most all of wood. The fort is demolished, but there is a good block-house, having some small cannon, erected in the middle of the town and sufficient to resist the Indians or incursions of Christians, but it could not hold out long.[98]

In time the sandy spit, where Fort Casimir stood, began to wash away ; the fort itself started again to fall apart, but this time it was not rebuilt. What remained of the old foundations was eventually buried in the bottom sands of the Delaware. Today there is nothing to mark the fort site, the river having encroached even farther on the shore line. The surviving original

[97] *NYCD,* 2 : 62.
[98] *Journal of a Voyage to New York in 1679–1680* (Danckers & Sluyter), Memoirs, Long Island Historical Society, 1 (1867), 228. The blockhouse referred to above was probably one built in 1672 to replace the old fort then " fallen to ruine & decay." Tiles, bricks, and other materials from the fort were used to build the blockhouse (*NYCD,* 12 : 474, 481, 482, 493).

frame dwellings in the " first row " were wiped out in the " great fire " which swept the Strand in 1824. The original residences in the " second row " weathered away or were torn down to make room for larger dwellings before and after the Revolution. Although interesting, rare, and unusual examples of American architecture of the colonial period can be seen today in the homes, churches, and civic buildings in New Castle that have withstood the attrition of time, there remains not one single structure that can be said with certainty to date from the Dutch period, that is, *prior* to 1664.

A brick house, having three stories and a stepped gabled roof, known as the "tile house," formerly stood at No. 54 in the Strand, but it was demolished in 1884. It bore on its façade the wrought iron date, 1687, and its first owner was John Boyer, son of Sander Boyer, interpreter between the Dutch and Indians. From the tile on its roof to the curved lintels over the windows and the stoop at the front door, the house was wholly Dutch in design, yet it was not built until after the close of the Dutch period.[99]

A much smaller brick house, with pent eaves and overhanging roof in the Dutch fashion, popularly known as " the old Dutch house," is still standing on Third Street between Harmony and Delaware Streets. It was purchased in 1939 by the Delaware Society for the Preservation of Antiquities and later turned over to the New Castle Historical Society, the present owner. A thorough study of the deed records of the property indicates the " old Dutch house " was erected *after* the Dutch period, probably between 1690 and 1704. It replaced an older log house, formerly

---

[99] See artist's sketch of house, frontispiece, back end-paper, *New Castle on the Delaware*. Cooperation and assistance of the Historical Society of Delaware is acknowledged in making available, from their files, notes and deed searches, by Jeannette Eckman.

owned by George Moore, which stood on the same lot as early as 1682 and was still standing in 1687.[100]

During the forty-year span — 1624 to 1664 — the Dutch had their day on the Delaware, with unlimited opportunity to colonize and develop the area. During the first ten years of their occupation, they faced no important competition, but their inattention to the territory became an open invitation to the Swedes to make it the site of their own settlement. If the Dutch had solidified their position and expanded their colony, as the English did in Virginia, it might have resulted in permanence of the colony. In this event, they possibly would have left a recognizable influence on the architectural pattern of the dwelling houses, churches, and civic buildings, as the French did at Quebec or the Spanish at St. Augustine. Other than the aforementioned " old Dutch house," one would be hard pressed to find specific elements in today's buildings in the Delaware Valley which could be said to be vestiges of the early Dutch period. This, to repeat what has already been said, is not due to weakness or lack of spirit on the part of the individual Dutch colonists ; their absentee employers simply did not encourage the expression of creative talents in their colony. As a result of the lack of what the sponsors of New Amstel would probably have considered a frivolous waste of their money, we have been disinherited of any architectural legacy from the early Dutch.

---

[100] Jeremiah Sweeney, former staff worker on the Delaware Writer's Project, made the deed search for the property. His notes were consulted by the authors; reference to George Moore's log house is in New Castle County, Del., *Deed Book*, B–1, p. 3 (1687).

IX

Dutch Maps and Geographical Names

The Dutch period of exploration and settlement on the Delaware started in 1609 and ended in 1664, when the English seized control. During this period of fifty-five years Dutch navigators and traders, and later, Dutch settlers, all had a hand in giving names to certain physical features in the Delaware Valley, as they did elsewhere in New Netherland.

In the process of place-naming, newcomers to an area often transfer names from their homeland ; they also make up new names, customarily using words from their own language. These are in addition to names taken over from the native population, for example, *Armenveruis, Arowamex, Matinakonk, Narraticonck, Sickoneysincks, Sankickans, Appoquinimink* — just to mention a few of the previously cited Algonkian place-names which are found in seventeenth-century Dutch records. Whatever their origin, geographical names, as a necessity of communication, are of immediate concern to the explorers who map out an area and to the settlers who come there to live. Some of the names first applied to a new territory often continue to be used by new generations, while other names become obsolete, new or modified ones taking their place.

The student of Dutch geographical names in the Delaware Valley must depend, to a considerable extent, upon the writings of explorers, promoters, colonizers, administrators, and travelers : to mention a mere half dozen, the works of de Laet, de Vries, Hartgers, and van de Donck, all previously cited, as well as the anonymous *Vertoogh* and *Kort Verhael*. Equally important as a source of information are the early maps and charts of the New Netherland area, to which attention will now be given.

Hudson's detention in England on his return from the third voyage brought knowledge of his discoveries to the drawing boards of English cartographers before the information reached the Netherlands. The first charting of Delaware Bay, as we saw in Chapter 1, appeared on an English map, a copy of which found its way to Spain and ultimately became known as the "Velasco Map." Since Hudson's exploration of the Delaware was confined to the mouth of the bay, the lines marking the bay on the "Velasco Map" break off inside the capes, and the shape of the upper stretches of the bay and river is left indefinite. The extension of these lines, and the detailing of the tributaries and the land they drained, had to await more thorough exploration. The data obtained after 1609 by successive Dutch explorers and traders permitted further delineation of the Delaware river system as each made his contribution.

In 1616, Hendricksen attempted to chart the full length of the Delaware on his "Figurative Map"; the data he furnished amplified the "Velasco Map," but more detailed mapping could only come with a fuller survey of the headwaters and tributaries. After the Walloons settled on Burlington Island in 1624, more of the middle section of the Delaware River became known, and when Fort Nassau was constructed in 1626, further geographical data about the eastern side of the river became available to Dutch map-makers. The settlement of Swanendael in 1631 brought knowledge of the southwestern sector of the bayshore ; the purchase by Hossitt of land on the opposite side of the bay added further to the fund of information. The Schuylkill region became better known as Dutch traders from Fort Nassau sought contact with the Minquas. Later, land routes between the Delaware settlements and Manhattan were established on the old

Indian paths. These, and other, developments permitted the charting of physical features not found on earlier maps.

When we examine the Dutch maps and charts made before 1675 on which Delaware Bay and River are fully delineated, we find they fall into three broad categories : (1) those which show a long stretch of coastline, including the middle Atlantic sector, (2) those which show only New Netherland, (3) those which show only a part of New Netherland — in this case the Delaware River area. Listed below are the maps in these three categories.

(1)

1614   [Figurative Map] (Block). Facsimile : *NYCD*, Vol. 1, facing p.13.

1630   Nova Anglia, Novum Belgium et Virginia (de Laet). Facsimile : Paullin and Wright, *Atlas of the Hist. Geog. of the U.S.*, Pl.21.[1]

c. 1630   Pascaert van Nieuw Nederlandt, Virginia, ende Nieuw Engelandt. Facsimile : F. C. Wieder, *Monumenta Cartographica*, Pl.77[2]. Wieder's date, 1639, is conservatively late.

c.1630-40   [A Chart of the Coast-line from Virginia to New England] (de Vries?). Facsimile : One of the two plates published in 1912 as a supplement to the Linschoten–Vereeniging edition of de Vries, *Korte Historiael*, ed. Colenbrander.

c. 1635   Nova Belgica et Nova Anglia (Blaeu). Facsimile : Stokes and Haskell, *Amer. Hist. Prints*, facing p.7.

---

[1] There is a copy in the Hexham translation of the Mercator-Hondius-Jansson *Atlas* (1636), and another in Hartgers' *Beschrijvinghe van Virginia* (1651) ; both show alterations.

[2] This chart should be compared with a facsimile made in the 1660's of a map of Minuit's time, c. 1630 (*Iconography*, 2 : C.Pl.39) ; also with the facsimile of a copy made in the 1660's of a survey likewise done in Minuit's time (*ibid.*, 6 : Pl.81 b).

1647–51 Belgii Novi, Angliae Novae, et Partis Virginiae Novissima Delineatio. Facsimile : Fite and Freeman, *A Book of Old Maps*, facing p.147.[3]

c.1653 Pas caarte van Nieu Nederlandt (Colom). Facsimile : *Iconography*, 2 : C.Pl.48.[4]

1661 Pas caerte van Niev Nederland en de Engelische Virginies; van Cabo Cod tot Cabo Canrik (van Loon).[5]

(2)

1616 [Figurative Map] (Hendricksen). Facsimile : *NYCD*, Vol. 1, facing p.11.

1630–4 [Map of New Netherland] (Minuit?). Facsimile : *Narratives, Jameson*, frontispiece.

c.1666 Paskaerte van de Zuydt en Noordt Revier in Nieu Nederlant Streckende van Cabo Hinloopen tot Rechkewach (Goos). Facsimile : *Iconography*, 2 : C.Pl.49.

1675 Pascaert van Niew Nederland streckende vande Zuijdt Revier tot de Noordt Revier en't lange Eijland (Roggeveen). Facsimile : *Iconography*, 2 : C. Pl.53.[6]

---

[3] This map is a good representative of the Jansson-Visscher series, which includes maps by Danckers, van der Donck, Allardt, and others. See the discussion in Stokes and Haskell, *Amer. Hist. Prints*, pp. 6–7 ; and for facsimiles and references see A. R. Dunlap, " A Checklist of Seventeenth-Century Maps Relating to Delaware," *Delaware Notes*, 18 : 68–76.

[4] Reprinted, with minor changes, in 1660 in Doncker's *De Zee-Atlas*. Colom published, in the 1660's, a map which also included Virginia and New England (cf. *Iconography*, 2 : 156-157).

[5] A chart with a similar title was published in Goos's *De Zee-Atlas*, 1666 ; for a facsimile, see A. L. Humphreys, *Old Decorative Maps and Charts*, Pl.63.

[6] This chart was published in 1675 in Part 1 of Roggeveen's *Het Brandende Veen* ; but even though it postdates the final period of Dutch political sway on the Delaware, it was probably prepared, at least in part, before 1675.

(3)

c. 1629 'Caerte vande Svydt Rivier in Nieu Nederland. Facsimile : *Dunlap & Weslager, 1958.*

c. 1630–40 [A Chart of the South Bay] (de Vries?). Facsimile : One of two plates published in 1912 as a supplement to the Linschoten - Vereeniging edition of de Vries, *Korte Historiael,* ed. Colenbrander.

c. 1630–40 [De Zuid-Baai in Nieuw Nederland] (de Vries?). Facsimile : see Figure 1, for a reproduction of the original, which is in the States Archives at 's-Gravenhage.

1643 Kaert vande Suyd Rivier in Niew Sweden.[8] Facsimile : F. C. Weider, *Monumenta Cartographica,* Pl.79.[9]

It is true in general that the maps in category (3) above — which show only a segment of New Netherland, usually in considerable detail — contain more Dutch geographical names for Delaware Valley features than the maps in categories (1) and (2). But since some of the names appearing on maps in categories (1) and (2) differ from those in category (3), maps of all three types must be studied with care in order to develop a list of Dutch geographical names which in any way approaches completeness.

---

[7] The date of this map is discussed in *Dunlap & Weslager, 1958.*

[8] A discussion of the different states of this map and their dates appears with F. C. Weider's facsimile. The word " Sweden, " as Wieder observes, is on a slip which has been pasted over the word " Nederlandt. " (For another map bearing the name " New Sweden, " see *Iconography,* 6 : Pl.81 a.).

[9] An unpublished Dutch map like those in this category, entitled " Caerte van de Suid Rivier, " might also be mentioned, although it dates from c. 1683. Accompanying the manuscript of the journal of the second voyage of Jasper Danckaerts (on deposit in the Long Island Historical Society), it throws light on conditions along the Delaware River in the decade after the last period of Dutch authority. The non-Indian names are all Dutch, but many of them are " back " translations of established names; for example, *Ende Kil* (Duck Creek), *Sloot* (Thoroughfare), and *Oudemans Kil* (Oldman's Creek).

As further comment on the maps listed above, it might be said that whereas the names of engravers and publishers sometimes got into the record, the names of few of the surveyors and original drafters are known. That Willem Verhulst was instructed to have Peter Minuit make a careful exploration of the Delaware as early as 1625 appears in a passage in the *Van Rappard Documents,* and Minuit's activities as a map maker have been taken for granted, as have those of de Vries.[10] It can also be assumed that Gillis Hossitt made a map of the Delaware River, as Samuel Godyn ordered him to do in the document dated June 1, 1629 (reprinted in Appendix A). And the Swedish governor, Johan Rising, shortly after his arrival on the Delaware in 1654, "caused [the river system] to be mapped, as well as it could be done in a hurry all the way from the bay even up to the falls, by one A. Hudden."[11] This was the same Andries Hudde mentioned earlier in this volume. For the most part, however, the surveying and drafting work for the maps destined to find their way to European engravers and publishers[12] is anonymous.

---

[10] *Iconography,* 1 : 136 ; 2 : 111-112, 142, 173 ff. ; cf. *Swedish Settlements,* 1 : 117–118. Note the reference in *Iconography,* 2 :116–117 to an unpublished sketch-map of Delaware Bay, possibly by de Vries, now in the State Archives at the Hague ; and see also the letter from Blommaert to Oxenstierna dated November 13, 1638, Kernkamp, *Zweedsche Archivalia,* p. 162.

[11] *Narratives, Myers,* p. 138; see fn. 2, where it is recorded that Rising paid Hudde twenty florins for "some maps of the river and other drawings"; see also *Swedish Settlements,* 1 : 516-517. In 1657, Hudde was employed as surveyor at Fort Amstel, and reference to one of his maps (the same one?) appears in the Bontemantel papers under date of August 16 : "Will try to send a map of the South River executed by Andries Hudde" ("Extract from the letter of the Director and Councillors from New Netherland dated August 16, 1657," *New Netherland Papers,* New York Public Library).

[12] It should be said that of a considerable number of maps mentioned in the records there is now no trace. See, for example, *van Laer,* p. 40; *NYCD,* 1 : 126, 262 ; 2 : 14-15, 224 ; 12 : 183, 643. But the loss in every case was not absolute. In a letter dated April 7, 1657, from the Directors to Stuyvesant occurs the statement that "The plan of the Southriver, given by

In view of the possibility of finding early Dutch geographical names on non-Dutch charts and maps of the area, it becomes necessary to broaden this survey to some extent. After the exploration of the Delaware by Thomas Yong in 1634, the bay and river were fully delineated on the maps of Cecill,[13] Dudley,[14] Daniel,[15] Farrer,[16] Seller,[17] and others. These maps, however, produce little of interest for the student of Dutch names. On the other hand, the map by Augustine Herrman is detailed enough to be worth close examination.[18] The maps of Peter Lindeström, who made his own surveys on the scene, must also be examined with care, even though it is sometimes difficult to say whether certain of the names he records are of Dutch or Swedish origin.[19,]

The Dutch names in the Delaware Valley, as revealed by the sources available to us, are given in the list below. In this list numbers and letters are keyed to the accompanying map (Figure 3). The names on the map are those of the early Dutch geographical names still in use.

Not included in the list is the major area name *Nieu Nederland* (1614) and the lesser area names *Swanendael* (1629) and *Jagers-*

the Director-General to Walewyn van der Veen, has been lost with other papers in the ship *de Otter* so that we expect a like draught on paper by the first chance from there " (*NYCD*, 12 : 183). On this general subject, see *Iconography*, 2 : 161 ff.

[13] Nova Terrae Mariae Tabula (1635) ; fascilile in *Narratives, Hall,* frontispiece.

[14] Carta Particolare della Nuova Belgica è Parte della Nuova Anglia (c. 1636) ; facsimile in *Doc. Hist. N.Y.*, 1, frontispiece.

[15] Facsimile in *Iconography*, 2 : c. Pl.34 a. Compare Evelyn's reference to this map in his letter to Mabel Plowden (1641), reprinted in C. A. Weslager, " Robert Evelyn's Indian Tribes and Place-Names of New Albion, " *Bulletin 9,* Archaeological Society of New Jersey, November, 1954, pp. 1-2.

[16] A Mapp of Virginia (1651) ; facsimile in *Winsor*, 3 : 465.

[17] A Mapp of New Jersey (c. 1664) ; facsimile in *Iconography*, 1 : Pl. 11 a.

[18] Virginia and Maryland (1670) ; facsimile in end pocket of P. L. Phillips, *The Rare Map of Virginia and Maryland by Augustine Herrman.*

[19] Lindeström's maps are listed in *Delaware Notes*, 18 : 69-70.

land [20] (1659). Also omitted are the Dutch names for Delaware Bay : *Zuyt Baye* (1624), *Nieuw Port May* (1625), and *Godins Bay* (1630–1640) ; and for the Delaware River : *Zuydt-Revier* (1624), *Willems Rivier* (1630–1640), *Prince Hendricx Riv[i]er* (1649), and *Nassaw Riv[i]er* (1659). These have all been cited earlier in this volume. [21]

The first group of names that follows includes those of Dutch (or occasionally German) provenience listed and discussed by Dunlap in his 1956 monograph on Dutch and Swedish place-names in the state of Delaware. [22] The date in parentheses following the name is that of the earliest form on record ; the spelling is also (as a rule) that of the earliest form, and thus may vary considerably from later forms of the same word. Where a translation of the word seems in order, the Dunlap translation is given. Multiple names for the same feature in the list are separated by commas ; when a number or letter represents a cluster of features, these features are separated by semicolons.

   1. *Cape Cornelius* (1625), *Zuijt Hoek* (1630) ("south cape"), *Cabo Hinloopen* (c.1629). [23]

[20] This word has not heretofore been mentioned in this volume. Apparently a territory name for the northeast corner of Maryland and parts of Delaware and Pennsylvania, it occurs first in Herrman's journal (*Narratives, Hall,* p. 314 [1659]), and later in a letter written in 1662 (*NYCD,* 12 : 409).

[21] These names, and others within the confines of the state of Delaware, were treated in *Dunlap, 1956.* Many of those in the Pennsylvania and New Jersey parts of the Delaware Valley were discussed in *Dunlap & Weslager, 1958.*

[22] Daggers precede the names that are of uncertain origin, though conceivably Dutch. Not discussed in this chapter, because of their narrow application, are certain seventeenth-century " sub-geographical names, " having Dutch association, e.g., *Alricks Swamp, De Lagranges Marsh, Gysbert Walravens Marsh, the fly (vly) of Hans Block, Hans Blocks Dyke, the Bowerie, Broad Dyke, the Strand,* and others.

[23] This name was applied to False Cape as early as 1625, but it later became the name of the Delaware cape at the entrance to Delaware Bay. For a discussion of the shift, see *Dunlap 1956,* pp. 31-33. The form given above appears on the map entitled *Caerte vande Svydt Rivier in Niew Nederland.*

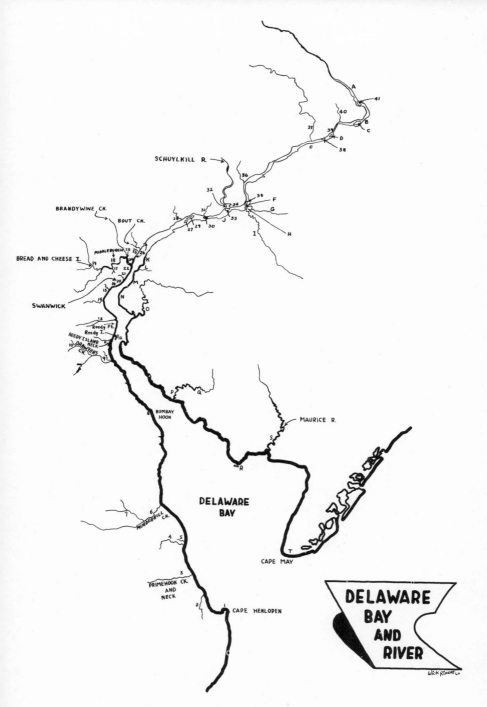

Figure 3. Dutch Geographical Names.

2. *Hinloopen Creek* (1629), *Bloemaerts Kil* (1630–40), *Hoeren-kil* (1640), *Haert Kill* (1654–55) ; *Kickout Neck* (1679) ("look-out neck ").

3. *Primehook Creek* and *Neck* (1670–80).

4. *New Sevenhoven* (the 1670's) (from *Zevenhoven,* a place in the Netherlands).

5. *Strunt Kill* (1739) (variation of *stront,* " dung ").

6.†*Murderkill Creek* (1654–55) ; *New Seavenhoven* (1679).

7. *Amsterdam* (1681/82) and *Amsterdam Branch.*

8. *Ruyge - Bosje* (1633) ("shaggy bushes " or "thicket "), *Boomptjes Hoeck* (1657) ("little-tree point").

9. *Knolbushaven* (1679) (" haven of round tufts ") ; *New Tiell* (1685) (from *Tiel,* a town in the province of Gelderland in the Netherlands) ; *Dreck²⁴ Creek* (1674), *Strunt Kill* (1686).

10. *Draijers Creek* (1671) ;²⁵ *New Utrick* (1677/78) (from *Utrecht,* a city and province in the Netherlands).

11. *Ariens²⁶ Kil* (1673/74) ; *Reeten²⁷ Point Neck* (1684) ; *Groeningen* (the 1670's) (named for a city in the Netherlands).

12. *Ret Eylandt* (c.1629) (" reedy island ").

13. *New Uytreght* (1683) ; *Reeden²⁸ Point* (1675).

14. *Apen²⁹ Island* (1663) ; *Knotsenburgh* (1684) (" retreat of clumps [tufts] ").

---

²⁴ A synonym for *stront,* " dung. "
²⁵ Meaning uncertain.
²⁶ Probably a Dutch personal name.
²⁷ " Reedy " (literally, " reeds ") Point Neck, which later came to be known as Reedy Island Neck.
²⁸ Reedy Point.
²⁹ Meaning uncertain.

15. *De Groote Kill* (1678) ("the great creek") ; *Ommelanden*[30] (1684) and *Omelanden Point*.

16. *Steenbackers Hoeck* (1656) ("brickmakers point") ; *Fort Casimir* (1651), *Santhoeck* (1651), *Nieuw Amstel* (1656) ; *Landerijen* (1667) ("landed property") ; *Smiths Boom*[31] (1701) ; *Vandiemans Land* (1682/83).

17. *Taswaijeeskijl* (1654–55) ("creek of the tufty meadow"), *Bosie* (1667) ("tuft" or "thicket") ; *Swart Nutten Island* (1667) ("black-walnut island").

18. *Middleburgh* (1684) (named for the capital of Zeeland in the Netherlands) ; *Buswick* (1685) ("district with tufts").

19. *Kees und Brodts [Eiland]* (1654–55) ("cheese and bread island") ; *Muscle Crupple* (1668) ("swampy thicket") ; *Claesburg*[32] (1677).

20. *Niew Clarelandh* (1654–55) ; *Strandwijk* (1654–55) ("strand district") ; *Jan Landemakers Hook*[33] (1668) (possibly the same as *Layman's Hook* [1669] or *Laymakers Hook* [1676]); *Swaenewyck* (1675) ("swan district").

21. *Forkins*[34] *Kill* (1665), *Pertdic Creek*[35] (1766); *Paerd*[36] *Hook* (1669).

22.†*Calcoen Island* (1683) ("turkey island") ; *Mill drope*[37] (1680).

---

[30] "Lands lying around a place," applied particularly to the country around Groeningen.

[31] *Boom* means "tree."

[32] An area presumably named for a settler called *Claes*.

[33] This feature may have been part of *Niew Clarelandh*.

[34] Meaning uncertain; perhaps "hog's creek."

[35] Evidently a form of *Paerd Hook*.

[36] Meaning of first element uncertain. *Paerd* means "horse" in Dutch, but *pert* or *pertti*, a Finnish dialect word meaning "cabin" or "bath-house," might have been etymologized by the Dutch (cf. *Dunlap, 1956*, pp. 46–48).

[37] *Drope* appears to be a metathesized form of Dutch *dorp*, "village."

23. *Elb-Revier* (1639) (named for a river in Germany, perhaps by Peter Minuit) ; *Fliegen Bourgh, Myggen Borgh, Rottn Bourgh, Slangen Borgh* (1654–55) (" fly burg," " mosquito burg," "rat burg," and "snake burg"); *Fort Altena* (1655); †*Brandywine*[38] *Kill* (1665); *Cuypers Eijlent* (1660) ("coopers' island "), *Jacob Vannivers Island* (1688) ; †*Young Keiricks (Yonkoraro?) Creek* (1744).

24. *Verdrietige Hoeck* (1655) (" tedious " or " troublesome hook ") ; †*Wilde Hook* (1668) ; *Carel Hook* (1680).

25. †*Honde Creek* (1673) (" dog creek ").

26. *The Bought* (1675) ("the bend [in a river]")—also *Bout Creek*.

The list continues with the names found on the west bank of the Delaware River above the present Delaware–Pennsylvania border, as well as those belonging in New Jersey on the east bank of the river (the latter are indicated by letter references). A number of the names, the ones followed by asterisks, were discussed by *Dunlap & Weslager, 1958,* and the definitions enclosed in quotation marks are those given in that work. To avoid repetition of the same date, the names marked with asterisks are all c. 1629. The remaining names, not included in either *Dunlap, 1956* or *Dunlap & Weslager, 1958,* are documented by footnote below.

27.†*Jaques Eylan[t].* *

28. *Wyngaerts Kill* (1633) (" creek of the vineyard ")[39]

29. *Doolhoff* * ("labyrinth"), *Bevers Eyl[ant]* (c. 1630),[40] *Island*

---

[38] Also Brainwend, Brandewyne, etc.

[39] *Narratives, Myers,* p. 22. De Vries, it should be noted, does not make a west-bank location unmistakably clear.

[40] *Pascaert van Nieuw Nederlandt* . . . ; for facsimile, see *Monumenta Cartographica,* Pl.77.

of *Kattenburgh*[41] (1656), *New Leyden* (1662).[42]

30. *Moder Eyland** (" mud island ").

31.†*Calcoone Hook* (1668) (" turkey hook ")[43] ; †*Andries Bonns Kill* (1669).[44]

32. *Schuylers Kil** (" creek of the hider ") — now the Schuylkill ; *Fort Beversreede* (1648) ;[45] *Mastemaeckers hook* (1648) (" mast-maker's hook ") ;[46] *New Hooven* (1648) (" new farm ") ;[47] *Kievits Hook* (1656) (" peewit's hook ").[48]

33. *Swaennen Eylandt** (" island of swans ").

34. *Creveceur* (1651) (" grief " — borrowed from French) ;[49] *t'vupebol* (1646); *t'vassebos* (1646).[50]

---

[41] *NYCD*, 12 : 132. In the *New Netherland Papers*, New York Public Library, a note occurs about the new form of the name in a MS entitled " 1657 July, Papers from New Netherland arrived with the ship Bever . . ." : " New Gottenburg, now named Cattenburg, is no fort, just a stately country house . . . " " Kattenburgh " is presumably a Dutch importation from the Netherlands, although it may have been brought to mind by the sound of its Swedish predecessor, " (New) Gottenburg."

[42] *NYCD*, 12 : 406.

[43] *PA*, 1st Series, 1 : 28.

[44] *Ibid.*, p. 29.

[45] *NYCD*, 12 : 38.

[46] *Ibid.*, p. 37.

[47] *Ibid.*

[48] *Ibid.*, 1 : 588. This name is often considered in the light of the context to be Swedish, but the context need not be so interpreted. Arguing in favor of the name's being of Dutch origin are these two points : (a) *kiewit* is a standard word in Dutch but a dialect word in Swedish ; and (b) the Dutch gave this name to a feature in New England (*ibid.*, p. 287).

[49] *Ibid.*, 1 : 598. Otherwise *Wicacoa*.

[50] Interpretations of *t'vupebol* and *t'vassebos*, the names of two features at the lower (?) end of *Wicacoa* (see the document recording Hudde's purchase of lands from the Indians September 25, 1646, Appendix B) are still to be worked out.

35. *'t Vogele Sant* (1646) ("bird-sand").[51] *Seutters Island* (1646).[52]

36. *Val** ("[water] fall").

37. *Draake Kijlen* (1654—55) ("dragon creek").[53]

38. *Peter Alricks Islands* (1667).[54]

39. *Onbekent Eyland** (" unknown island ").

40. *Wolve Kil** ("wolf creek").

41. *Verhulsten Eyland.**

A. *Val** : another feature with the same name as 37 above.

B. *Goutmijn* (1647—51) ("gold mine").[55]

C. *Houten Eylandt** ("wooded island").

D. *Hooghe eylant* (1624) ("high island"),[56] *Schoon Eyland** ("beautiful island"), *Bommelerweert* (1664) (from the island of *Bommelwaard* in Gelderland),[57] *Juniosa (Inniosa) Island* (1666) (named for Alexander d'Hinoyossa).[58]

---

[51] Some commentators have erroneously located this island in Delaware Bay. For a correction of this error, see *Dunlap, 1956,* p. 58. *Campanius,* p. 51, makes the following observation : "*Fogelsand* [*'t Vogele Sant*] is a white sand bank which is dry in summer. "

[52] This feature is near *'t Vogele Sant,* " over against " a creek at the upper side of *Wicacao* (see Hudde's purchase, Appendix B). It may possibly have been named for a Dutch trader or settler.

[53] *Lindeström,* Map A.

[54] In a land record dated 1667 (see *DYR,* p. 125) there is mention of two islands patented to Peter Alricks (cf. Chapter 3 above, wherein reference is made to Peter Alricks' owning four different islands in the Delaware at different times).

[55] Maps in the Jansson-Visscher Series ; on the 1639 chart reproduced in *Monumenta Cartographica,* Pl. 77, as well as on similar ones reproduced in *Iconography,* 2 : C. Pl.39, and 6 : Pl/81 b., this name appears simply as " Mine. "

[56] *Van Laer,* p. 51.

[57] Cf. Chapter 10 below.

[58] Cf. Chapter 3 above.

E. *Pruym Hoeck** (" plum hook ").

F. *Gansen Eylandt** (" geese island ").

G. *Timmer Kil** (" timber creek ").[59]

H. *Fort Nassau* (1626).[60]

I. *Verkeerde Kil** (" wrong creek," " turned-about creek ").

J. *Roden hoeck** (" red hook ").

K. *Einboome* [*hoeck*] (1675) ("one-tree hook");[61] *Bout-towne* (1683) ("bight-town").[62]

L. *Steurvangers kil* (1643) ("sturgeon[shad?]-catcher's creek"),[63] *Cameelkijlen* (1654–55).[64]

M. *Swart-hooke* (1668) (" black hook ").[65]

N. *Pompion Hook* (1675) (" pumpkin hook ").[66]

O. *Verckens Cil** (" hog creek ").

P. *Colake hoeck* (1675).[67]

Q. *Graef Ernsts riuier* (1630 – 40) (" Count Ernst's River ").[68]

R. *Cammens Eijlandh* (1654 – 55),[69] *Hammen Eylant* (1675).[70]

---

[59] Not to be confused with present Timber Creek: cf. Chapter 5 above.

[60] Cf. Chapter 5 for date and location.

[61] *P.A.* 1st Series, 1 : 34.

[62] *Ibid.*, p. 57.

[63] Map entitled Kaert vande Suyd Rivier, reproduced in *Monumenta Cartographica*, Pl. 79.

[64] *Lindeström*, Map A ; meaning of first element uncertain, and it may not be the same stream as the one named *Steurvangers Kil*. Somewhere near this waterway was a feature named *Steen-hooke* (1677), " stone hook, " the property of John Paul Jacquet (*PA*, 1st Series, 1 : 37).

[65] *Ibid.*, p. 35.

[66] *Ibid.*, p. 34.

[67] *Roggeveen's Chart*: meaning of first element uncertain.

[68] Cf. Chapter 5 for names of prominent members of the house of Nassau.

[69] *Lindeström*, Map A : meaning of first element uncertain

[70] *Roggeveen's Chart* : meaning of first element uncertain.

S. *Graeff Hendricx Rivier** (" Count Henry's River "), *Prince Maurice R.[iver]* (1670)."

T. *Cabo May** (" Cape May ").

Like names in other times and places, the seventeenth-century Dutch names in the Delaware Valley may be classified according to certain types. The Stewart method of classification is followed here." Where there is still some question that a word may not be Dutch, it is preceded in the list below by a dagger.

1. DESCRIPTIVE NAMES, those which originate from some quality of the place : *Boomptjes Hoeck, Bosie, the Bought, Buswick* (possibly belongs in class 4), *Doolhoff, Dreck Creek, Einboome [Hoeck], De Groote Kill, Hooghe eylant, Houten Eylant, Knolbushaven, Knotsenburgh, Landerijen, Mill drope, Moder Eyland, Muscle Crupple, New-Hooven, Niew Clarelandh, Pompion Hook, Primehook Neck, Pruym Hoeck, Reeden Point, Ret Eylandt, Roden hoeck, Ruyge-Bosje, Santhoeck, Schoon Eylandt, Steenhooke, Strandwijk, Swart-hooke, Strunt Kill* (occurs twice), *Swart Nutten Island, Taswaijeeskijl, Timmer Kil, Val* (occurs twice), *Verkeerde Kil, 't Vogele Sant* (possibly belongs in Class 3), *Wyngaerts Kill, Zuydt-Revier.*

2. POSSESSIVE NAMES, those applied because of a feeling that someone owned a particular place : *Peter Alricks Islands, Ariens Kil, Bloemaerts Kil, †Andries Bonns Kill, Carel Hook, Claesburg, Godins Bay, Juniosa Island, †Jaques Eylan[t], Jan Landemakers Hook, Laymakers (Laymans) Hook, Smiths Boom, Vandiemens Land, Jacob Vannivers Island, Verhulsten Eylandt,* and possibly *Seutters Island.*

3. INCIDENT NAMES, those which identify a place by means of some incident which occurred at or near it (this class includes

---

⁷¹ *Herrman's Map* : cf. Chapter 5.
⁷² George R. Stewart, " A Classification of Place-Names, " *Names,* Journal of the American Name Society, 2 (March, 1954), 1-13.

animal names, although some of these may also be considered descriptive) : *Bevers Eyl[ant]*, †*Calcoen Island*, †*Calcoone Hook*, *Cuypers Eijlent*, †*Draake Kijlen*, *Fliegen Bourgh*, *Fort Bevers-reede*, *Gansen Eylandt*, *Goutmijn*, *Hoeren Kil*,[72] †*Honde Creek*, *Kickout Neck*, *Kievits Hook*, *Mastemaeckers hook*, †*Murderkill Creek*, *Myggen Borgh*, †*Paerd Hook*, *Rottn Bourgh*, *Slangen Borgh*, *Steenbackers Hoeck*, *Steurvangers kil*, *Swaenewyck*, *Swaennen Eylandt*, *Swanendael*, *Verckens Cil*, †*Wilde Hooke*, *Wolve Kil*, and possibly *Forkins Kill*, and *Jagersland*.

4. COMMEMORATIVE NAMES, names of places or people which are given a new application for honorific ends : *Amsterdam*, *Bommelerweert*, *Cape Cornelius*, *Cabo Hinloopen*, *Cabo May*, *Elb-Revier*, *Fort Altena*, *Fort Casimir*, *Fort Nassau*, *Graef Ernsts riuier*, *Groeningen*, *Island of Kattenburgh*, *Middleburgh*, *Nassauw Riv[i]er*, *New-Leyden*, *New Seavenhoven*, *New Sevenhoven*, *New Tiell*, *New Utrick*, *New Uytreght*, *Nieuw Amstel*, *Nieu Nederland*, *Nieuw Port May*, *Ommelanden*, *Graeff Hendricx Riv[i]er*, *Prince Hendricx Rii[i]er*, *Prince Maurice R.[iver]*, *Willems Rivier*.

5. SHIFT NAMES, those shifted from one feature to another in the same general vicinity : *Amsterdam Branch*, *Bout Creek*, *Bout-towne*, *Hinloopen Creek*, *Omelanden Point*, *Pertdic Creek*, *Primehook Creek*, *Reedy Island Neck*, *Zuijt Hoek*, *Zuyt-Baye*.

The following names of uncertain origin or meaning are left unclassified : *Apen Island*, †*Brainwend (Brandywine) Kill*, *Cameelkijlen*, *Cammens Eijlandh*, *Colake hoeck*, *Creveceur*, *Draijers Creek*, *Haert Kill*, *Kees und Brodts [Eiland]*, *Onbekent Eyland*, *Schuylers Kil*, *t'vupebol*, *t'vassebos*, *Verdrietige Hoeck*, †*Young Keiricks Creek*.

A study of the above names by chronological periods reveals interesting changes in the patterns of Dutch name-giving on the

---

[73] A.R.D. thinks this should be included among names of uncertain origin, whereas C.A.W. believes it to be an incident name.

Delaware. In general, names tended to change in this sparsely settled valley with the changing conditions of promotion. As the posts for whaling and fur-trading gave way to settlements of a somewhat more permanent nature, new names appeared, not only for features in areas previously unoccupied by the Dutch, but also for some of the features already named — as the replacement of names like *Cape Cornelius, Godins Bay, Bloemaerts Kil, Elb-Revier, Wyngaerts Kill,* and so on, bears witness. More specifically, it might be pointed out that before 1651 (the date of the founding of Fort Casimir) there was a larger proportion of names commemorating prominent people than in the rest of the Dutch period ; and that after 1651 the proportion of names given for places in the homeland became greater than before. Among these new names were a number to remind their users of such familiar places across the Atlantic as *Amsterdam, Groeningen, Leyden, Middleburgh, Tiel, Utrecht,* and *Zevenhoven.*

In concluding this chapter, it might be observed that, of the names presented, only the following have preserved some or most of their Dutch character : Cape Henlopen, Primehook Creek and Neck, Bombay Hook (from *Boomptjes Hoeck*), Drawyers Creek (from *Draijers*), Swanwick,[74] Middleburgh, Bout Creek, Schuylkill River, Maurice River, and Cape May. An additional group has survived in translation : Reedy Point, Reedy Point (Neck), Reedy Island, Bread and Cheese Island, and possibly (Big) Timber Creek and Red Bank.[75] Added together, these survivors

---

[74] The current name, however, may be an example of revival rather than survival.

[75] The stream known in the seventeenth century as Timmer Kill and present Big Timber Kill are not identical, as was pointed out in Chapter 5. The name might have shifted from one stream to the other, since they are close neighbors, but another possibility is that their Dutch names were both replaced by English names, the recurrence of " Timber " being fortuitous. It is also possible that the first element of present Red Bank goes back to the first element of *Roden Hoeck,* but Red Bank could be entirely English in origin. Other names which, if clearly of Dutch origin, might be put in this group are Murderkill Creek and Brandywine Creek.

constitute about 15 per cent of the total list, but the reader will immediately recognize that they form an exceedingly small percentage of the names now in use in the Delaware Valley ; our linguistic heritage of Dutch seventeenth-century geographical names has not been a rich one.

X

The End of the Dutch Era

Each English attempt to gain a firm foothold on the banks of the Delaware had been blocked by the Dutch, assisted after 1638 by the Swedes. The major efforts had been made successively by a small party of Englishmen from Virginia, by merchants from the New Haven colony, and by the organizers of a Delaware Company in the Massachusetts Bay colony. A lesser-known attempt at settlement on the Delaware had also been made by Sir Edmund Plowden, as part of his plan to found New Albion, but it, too, failed. In 1659, another English voice was heard — that of Cecil Calvert, Lord Baltimore, who claimed that the charter of Maryland, granted to him in 1632 by Charles I, included the territory on the western side of Delaware below the fortieth parallel.

The reader has already seen that prior to 1634, the time Lord Baltimore's colonists arrived in Maryland, the Dutch had started colonies on Burlington Island and Swanendael ; they had also built Fort Nassau and Fort Beversreede. The Maryland settlers were not well informed about this prior Dutch activity on the Delaware River. By 1659, the governor and council of Maryland awakened to the fact that the Dutch were on the Delaware and that the principal place of their settlement, New Amstel, was within the limits of the Maryland grant. Colonel Nathaniel Utie, a member of the council, was sent to New Amstel to tell the intruders to leave !

Utie's instructions directed him to require the trespassers either to depart from the Delaware or to acknowledge Lord Baltimore's authority and become his obedient subjects.[1] When Utie arrived in Director Alricks' presence, he became more arrogant and demanding than his instructions provided ; in fact, he issued an ultimatum. If the Dutch did not comply, he said, he would not hold himself responsible for the blood that would be spilled. He pointed out that Lord Baltimore had power to make war and peace without consulting anyone. He consented to give Alricks three weeks to consult his superiors and submit, after which he threatened to invade the Delaware settlement.[2] Alricks was not prepared for trouble or war, nor was Stuyvesant, to whom he turned for assistance. After all, the Company had sold to the City of Amsterdam land that was supposed to be unincumbered, and Alricks held Stuyvesant responsible. The result was that a Dutch diplomatic mission, consisting of the brilliant surveyor and geographer, Augustine Herrman, and Resolved Waldron, was sent to Maryland to represent the Dutch in conversation with the English authorities. Stuyvesant also sent Cornelis van Ruyven and Captain Martin Creiger to New Amstel as his commissioners with fifty soldiers to prepare a defense.[3] Herrman and Waldron conferred with Governor Josias Fendall, Philip Calvert (a younger half-brother of Cecil, Lord Baltimore), who was destined to succeed Fendall, and the members of the council. They presented a communication from Stuyvesant and also made their own representations, from which the following is excerpted :

And as for the Sowth River or as it is called by the English Delaware int particular : The said River was in the primitive tyme likewise possessed, and a collony planted in the Western Shore within the mouth of the Sowth Cape called the Hoore Kill to this

---

[1] *Maryland Archives,* 3 : 365 ; Fendall had earlier warned Alricks to leave (*NYCD,* 2 : 67).
[2] *NYCD,* 12 : 252, 262.
[3] *Narratives, Hall,* p. 314 ; *NYCD,* 12 : 259.

day, The Dutch Nation erecting there and all over the Countrey
their States Armes and a little fforte, but after some tyme they were
all slain and murthered by the Indians. Soe that the possessions and
propriety of this River at the first in his Infancy is Sealed up with
the blood of a great many Sowles. After this in the yeare 1623 [sic.]
the fforte Nassaw was built about 15 leagues up the River on the
Eastern Shore, besides many other places of the Dutch and the
Dutch Swedes to and againe settled.[4]

By the " Dutch Swedes " they meant those colonists brought
from Sweden in 1638 by Minuit, because "the greatest number
of them were partners of Dutchmen," but (Herrman said) they
became so insolent that the Stuyvesant government was compelled to put them in their place.[5]

At several meetings with Fendall and his associates, Herrman
and Waldron argued eloquently and logically for the Dutch right
to occupy the Delaware. Fendall rebutted with what he believed
was equally logical argument in support of the English position.
In the heat of the discussion, the English made the error of showing the Dutch ambassadors a copy of Baltimore's Maryland
patent and giving them an opportunity to make an extract of it.
It is not known whether it was Herrman or Waldron who pounced
on the technicality of a Latin phrase in the charter which Fendall
had overlooked, so history must credit both of them for exposing
the words *hactenus inculta* (" not yet cultivated and planted ").
These words would become the basis of litigation between the
Calverts and Penns over the boundary question for years to
come. There was no doubt that the Dutch had " cultivated and
planted " the western side of the river at Swanendael before
Charles I issued the charter to Cecil Calvert. Therefore, Herrman and Waldron argued, Lord Baltimore had no right to this
land under the terms of his charter.

---

[4] *Maryland Archives,* 3 : 370.
[5] *Narratives, Hall,* p. 331.

Waldron returned to Manhattan with reports, papers, and documents respecting the negotiations and a polite letter from Fendall to Stuyvesant protesting Dutch occupancy of the Delaware. Herrman went to Virginia to solicit moral support there for the Dutch cause. But no English attack came at New Amstel as Utie had threatened, and the Dutch settlers pursued their daily activities in peace. Back in England, Cecil Calvert sent, as his attorney, Captain James Neale, to protest to the Assembly of XIX at Amsterdam, but New Amstel still remained in Dutch hands.[6]

After Neale's visit, the Assembly of XIX appealed to States General to request the Dutch ambassador in England to order Lord Baltimore to desist from his pretension. Meanwhile, Lord Baltimore sent Captain Neale to his colony with a message to the officers of his government urging them to cooperate and to "think upon some speedy and effectual waye for Reduceing the Dutch in Delaware Baye. The New England men will be assisting in itt and Secretary Ludwell of Virginea assured me before he went from thence that the Virgineans will be soe toe . . . ."[7] But the Maryland council, with or without the assistance of the New Englanders, was not eager to start a war with the Dutch in New Netherland, with whom Maryland was then enjoying profitable trade relations ; the Dutch were furnishing much-needed negro slaves and other commodities in exchange for tobacco. Furthermore, the council, not having the benefit of an accurate land survey, had some doubt whether New Amstel was actually within the bounds of Lord Baltimore's patent,[8] Philip Calvert, who succeeded Fendall, became very friendly with his Dutch neighbors, and so the relations between Maryland and New Netherland during this period were amicable. Thus, the Dutch continued to

---

[6] *PA,* 2nd Series, 5 : 399.
[7] *Maryland Archives,* 3 : 426.
[8] *Ibid.,* p. 427.

remain in control of the Delaware, but dark clouds were beginning to gather on the horizon.

On March 12, 1664, Charles II granted to his brother James, Duke of York (who would later become James II), a patent conveying proprietary rights to the land in America from the St. Croix River in New England to and including the east side of Delaware Bay. The grant embraced most of New Netherland, as well as part of the New Albion tract granted Sir Edmund Plowden in 1634, but which he had not succeeded in colonizing. The grant to the Duke did not, however, include New Amstel, the Hoerenkil, nor the other territory occupied by Dutch, Swedes, and Finns along the *west* side of the Delaware. War was then in the making between England and Holland (it broke out April 20, 1665) and the Duke was not deterred by any fear of antagonizing the Dutch, with whom relations were already strained almost to the breaking point. Furthermore, he ignored Plowden's rights to New Albion, whose charter, incidentally, had been inherited by Thomas Plowden, Sir Edmund's son. Indeed, the Duke didn't seem concerned if he overlapped the territory of the Baltimores. Therefore, when he sent over a fleet from England to seize and exercise ownership over his grant, he instructed his officers to capture *all* of New Netherland, including the western side of the Delaware River.

Governor Stuyvesant surrendered New Amsterdam, as the Dutch then called their town on Manhattan Island, to the superior English force consisting of four warships. Colonel Richard Nicholls, " a groom of the Duke's bedchamber," who was in command of the expedition, was also the deputy-governor, appointed by the Duke as his chief administrator in the new territory. Assisting Nicholls were three commissioners, one of whom, Sir Robert Carr, an ambitious but impecunious nobleman, was to play an important part in bringing English rule to the

Dutch settlements on the western side of the Delaware. The commission given to Sir Robert Carr on September 3, 1664, read in part as follows :

Whereas we are enformed that the Dutch have seated themselves at Delaware bay, on his Maty of great Brittaines territoryes without his knowledge and consent, and that they have fortifyed themselves there, and drawne great trade thither . . . . . . And by these do order & Appoint that his Maties ffrygotts, the *Guinney* and the *William & Nicholas* and all the Souldyers which are not in the Fort [at New York] shall with what speed they conveniently can go thither, under the command of Sr Robert Carr to reduce the same.[9]

The *William & Nicholas* was an armed merchant ship under command of Captain Thomas Morley. The *Guinney,* Sir Robert's " flagship," was a large, fully armed man o'war carrying forty guns, under the command of Captain Hugh Hyde.[10] Lieutenant John Carr (promoted to the rank of captain before the campaign ended) and Ensign Arthur Stocke were two of the officers in charge of more than one-hundred foot soldiers transported by the vessels.

The Duke's objective was to effect a change of masters on the Delaware (as had been done at New York) with a minimum of bloodshed and as little disturbance as possible to the social and economic systems. Carr had been carefully instructed how to handle Charles Calvert, Cecil's son, who had succeeded Philip two years before as governor of Maryland, in the event he offered objection or resistance. Carr was to inform him that his majesty had, at great expense, sent ships and soldiers to reduce all foreigners in these parts ; that he was instructed to keep possession of the place for his majesty's own behoofe ; and " that if my Lord Baltimore doth pretend right thereunto by his patent (which is a doubtfull case) you are to say that you only keep possession till his Majesty is informed and satisfyed otherwise."[11]

To reduce the Dutch, Nicholls had carefully planned the strategy that he outlined in the instructions issued to Carr : He would first make peace with the Swedes and Finns ; next he would assure the Dutch farmers and burghers that if they submitted to English rule they would not be harmed and their lands, homes, and possessions would be unmolested. Carr knew that if he could win the support of the citizenry, Governor Alexander d'Hinoyossa, the thirty-five-year-old ranking officer in the City of Amsterdam's colony would be " disarmed of their assistance and left to defend his inconsiderable fort with less than fifty men."[12] Actually the garrison at Fort New Amstel, including officers, numbered only thirty, but Carr did not know this until the attack.

The shoals in the Delaware caused Carr's vessels difficulty, as they had arrested Hudson fifty years before, and would block another English invader, Sir William Howe, one hundred years later. Nevertheless, Carr carried out his assignment completely and efficiently. He remained aboard the *Guinney* during the early phases of the attack on New Amstel, but went ashore in time to commandeer the supplies and material in the fort. The fort, its equipment, weapons, and provisions, as well as the houses, arms, slaves, livestock, and personal possessions owned by the City's officers or soldiers — these were all legitimate spoils of battle belonging to the conqueror. Strictly speaking, all the pillage was the property of the Duke of York, but Sir Robert knew that the Duke had no patent for the *west* shore of the Delaware. As the commanding officer who had risked his life and the lives of his soldiers and officers in the engagement, he had his own ideas about the disposition of the spoils, as we shall soon see.

A number of versions of the English attack have been published

[11] *NYCD*, 12 : 457-458.
[12] *PA*, 2nd Series, 5 : 569

in secondary sources, some less accurate than others, but most are incomplete. The following eyewitness story gives the important details from the Dutch viewpoint. It was discovered by the historian van Laer in the notary records of Amsterdam and translated by him into English :

On this day, the 16th of June, Anno 1665, before me, Hendrick Rosa, notary public, etc., in the presence of witnesses hereinafter named, appeared Godefro Meyer van Cloppenburgh, about 40 years of age, formerly sergeant, Steffen Ottingh van Loo, about 29 years of age, and Jan Janss. van Loo, about 32 years of age, both formerly farm laborers, and all three of them having been in the service of the Hon. Commissaries of the South River in New Netherland, [i.e. commissioners of the city's colony] who, at the request and urging of the said Hon. Commissaries by true words, in place and under proffer of an oath deposed, declared and attested that [the following] is true and well know to the deponents.

First, they, Godefro and Jan Janss. van Loo [two of] the deponents jointly [declared] that on [the first day of] the month of October of last year, 1664, towards evening, while they, the deponents were staying at Fort New Amstel on the South River, there came and arrived a large warship of the King of Great Britain, mounted with more than forty guns, accompanied by an English merchant vessel with soldiers, and that immediately three members of the council from the fort [Peter Alricks, Gerritt van Sweringen were two of them and possibly Joost de Lagrange was the third] went on board the English ship to demand of the commander for what purpose these ships had arrived there, as they were not accustomed to see such flags in their country. The admiral or commander [Sir Robert Carr], showing them certain sealed letters from the King of England, said that they had come to take possession of the country for the King, either by agreement or by force, whereupon the said three members of the council returned to the fort and reported the same.

The next day, very early in the morning, the first deponent

[Sergeant Godefro Meyer] was sent by their governor, Alexander Innejose, to their gunner, Hans [Block], residing a gun shot's distance from the fort, to order him to roast immediately four chickens and to boil a ham, as the governor and the English commander, each accompanied by four soldiers, but without the presence of other people, were to meet on land, outside the fort, in order to come to an agreement. Accordingly, that morning, at nine o'clock, after one of our four soldiers had fired his gun, the English admiral came ashore and he, the deponent, fired a salute of nine guns from the battery. The governor of the fort and the English admiral, alone, then walked away a short distance from the fort and remained together for about an hour and a half. The English admiral then returned aboard and the governor returned to the fort, where he ordered the deponent to load the pieces with shrapnel and to supply the soldiers with muskets and double [side]arms. The governor also asked all the soldiers whether they were resolved to fight, to which they all said, Yes, as long as they could stand up.[13]

The next day, about 8 o'clock in the morning, about one hundred and thirty English soldiers from the warship, as well as from the merchant vessel, landed, as they both declare, and marched around the castle to the rear of the farmhouse of the castle. At about three o'clock in the afternoon, some cannon shots were fired from the ship through the roofs of the houses in the fort and the soldiers who were on land climbed over the rear wall, whereupon Schout van Sweringen and Ensign Pieter Alderts, both of whom were of the council, jumped over the walls and began to run and when he, the deponent, asked the governor whether he should fire on the ship, the governor forbade him to do so and ordered him not to shoot. In climbing over the wall of the fort, the English in their fury cut down some of the people and wounded many. Thus, at four o'clock in the afternoon, the fort was taken by the English by storm and they, the deponents, and all the other people were plundered. They

---

[13] Of his conference with d'Hinoyossa the day before the battle, Carr wrote that d'Hinoyossa refused to accept his proposition for surrender (*ibid.,* p. 577).

also declare that there was then not a day's ration of bread for the people in the fort.

The two deponents further declare that eight or ten days before the loss of the fort, after word had been received that the Manades [Manhattan Island] had surrendered to the English, a general muster of the burghers and farmers and those in the fort showed that the burghers and farmers were ninety strong and that in the fort the number of officers and others was thirty.

The deponents also declare that the same afternoon that the two English ships arrived as above stated, the burghers and farmers who were outside the fort agreed with the English and retained their possessions, without being molested by the English in any way.

They also declare that at the time of the surrender of the fort, there was so much merchandise in the fort that the first deponent's house was filled with merchandise from top to bottom, so that no more could be stowed in it, including cloth, linen, wine, brandy, Spanish wine, stockings, shoes, shirts, and other goods.

The first deponent further declares that three or four months before the surrender of the fort, the aforesaid Governor Alexander Innejose traded with the English in Maryland Spanish wine, brandy, Rochelle [wine], linen, stockings, shoes, shirts, etc. for tobacco of the best quality, at two stivers a pound, which the English were to deliver at the proper season, and that thus he has sold some hundreds of guilders worth of merchandise to the English, for which as yet no payment has been received.[14]

The three deponents also declare that they saw in the Virginis,

---

[14] D'Hinoyossa had been trading merchandise belonging to the City of Amsterdam in his own interests. See the reference below to his taking delivery of Maryland tobacco in London. Beeckman had written prior to the attack that although trade in peltries and tobacco was reserved for the City of Amsterdam, d'Hinoyossa was taking one-half of it (*NYCD*, 12: 450). He also accused d'Hinoyossa of selling the City's millstones for one-thousand pounds of tobacco and a brew kettle for seven-hundred to eight-hundred pounds (*ibid.*, pp. 375, 379). In 1662, van Sweringen went to Maryland, "to collect tobacco belonging to both of them which they bartered for the City's millstones, the galiot and other City property" (*ibid.*, p. 422).

and the last two deponents that they helped loading into the ship of Jan Telly for the aforesaid Alexander Innejose, fifty-nine elk skins, a chest and a trunk packed with some others and various sorts of peltries and two beggar bags full of raccoons and he, the deponent, Godefro, [declares] that with the aforesaid commander and his family and the carpenter and the secretary he arrived about fourteen days ago with the aforesaid ship and goods at London.[15]

The deponent, Jan Janss, declares that he arrived from the Virginis in England on the ship *Coninck Salomon* ["King Solomon"] and that the said Mr. Innejose had some hogsheads of tobacco in her, as he was told by the crew; all three of the deponents declaring also that they heard from the Commander Innejose's own mouth at London that he had some hogsheads of tobacco in the aforesaid ship *Coninck Salomon,* saying that he must look after them.

The deponent, Steffen Ottingh, declares that he served on the island *Bommelerweert*[16] as foreman of the farmhands when the English with a small vessel with soldiers came up the river and overpowered the inhabitants and that the English plundered and took everything, even the bedding from under the people's bodies, and carried away everything, except what they kept for their own needs. The said deponent arrived in England in the ship of Captain Gilmer and all the deponents together came last Saturday, a week ago, on the Ostend convoy ship from London to Ostend and thence hither. Done at Amsterdam in the presence of Johannes Basse and Johannes Outhuysen, as witnesses.[17]

Van Sweringen in a later deposition stated that Carr also sent

---

[15] In an undated letter written from Thomas Howell's home in St. Mary's (present-day Annapolis) d'Hinoyossa asked Nicholls to restore his Delaware estate, which Carr had seized. He indicated he would remain in Maryland for two or three months and would then go to England. The above deposition indicates that d'Hinoyossa arrived in London early in June of 1665 (*PA,* 2nd Series, 5 : 587). He returned to America from England, and he, his wife and children became naturalized citizens of Maryland in 1671 (*Maryland Archives,* 2 : 282).

[16] This appears to be another name for d'Hinoyossa's Island (Burlington Island).

[17] The above deposition is given in *Iconography,* 6 : 19.

a boat to the Hoerenkil, where the English soldiers pillaged that settlement, including the homes of Plockhoy and his followers (see Chapter 4). Whether the Dutch residents there resisted the invasion, and were punished by having their belongings confiscated, or whether the attackers considered everything there as the property of the City of Amsterdam, and thus legitimate spoils, is not made clear in the deposition. In any event, the Hoerenkil was taken and also fell under the Duke's rule.

The English surrender terms were more generous than the Dutch had reason to expect — the burghers, farmers, and other private citizens at New Amstel, who had cooperated with the attackers, were permitted to retain their homes and personal property. Any Dutchman who did not want to live under English rule was free to depart unharmed within six months ; everyone was guaranteed freedom of conscience in church discipline; the Dutch magistrates were allowed to continue in office ; all the magistrates and inhabitants, Swedes and Dutch alike, were told they must submit to the King and take an oath of allegiance to " his Majtie of great Brittaine." [18] This seemed to impose no hardship on anyone, because there had been no strong loyalties to the deposed Dutch government. As a matter of fact, many of the citizens were doubtless glad to be rid of d'Hinoyossa, who had been a tyrannical, unprincipled administrator primarily interested in his own personal gain.

The plunder that Carr took from the Dutch was itemized as follows in van Sweringen's deposition :

One hundred sheep & thirty or forty horses, fifty or sixty cowes and oxen, the number of between sixty and seventy negroes, brewhouse, stillhouse, and all materials thereunto belonging, the produce of the land for that yeare, as corne hay &c were likewise seized by Sr Robert Carr for the use of the King and likewise the cargoe that

---

[18] *NYCD*, 3 : 71.

was unsold, and the bills for what was sold. They also got in their custody, being all, to the value so neere as I can now remember of foure thousand pounds sterling, likewise armes and powder and shott in great quantity, foure and twenty great guns were, in the greatest part, transported to New Yorke. The Dutch soldiers were taken prisoners & given to the merchant-man that was there, in recompence of his service, and into Virginia they were transported to be sold, as it was credibly reported by Sir Robert Carrs officers and other persons there liveing in the town. All sorts of tooles for handicraft tradesmen and all plowgeer and other things to cultivate the ground which were in the store in great quantity, as likewise a Saw Mill to saw planke ready to sett up, and nine sea buyes [buoys] with their iron chaines, great quantities of phisicall meanes besides the estate of Governor Debonissa and myself, except some household stuff and a negro I gott away and some other moveables Sr Robert Carr did permit me to sell.[19]

Sir Robert's account of the engagement is contained in a letter he wrote to Colonel Nicholls from Fort New Amstel, which he now called " Dellawarr Fort." Essentially it tells the same story told by van Sweringen in his deposition. Carr adds that after d'Hinoyossa had refused to surrender

I landed my soldiers on Sonday morning following & comanded ye shipps to fall downe before ye Fort withn muskett shott, wth directions to fire two broadsides apeace uppon yt Fort, then my soldiers to fall on. Which done, the soldiers neaver stopping untill they stormed ye fort, and soe consequently to plundering : the sea-

---

[19] *Ibid.,* pp. 345–346. Van Sweringen removed to Maryland after the attack and in 1669 he, his wife, Barbara, and his children, Elizabeth and Zacharias (both born at New Amstel) were naturalized as citizens of Maryland (*Maryland Archives,* 2 : 205). Van Sweringen had arrived in New Amstel on the vessel *de Purmerlander Kerck* February 3, 1662, (*NYCD,* 12 : 360). Since he was in office there for only two years, his children must have been born between the time of his arrival and the English attack in 1664. For names of other passengers on the vessel, see A. R. Dunlap, " Three Lists of Passengers to New Amstel," *Del. History,* **8** (March, 1959), 310-311.

men, noe less given to that sporte, were quickly wthin, & have gotten good store of booty; so that in such a noise and confusion noe word of comand could be heard for some tyme; but for as many goods as I could preserve, I still keep intire. The loss on our part was none; the Dutch had tenn wounded and 3 killed. The fort is not tenable although 14 gunns, and wthout a greate charge wch inevitably must be expended here wilbee noe staying, we not being able to keepe itt. Therefore what I have or can gett shalbee layed out upon ye strengthening of the Fort. Wthin these 3 dayes Ensign Stock fell sick soe that I could not send him to you to perticulerise things, but on his recovery I will send him to you, etc.[20]

Sir Robert was very generous in dividing certain of the booty among the officers on his staff. He gave van Sweringen's house, servants, lands, and personal possessions to Captain John Carr ; he rewarded Ensign Stocke, who was promoted to serve as commissary, with Peter Alricks' houses and possessions, including eleven negro slaves.[21] He granted Captain Hugh Hyde and Captain Thomas Morley a large tract of land, near the head of the Delaware River, to be known as the Manor of Grimstead.[22] This transfer leaves no doubt of Sir Robert's authority ; it refers to him as " sole and chiefe commander & disposor of the affayres in the behalfe of his Majesty of Great Britaine, of Delaware Bay and Delaware River." Sir Robert kept the richest prize for himself, d'Hinoyossa's estate on the " best and largest island in the South River," i.e., Burlington Island, with its gardens, dykes, houses, cultivated fields, livestock, and servants. D'Hinoyossa had lived there in luxury with his wife and his Holland-born children, Alexander, Johannes, Peter, Maria, Johanna, Christina, and

---

[20] *PA,* 2nd Series, 5 : 577.
[21] *Ibid.,* p. 602. An Island seven miles below New Castle, owned by Peter Alricks, was given to William Tom, a member of the expedition (*DYR,* p. 26).
[22] *Ibid.,* p. 575.

Barbara.[23] Among d'Hinoyossa's servants were a number of negro slaves that the city of Amsterdam had shipped over at his request. Carr reshipped all the negroes seized in the attack to Maryland to be sold to the English planters in exchange for " beefe, pork, corne & salt, etc."

Sir Robert did not bother to obtain from his superiors permission for his program of sharing the Dutch wealth. To him the spoils belonged to the victor in a very personal sense! Colonel Nicholls in New York was grieved to learn of Carr's actions, and he reported to his superiors in London that Sir Robert had reportedly said of the loot taken on the Delaware, " 'Tis his owne, being wonn by the sword." In the same report, Nicholls added :

I cannot but looke upon it as a great presumption in Sr Robert Carr who acted there, or at least ought to have done, as a private Captain to assume to himself the power not onely of appropriating the prize to himselfe, but of disposing the confiscations of houses farms and stock to whom he doth thinke fitt.[24]

Nicholls was so annoyed with Carr's actions that he added that he intended to go to Delaware to take charge and dispose of the plunder for his majesty's service, " and not for private uses." A few days earlier he had said he would send Captain Robert Needham to command there, but on October 24, 1664, a commission was drawn up and signed by two of the commissioners, ordering Nicholls to go to Delaware and take charge.[25] The records do not clearly state that he went to Delaware—if so, he did not take charge, for Carr remained there as the ranking English officer until February of the following year. Nicholls' communications reflected his doubt about the Duke's authority on the Delaware,

[23] *Maryland Archives*, 2 : 282.
[24] *PA*, 2nd Series, 5 : 569.
[25] *Ibid.*, p. 579. Van Sweringen stated several years later that he was informed Nicholls had gone to Delaware " being on the way for Maryland " (*NYCD*, 3 : 346).

and he usually referred to his taking certain action on a tentative basis only, pending the King's orders.

Later, Nicholls was persuaded that Carr, despite his private interests, had rendered meritorious service in his country's interests. On April 10, 1666, he wrote the Earl of Arlington, then Secretary of State, requesting that confirmation be given to Carr and his officers for their land acquisitions on the Delaware, which they then had already possessed for almost two years![26]

Sir Robert evidently enjoyed his role of conqueror on the Delaware — as well as the personal satisfaction and luxury of living on d'Hinoyossa's island estate. Carr ignored orders signed by Nicholls and the other commissioners that he return promptly to New York. His original instructions had empowered him to keep possession in the King's name and to exercise his own discretion in so doing.[27] As he saw it, duty, as well as his personal interests, called on him to remain! Since Carr's authority was equal to that of the other two commissioners, who had not even participated in the engagement on the Delaware, he probably felt that he alone had the right to make the decisions there. Some of the English soldiers in Carr's forces, as well as those who followed during the next few years, liked it so well on the Delaware that they remained, too, and were given lands for their service. Among these were Charles Floyd, John Henry, William Tom, John Ogle, Thomas Wollaston, James Crawford, John Askus, and others.

On January 16 (more than three months after the attack) George Cartwright, one of the commissioners, wrote from Boston,

. . . Mr. Maverick and my selfe have had nothing to doe but observe His Majesties commands in visiting the English colonies;

---

[26] *PA*, 2nd Series, 5: 599-600.

[27] See his instructions, *NYCD*, 12: 458. V. H. Paltsits called Carr an "impecunious royalist knight" ("The Transition from Dutch to English Rule, 1664-1691," *History of the State of New York*, ed. A. C. Flick, vol. 2, Columbia University Press, 1933).

but we have not had power to doe anything ; for together he and I cannot act without a third man though each of us single may act with Colonell Nicholls; but he is detained at New York with the affaires of his government, and Sr Robert Carre cannot be perswaded to leave Delaware as yet. And if they should not be spared from their governments, the next spring (wch I fear they cannot) we shall be in a great straight. . . . I have neither credit here to take up money nor an estate in England to pay it with."[28]

Nicholls finally prevailed upon Sir Robert to return to New York and pursue his duties as commissioner elsewhere in the colony, where there was work to be done in the Duke's interests, and on February 4, 1665, Carr arrived in Boston. In the fall of the same year he was still in Boston, complaining of a leg injury he had received on the Delaware which prevented his wearing a boot. In December, he wrote bitterly, " That little which I had gotten at Delaware, & for which I had hazarded my life, I am told is given away, and one is now come to take possession of it. Wherefore I humbly pray you [the Secretary of State] to assist my sonne that I may have this land above mentioned, granted to me by patent."[29] The land to which he referred was a tract on the Sagatucket River in the Narraganset country that he desired to settle on.

Commissioner Samuel Mavericke also had his own cause for complaint. He wrote that he had " not one farthing worth of all the plunder taken at Delawar it was worth they say about Ten

---

[28] *PA,* 2nd Series, 5 : 598. Nicholls himself complained that he, too, was " utterly ruin'd in my small estate and credit, " and that the other commissioners had neither money nor credit (*ibid.,* p. 599).

[29] *NYCD,* 3 : 110. This quotation is O'Callaghan's authority for indicating in the Index of the *NYCD* (see 11 : 120) that Captain John Carr was a son of Sir Robert ; the present authors have failed to find evidence to support this assumption. Gabriel Thomas, writing in 1698, said that Sir Robert was a cousin of Captain John Carr (*Narratives, Myers,* p. 316). Myers, without giving authority for his statement, said that the two men were brothers, not cousins (*ibid.,* fn. 6). The relationship is still in doubt.

thousand pounds, but how squandered away or to whom giuen
we know not, a runagot seruant of his confessed he had 400.
I mean Sr Robt Carr, he heares he is not to haue the gouermt
of Delawarr and therefore now moues the Inhabitants of the
prouince of Mayne to petition that he may be Gouernor ouer
them he indeavors to bee very popular . . . ."[30]

The following year Carr returned to New York, where he was
taken ill, and a letter written October 24, 1666, reported that he
had been abed for ten weeks. The nature of his illness was
described thus : " got in his travills to Delaware & Maryland a
Feavor, & Ague."[31]

Possibly Sir Robert returned for a while to the Delaware following his sickness in New York, as intimated by Fisk, but this is
not a certainty.[32] The Delaware was certainly no longer under
his jurisdiction ; indeed, on April 9, 1666, Nicholls had written
to Lord Arlington, " After a long expectation of His Maties
further directions towards the settlement of Delaware River for
which I heare not of any patent yet graunted, till wch time it
must and hath remained under my care and to my great charge,
etc."[33]

Sometime in 1667, Sir Robert Carr departed from Boston for
England, but upon the vessel's arrival he " dyed in Bristoll and
never got to London."[34] Any claim that Sir Robert had to property
on the Delaware evidently died with him. After his return to
England, Captain John Carr, who remained at New Castle with
the occupation forces, released Carr's Island (Burlington Island)
to Peter Alricks (see Chapter 3). Later the island was repossessed
by the English authorities.

On April 21, 1668, there was issued to Captain John Carr

[30] *Colls. N.Y. Hist Soc.*, 2 : 81 (1869).
[31] *Ibid.*, pp. 125-126, 128.
[32] John Fisk, *The Dutch and Quaker Colonies in America,* 1903, 2 : 11.
[33] *NYCD*, 3 : 113.
[34] *Ibid.*, p. 161.

" Resolutions and Directions for the Settlement of the Government in Delaware," authorizing him, as Sir Robert's successor, to command the English army of occupation (about twenty soldiers), and to become head of a governing council composed of Dutch and Swedish civil magistrates.[35]

The successful attack by Sir Robert Carr was the culmination of Dutch–English rivalry for possession of the Delaware Valley that had begun many years before and had seen a succession of English failures. The English threat had annoyed the Dutch, but with the assistance of the Swedes they thwarted the English when settlement attempts were made by those from New Haven, Virginia, and Massachusetts Bay. The Dutch did not allow this rivalry to become a blood battle ; it was a fencing match, to use Pomfret's analogy, that did not draw blood. Pomfret also suggested that neither Holland nor England wanted to risk straining relations while Spain presented a common danger.[36] There can be no question that European politics had an important influence on Dutch and English relations in America. Under Charles I the English had entered an alliance with the Dutch, and the quarrel between Charles I and his Parliament absorbed attention ; small heed was paid to Dutch activity in New Netherland until the times of Charles II. When the common enemy, Spain, lost her power, the commercial rivalry between England and the United Netherlands became keener than before; the war between them broke the friendly ties and each nation aggressively pursued its own national interests.

Although Dutch power had ended in America, New Castle, an English name given to New Amstel, remained predominantly Dutch in character for a number of years. George Fox, visiting

---

[35] *Ibid.*, 12 : 461-462.
[36] John E. Pomfret, *The Province of West New Jersey, 1609-1702,* Princeton University Press, p. 11. Fisk (*op. cit.,* p. 105) had earlier made the same observation.

seven years after the English had assumed authority, wrote in his journal, " The Town we went to was a *Dutch* Town, called New Castle."[37] Some of the Dutch officers were reappointed during the English administration, but as time went on English laws and mores were gradually introduced. The brief period — from August 8, 1673, to February 19, 1674 — when the Dutch were again in control made no important or lasting difference in the sweep of social and economic history on the Delaware.[38] Under the Treaty of Westminster, English rule soon returned and continued until the dawn of the American Revolution.

Prior to the English period, which started with Carr's attack in 1664, land on the eastern (present-day New Jersey) side of the Delaware had only been sparsely settled. After the abandonment of Fort Nassau, neither the Company nor the City of Amsterdam paid much attention to that side of the river. On June 24, 1664, four months before Carr's attack, the Duke of York presented this territory (which was to be called West New Jersey) to Sir John Berkeley and Sir George Carteret. The Indian inhabitants in the West New Jersey territory had become very unfriendly toward the English. When Sir Robert Carr arrived at New Amstel he wrote Nicholls that these Indians living on the eastern bank of

---

[37] *Narratives, Hall,* p. 395.

[38] In the *New Netherland Papers,* New York Public Library, there is a folder containing Dutch MSS relating to the Dutch recapture, with translations by Paltsits, which have not been published. Among these are two sets of secret instructions, cipher code, and the names of English vessels taken or burnt. The following extract from the Register of Secret Resolutions of the States General on October 25, 1673, explains why so little has been written about this interlude : " . . . that the Lords of said Board of Admiralty at Amsterdam had received confirmation about the recovery of New Netherland, but that unfortunately all letters had been lost, on account of the capture of the little vessel, sent by Capts. Binckes [Jacob Benckes] and Evertsz [Cornelis Evertsen] to convey the news ; in obedience to orders the Pilot had thrown [said letters] overboard ; consequently their honors were entirely in the dark . . . " Benckes and Evertsen appointed Anthony Colve as " Governor-General " (William Smith, *History of New York,* Albany, 1814, p. 59 ; also *NYCD,* 2 : 569, 609).

the river were then so strong that " noe Christian yett dare venter [venture] to plant on that side."[39] This was slightly exaggerated because a few scattered farmers, mostly Swedes and Finns, were living there. However, no organized colonization effort took place until later when the Quaker, John Fenwick, purchased Berkeley's interest and brought a contingent of settlers from England. This is still another phase of the English activity on the Delaware that remains to be fully told.

To understand why the Dutch colonization effort in the Delaware Valley failed, it is important to remember that in the seventeenth century commercial interests dominated the United Netherlands. Not rich in natural resources, the country had prospered through commerce. Her fleets of armed merchant vessels sailed the known trade routes in the seven seas and laid out new ones to lands discovered by Dutch navigators. The woolens of Friesland, lace and linens of Holland, pottery, tile, Delftware, cheese, and other commodities were exported from the busy water towns and cities of the low countries. Vessels, both large and small, anchored in Dutch seaports to unload their cargoes of lumber, silks, furs, spices, wines, whale oil, and other merchandise from Surinam and Curaçao, Greenland, South Africa, and the East Indies, as well as from North America. These imports were not all consumed by the people of the Netherlands — large quantities were sold and reshipped to neighboring European countries. Hundreds of persons were employed on the quays and in the warehouses and counting houses of the merchants in whose offices decisions were made that affected not only international trade but the economic and political life of Europe.

Although Holland was well populated, her cities and towns were not yet overcrowded. Her industrious people had rehabilitated the lands that had been under water with an intricate

---

[39] *PA,* 2nd Series, 5 : 578.

system of dikes and canals to form polderlands. It was an accomplishment in hydraulic engineering for the benefit of agriculture and commerce unsurpassed anywhere in the world. The dikes were also of military importance ; they could be opened and a sea unleashed against an attacker. The country was known for political and religious freedom as well as for social tolerance. There were few titles of nobility and no king or queen. There had come into existence a solid and content middle class of burghers having an attachment to the fatherland, and lacking motivation to leave their comfortable homes in a prosperous economy to settle distant lands. A successful colonizing effort usually requires a group of people with a common interest in escaping the social, religious, or political pressures and willing to endure hardship to found new settlements and wrest a living from the soil. The usual causes of such group migration — overcrowding, soil exhaustion, food shortage, religious or political persecution — did not prevail in this era when Holland ranked highest among the great mercantile nations.

The reader has seen how the successive trials by the Dutch to colonize the Delaware between 1623 and 1651 had all ended in failure. The final attempt at New Amstel, although of larger proportions and having greater support than the earlier ones, was also doomed for the same reasons that caused the others to fail. The sponsors were so beset with commercial interests and so eager for financial gain that colonization as an extension of Dutch life to the Delaware Valley was never their aim. They carefully weighed expenditures against probable returns, a sound principle of trade, but an unrealistic approach to the initial problems of colonization. The settlers were town dwellers, traders, and tradesmen, not tillers of the soil, and therefore lacking in disposition and experience an interest in agriculture so necessary to permit a growing colony to feed itself.

Divided opinions developed among the directors and stockholders of the West India Company — as well as among the burgo-masters of Amsterdam — which led to misunderstanding, petty bickering, and open animosity. This was accompanied by errors of judgment, confusion, and mismanagement which further blighted efforts to make even a commercial settlement a success, whether under the auspices of the Company, the patroons, or the City. When New Netherland changed allegiance, the entire population was not more than ten thousand, according to Colenbrander, in contrast to an English population of about one hundred thousand in New England, Maryland, and Virginia.[40] Yet the Dutch were fully entitled to whatever credit a nation can claim for exploring, first settling, and first exploiting the resources of the Delaware Valley. Their presence along this waterway before English and Swedish settlers appeared on the scene, casual though it was, gave them the right to have their people, their arts, and their industries transplanted to the New World. History, so full of paradoxes, would not have it so, and the Dutch lost their opportunity, with the result that the English wave swept westward across the Atlantic, engulfed them, and eventually all that remained was a dim memory of their failures.

---

[40] H. T. Colenbrander, "The Dutch Element in American History," *Annual Report, 1909,* American Historical Association, Washington, 1911, pp. 193-201.

Appendixes

APPENDIX A

SWANENDAEL DOCUMENTS

NOTIFICATION BY SAMUEL GODYN, KILIAEN VAN RENSSELAER, AND SAMUEL BLOMMAERT THAT THEY ARE SENDING TWO PERSONS TO NEW NETHERLAND TO INSPECT THE COUNTRY

Extract from the register of resolutions of the West India Company, Chamber of Amsterdam, the 13th of January 1629[1]

President Godyn and Mr. Rensselaer notify the Chamber that their honors together with Mr. Blommaert by the ships now going to New Netherland send two persons, one named Gillis Houset, sailor, and the other Jacob Jansz Cuyper, with the intention, in case they make favorable report to their honors, of planting a colony there in accordance with the conditions drawn up by the Assembly of the XIX.

---

[1] *VRB*, pp. 50, 154.

GILLIS HOSSETT'S PURCHASE OF LANDS FROM THE INDIANS FOR
THE SWANEDAEL COLONY[1]

June 1, 1629

In Ye Yeare Ao 1629 hath afsd. Gillis Housett by order and for
Samuell Godyn (as per Octroy of ye Westindia Company Art
XXVII of ye gifts and freedome obtained from them by the Patrons
of ye Collonies) bought of ye Ciconicins in a full Councell gathered
togather, where being prsent ye undermentioned head officers or
Patrons vizt Aixtamin, Oschoesien, Choqweke, Menatoch, Awij-
kapoon Mehatehan Nehatehan Atowesen Ackseso Maekemen
Queskakons and Eesanques, as also all ye Generation both young
and old Inhabitants, out of their Villages compassed within ye
Zouth Corner of ye Baay of the Zouth river & they have actually
sold to the aforesaid Gillis Houssett in Manner and quality as aboue-
said, ye Land now Called Swanendale or Swansdale in ye Length
of [blank] from seashore of ye aforesaid Zouth Corner or Creek
Called Hinloopen to ye Coming in or first narrow of ye Zouth riuer
about 8 Large miles & of ye breath (Landwaes in) about $\frac{1}{2}$ a mile
goeing upwards till you [?] Come to A Certaine Lownesse or Valley
whereby ye same Can bee Clearly separated, as it is done in this
Caard [Map] by stips [dots] parked [encircled?] and with a kind of
reddnesse made there ; It is easie to be deserned from ye other Land,
said Commiss : Gillis Housett paying and satisfying them, afsd

---

[1] This document may be found in vol. 15 of the *Penn Mss, Papers Relating
to the Three Lower Counties,* Historical Society of Pennsylvania, p. 15. It
is an English translation of a missing Dutch document. Immediately above
the translation appears the following statement : " A Caard of ye South
river in New Netherland made upon a newer View of itt done in ye yeare of
our Lord Anno 1629 by order of Samll Godi jn by his Commiss. Gillis
Housett in divers places amended and Corrected by Hendrick Gerratsen.
Upon ye 28th Aprill." The map herein referred to was unfortunately not
copied by the translator. " Hendrick Gerratsen " may be an erroneous form
of the name of the Dutch cartographer, Hessel Gerritsz, who made maps
for the East India Company. The above document was first published by
A. R. Dunlap, " Dutch and Swedish Land Records Relating to Delaware,"
Del. History, 6, No. 1 (March, 1954), 27-28 ; see *Dunlap & Weslager, 1958,*
for a map reproduction which may be the map herein referred to.

patrons for itt ye same day who have with a full satisfaction declared ye payment yrof [thereof] to bee good Mrchandize, as Cloath axes edges [adzes] Corralls with severall more such like Mrchandize well worth Bevers — whereupon following the undermentioned Counsells being then present, their Sakmah or King under years[2] [the chief was still a minor] where they deputed queskakons & Eesanques to goe for ym [them] and in their behalf and appeare before ye Dirrector Peter Minuitt both Director and Counseler of ye Isle ye Manhatans to the purpose, that they might there solemnly declare to be fully satisfied of this sale and due bills of sales, acquittances &ca. should be passed & made as was done by them upon ye first day of ye month called June Ao 1629 as abovesaid. [Signature missing, except for the letters *Uerte*]

---

[2] Not without precedent among the eastern Algonkian. In 1635 Leonard Calvert sailed to Patowmeck Indian town, " where the Werowance being a child, Archihau his unckle (who governed him and his Countrie for him) gave all the company good wellcome, etc. (*Narratives, Hall*, pp. 71-72).

REGISTRATION BY SAMUEL GODYN OF THE COLONY OF SWANENDAEL
ON THE BAY OF THE SOUTH RIVER

Extract from the register of resolutions of the West India Company, Chamber of Amsterdam, the 19th of June 1629[1]

Mr. Samuel Godjin having heretofore caused it to be registered here that he intended to plant a colony in New Netherland and that to that end he had engaged two persons to go thither to inspect the situation of the country, declares now that he agrees to occupy in the capacity of patroon the bay of the South River, on the conditions ratified at the last session of the XIX, of which he also advised Director Pieter Minuict by the last ships and charged him to register the same there.

---

[1] *VRB*, p. 155.

REGISTRATION BY ALBERT COENRAETS BURGH AND OTHERS OF A
COLONY ON THE EAST SIDE OF THE SOUTH BAY

Extract from the register of resolutions of the West India Company, Chamber of Amsterdam, the 1st of November, 1629[1]

Mr. Albert Coenraets and Company declare themselves from now on as patroons of the east side of the South Bay, beginning at the mouth of the bay [and extending] to the narrows of the South River opposite the land which Gillis Houset bought for his masters, intending to send a colony thither at the first opportunity in accordance with the articles ratified by the Assembly of XIX.

[1] *VRB*, pp. 164-65.

FIRST COMBINATION OF COLONIES IN NEW NETHERLAND AND SHARES
EACH PARTNER IS TO HAVE IN THEM[1]

February 1, 1630

Original draft of the first combination of the colonies and of what shares each one is to have in the others' colonies, the direction of each colony being reserved to the patroon by whom the colony was registered and in whose name it was bought of the owners according to the sealed instruments

Remarks on the colonies in New Netherland,
this first of February 1630

Participants in the said colonies

Mr. Coenradus on the east side of the bay of the South River	2/5	
Samuel Godyn ditto	1/5	[This colony was
Samuel Blommaert	1/5	abandoned and not
K. V. rensselaer	1/5	established.]
Total	5/5	

Hereof Mr. Coenradus is to have the management in his name.

Mr. Samuel Godijn on the west side of the bay of the South River	2/5	[This colony, to which
Mr. Coenradus	1/5	other participants were
Blommaert	1/5	added, was begun and
rensselaer	1/5	finally sold to the West
Total	5/5	India Company.]

Hereof Mr. Godijn is to have the management in his name.

[The above four patroons also planned colonies on the Connecticut River and at Fort Orange, near present Albany, with Blommaert the major share holder on the Connecticut and Van Rensselaer the major owner at Albany. The Connecticut River colony was not established, but the latter became known as Rensselaerswyck.]

---

[1] *VRB, pp.* 164-65.

AGREEMENT BETWEEN THE PATROONS, SAMUEL GODYN, ALBERT
COENRAETS BURGH, SAMUEL BLOMMAERT, AND KILIAEN VAN
RENSSELAER[1]

October 1, 1630

In the name of the Lord, Amen. Whereas we, the underwritten, are inclined to plant some colonies in New Netherland as elsewhere within the limits of the charter of the West India Company according to the Freedoms and Exemptions granted by the Assembly of the XIX of the said Company to all participants, and for this purpose have already had several colonies registered.

First, along the bay of the South River with the land on the west side thereof, which has been bought for us from the natives by Gillis Houset.

Secondly, on the east side of the South Bay from the mouth of the bay to the narrows of the said South River.

[The document goes on to describe other colonies registered by the same individuals and outlines the basis on which they would share profits or losses; how they would take turns at presiding at their meetings; that the capitalization of their company would be twenty thousand guilders with each paying an equal share of five thousand guilders, etc. Other references in the agreement to the South River are given below.]

Whereas . . . we have agreed, without prejudice to our ownership, right and interest in the said colonies, that Samuel Godijn for himself, his heirs, successors and assigns, shall bear the title of patroon of the colony on the west side of the bay of the South River and give to the same and to the places within its jurisdiction such names as he shall see fit.

---

[1] *VRB,* pp. 171-175.

Albert Coenraets Burgh shall on the above conditions bear the title of patroon of the colony on the east side of the aforesaid bay of the South River.

[Here follow details about the other colonies.]

Thus done and approved, after previous reading of the decisions, and in testimony of the truth four copies of like tenor have been made hereof, signed by each of us with his own hand, without guile or deceit, in Amsterdam, the 1st of October 1630 : and was signed with the several hands, S. Godijn, S. blomaert, K V Rensselaer. Underneath was further written as follows : Whereas Mr Albertus Conradj had before this ceded me his half and his wife now in his honor's absence[2] neglects matters entirely, I have signed for one fourth, but with this understanding that if his honor on his return home thinks that he sees anything to his detriment herein, I submit myself to the decision of the aforementioned three gentlemen; and was signed, J. de Laet.

[There then follows this note in the handwriting of Kiliaen van Rensselaer, dated 2d of March 1639 in Amsterdam.]

Inasmuch as three of the above mentioned four colonies have come to an end, to wit, the colony on the west side of the bay of the South River whereof Samuel Godijn was the patroon; also, the colony on the east side of the aforesaid bay of which albertus Coenradus or Jehan de Laet was the patroon, both of which colonies have been sold and turned over to the West India Company; third, the colony on the Fresh River [Connecticut] and the island of St. Martijn of which Samuel blommaert was to be the patroon but

---

[2] Burgh's absence is explained in a statement signed by him August 4, 1647, " . . . about the year 1630 when I departed for Russia, since which time, or since my return when I found that my share had been ceded to Mr. Jehan delaet, I have not troubled myself further about it " (*VRB*, p. 725). Burgh was ambassador at the court of Muscovy 1631-1632, (*van Laer*, p. 268, note 14).

which was not begun at all ; there remains at present of the said four colonies only that on the North River, lying above and below Fort Orange now named Rensselaerswyck, of which Kiliaen van Rensselaer and his heirs are patroons, holding, with the purchased tenth share of the heirs of Samuel Godijn, deceased, five tenth shares or the exact half, Samuel blommaert and adam bessels each one tenth share, Jehan de laet and [Toussaint] Mussaert in place of Albertus Coenradj each one tenth share and Jacob and hendrick Trip together one tenth share.

PATENT TO SAMUEL GODYN FOR LAND ON WHICH SWANENDAEL
WAS INTENDED TO BE LAID OUT[1]

July 11, 1630

We, Director and Council of New Netherland, residing on the Island of Manhattan at Fort Amsterdam, in the jurisdiction of Their High Mightinesses the Lords States-General of the United Netherlands and the Incorporated West-India Company, Department of Amsterdam, attest and declare herewith, that this day, as underwritten presented themselves and appeared before us Quesquaekous, Eesanques and Siconesius[2] and inhabitants of their village, situate on the Southhook of the Southriver-bay, who declare of their own accord and deliberately, by special authority of their superiors and with the consent of the community there that on the first day of the month of June of the last year 1629 and in consideration of a certain quantity of goods, which they acknowledge to have received and taken possession of to their fullest satisfaction before the passing hereof, they have transported, ceded, surrendered and conveyed as lawful true and free possession, as they herewith transport, cede, surrender and convey to and for the behoof of the Noble, Honorable Samuel Godyn (who is absent and for whom we ex officio, subject to usual reservation accept it) to wit the land belonging to them, situate on the South side of the aforesaid bay, called by us the bay of the Southriver, running along the same from Cape Hinlopen to the mouth of the South river aforesaid for about eight great miles [Dutch miles equal to approximately thirty-two English miles] and inland half a mile in width, reaching to a certain low place or valley, by which valley these limits can be distinguished with sufficient clearness, with all the appurtenances, rights, privileges,

---

[1] NYCD, 12: 16-17.
[2] The phraseology would indicate that "Siconesius" was a third Indian, which is not the case. It was inserted as an appositive to identify the two chiefs but misconstrued by the scribe. See C. A. Weslager, "Indians of Lewes, Delaware." *BASD*, 4, Nos. 5 (January, 1949), 7. In the document dated July 15, 1630, which follows, the phraseology is correct. For a discussion of the relationship of the two documents, see A. R. Dunlap, "Dutch and Swedish Land Records," pp. 46-47.

which belong to them in their aforesaid quality, constituting and delegating the said Honorable Samuel Godyn in their stead and place as real and actual owner thereof and at the same time giving full and irrevocable power, authority and special charge, that *tamquam actor et procurator in rem suam ac propriam* the aforesaid Noble Mr. Godyn or those, who herafter may receive his property, may enter upon, peacefully settle, inhabit, use, keep, do with, trade and dispose of the said land, as his Honor would be allowed to do with his own land, acquired honestly and by lawful titles without that they, the conveyors, shall have, reserve or keep in the least degree any particle of claim, right or privilege thereon, be it of ownership, authority or jurisdiction, but for the reasons as above they desist, give up, abandon and renounce herwith now and forever all the aforesaid, promising further not only to keep, fulfill and execute firmly inviolately and irrevocably until the day of judgment this their compact and what might hereafter be done on the authority thereof, but also to deliver the said tract of land and keep it free against everybody from claim, challenge and care, which anybody might intend to create; all in good faith and without deceit or fraud. In testimony whereof this has been attested with our usual signature and with our seal appended. Done on the Island of Manhattan, this 11th of July, 1630.

PATENT TO MESSRS. GODYN AND BLOMMAERT FOR A TRACT OF LAND
ON DELAWARE BAY[1]

July 15, 1630

We, the Director and Council in New Netherland, residing on the Island Manahatas and in Fort Amsterdam, under the authority of their High Mightinesses the Lords States General of the United Netherlands, and of the Incorporated West India Company, Chamber at Amsterdam hereby acknowledge and declare, that on this day, the date underwritten, came and appeared before us, in their proper persons, Queskakous and Eesanques Siconesius, and the inhabitants of their village, situate at the South cape of the Bay of the South River, and freely and voluntarily declared, by special authority of the rulers and consent of the Commonalty there, that they already, on the first day of the month of June of the past year, 1629, for and on account of certain parcels of cargoes, which they, previous to the passing hereof, acknowledged to have received and got into their hands and power, to their full satisfaction, have transported, ceded, given over and conveyed in just, true and free property, as they hereby transport, cede, give over and convey to, and for the behoof of, Messrs. Samuel Godin and Samuel Blommart absent; and for whom We, by virtue of our office, under proper stipulation, do accept the same, namely : the Land to them belonging, situate on the South side of the aforesaid Bay, by us called The Bay of the South River, extending in length from C. Hinlopen off unto the mouth of the aforesaid South River, about eight leagues (*groote mylen*) and half a league in breadth, into the interior, extending to a certain marsh (leegte) or valley, through which these limits can be clearly enough distinguished. And that with all the action, right and jurisdiction to them in the aforesaid quality, therein appertaining, constituting and surrogating the said Messrs. Godin and Blommaert in their stead, state, real and actual possession thereof; and

---

[1] *NYCD*, 1 : 43. The date given on the previous page was July 11, 1630, whereas the above is dated July 15, 1630. The latter date is the one in the original (facsimilie in Historical Society of Delaware). Note that Blommaert's name appears only in original dated July 15.

giving them, at the same time, full and irrevocable authority, power and special command, to hold in quiet possession, occupancy and use, *tanquam Actores et Procuratores in rem propriam,* the aforesaid land acquired by the above mentioned Messrs. Godin and Blommaert, or those who may hereafter obtain their interest; also to do, barter, and dispose thereof, as they may do with their own well and lawfully acquired lands. Without they, the Grantors, having, reserving, or retaining for the future, any, the smallest part, right, action or authority, whether of property, command or jurisdiction therein; but now, hereby, for ever and a day desisting, retiring from, abandoning and renouncing the same for the behoof aforesaid; promising further not only to observe, fulfill and to hold fast, unbroken and irrevocable, this their conveyance and whatever may be done in virtue thereof, but, also, the said parcel of land to maintain against every one and to deliver free of controversies, gainsays and contradictions, by womsoever instituted against the same. All in good faith without guile or deceit. In Witness is this confirmed with our usual signature and with our seal dependant therefrom. Done on the aforesaid Island Manahatas, this fifteenth of July, XVI and thirty. (Signed)

Peter Minuit, Director	Jacob Elbertsen Wissinck[4]
Pieter Bylvelt[2]	Symon Dircksen Pos[5]
Jan Jansen Brouwer[3]	Reyner Harmensen[6]
	Jan Lampe, Sheriff[7]

---

[2] Bylvelt was a prominent member of Minuit's council ; he was recalled to Holland with Minuit in 1632, before the expiration of his term (*VRB,* p. 295 ; cf. Chapter 7). Following that, he applied to van Rensselaer for the position of commis for the fur trade in Rensselaerswyck, stating, " for a considerable number of years has filled the office of commis of the honorable directors of the West India Company, had the management of furs and merchandise " (*VRB,* p. 234). He signed his letter *Pieter Bijlvelt.* Prior to his return to Holland he owned considerable livestock at Manhattan, which he sold to van Rensselaer (*VRB,* pp. 192, 225). He is referred to elsewhere as a skipper (see " Pieter Pietersz Billevelt," in de Rasière's letter, *van Laer,* p. 248).

[3] Brower (Brouwer), another council member, was the same skipper mentioned in Chapter 2. He had made a number of voyages to New Netherland, having " long ranged these coasts as skipper and trader " (*van*

Laer, p. 262, note 13). The shipmasters present at the time business was transacted served the director as councillors ; this was Brouwer's function in signing the above document. He lived in Hoorn (A. Eekhof, *Jonas Michaëlius. Founder of the Church in New Netherland,* A. W. Sijthoff's Publishing Co., Leyden, 1926, p. 49).

⁴ On August 13, 1630, he had also signed the certificate of purchase of land from the Indians on the west side of the Hudson, writing his name *Jacob Elbertsz Wissinck.* Other members of the council who signed this document were " Pieter Bijvelt, Ian Uanssen Brouwer, Sijmon Dircks Pos, Reynier Harmensen, and Peter Minuit, Director " (*VRB,* pp. 166-167).

⁵ His letter to van Rensselaer of September 16, 1630, which he signed *sijmon dircxz pos,* reports how Director Minuit and the secretary, Johan van Remunde, were embittered against each other (*VRB,* pp. 169-170). Remunde had reported grievances, both true and false, concerning Minuit to the directors ; he appears to have been a chronic troublemaker. He returned to Holland in 1632 with Minuit and other officials ; see the note in the memorandum book of Arnoldus Buchelius reading : " Johan van Voorst coming hither from New Netherland was on arriving in England detained there for more than four months. . . . with the same ship came over also all the authorities, the governor, director, secretary, and minister, not being able to get along together " (*van Laer,* pp. 272-273, note 17 ; p. 266, note 3). Minuit, like Bylvelt, had considerable livestock at Manhattan, including sheep, cows, mares, hogs, chickens, pigeons, etc., which he sold to van Twiller and van Rensselaer (*VRB,* pp. 223-224).

⁶ Also referred to as *Master Reyn Harmanssen,* indicating he, too, was a skipper and *ex officio* member of the council (*VRB,* p. 160).

⁷ Lampo, an Englishman from Canterbury, was one of the earlier Verhulst colonists (*van Laer,* p. 90). He was appointed the first schout-fiscal (chief law officer and prosecutor, an *ex officio* member of the council who had no vote) and served under Minuit (*van Laer,* p. 265, note 20). He returned with Minuit to Holland in 1632 on the *Eendracht* (*NYCD,* 1 : 51). Lampo was succeeded by Coenraed Notelman, van Rensselaer's nephew, who had brought the papers ordering the recall of Minuit and the other officials.

PATENT TO SAMUEL GODYN AND SAMUEL BLOMMAERT OF THE EAST
SIDE OF DELAWARE RIVER (NOW IN CAPE MAY COUNTY, N.J.)[1]

June 3, 1631

We, Director and Council of New-Netherland, residing on the
Island at Fort Amsterdam, under the jurisdiction of Their Noble
High Mightinesses, the Lords-States-General of the United Netherlands and the Incorporated West-India Company, Department of
Amsterdam, attest and declare herewith that today, date underwritten, appeared Peter Heyssen, skipper of the Ship *Walvis* at
present lying in the Southriver, and Gillis Hosset, commissary on
the same, who declare, that on the 5th day of May, last past, before
them appeared personally Sawowouwe, Wuoyt, Pemhake, Mekow-
etick, Techepewoya, Mathamek, Sacook, Anehoopen, Janqueno and
Pokahake, lawful owners, proprietors and inhabitants of the east
side of Goddyn's East Bay, called Cape de Maye, who for themselves in proportion of their own shares and for all the other owners
in regard to their shares of the same land, declared of their own
accord and deliberately in their said quality, to have transported,
ceded and conveyed as lawful, unalienable and free property by
virtue and title of sale and in consideration of a certain quantity
of goods, which they, the conveyors, acknowledge in their said
quality to have received and accepted before the passing of this
contract, and they herewith transport, cede and convey, to and in
behoof of the Noble Honorable Samuel Godyn and Samuel Bloemmaert (who are absent and for whom they had accepted the hereafter described land subject to the usual reservation) to wit : the
eastside of Godyn's Bay or Cape de May, reaching 4 miles [Dutch
miles] from the said Cape towards the bay and 4 miles along the
coast southward and another 4 miles inland, being 16 square miles,
with all interests, rights and privileges, which were vested in themselves in their aforesaid quality, constituting and delegating the

---

[1] This patent and the previous one, dated July 11, 1630, were both issued
by Peter Minuit, then Director-General of New Netherland (*NYCD*,
12 : 17-18).

aforesaid purchasers in their own stead as real and actual owners thereof and giving and surrendering at the same time to their Honors, full, absolute and irrevocable power, authority and special charge, that *tamquam actores et procuratores in rem propriam* the Noble Messrs. Godyn and Bloemmaert or those, who might hereafter receive their property, enter upon, possess in peace, inhabit, cultivate, keep, use, do with, trade and dispose of the aforedescribed land, as they would do with their own inherited lands and fiefs, without that they, the conveyors, shall have, reserve or keep in the least degree any particle of claim, right or privilege thereon be it of ownership, authority or jurisdiction, but for the behalf as aforesaid they herewith entirely and absolutely desist from, give up, abandon and renounce it now and forever, promising further not only to keep, fulfill and execute firmly, inviolately and irrevocably in infinitum this, their contract and what might be done hereafter on the authority thereof, but also to deliver the said tract of land and keep it free against everybody, from any claim, challenge or incumbrance which anybody might intend to create; as well as to have this sale and conveyance approved and confirmed by the remainder of the co-owners, for whom they are trustee; all this under the obligations required by law, in good faith, without evil intent or deceit. In testimony whereof this has been confirmed by our usual signature and our seal appended thereto. Done on the aforesaid Island of Manhattan at Fort Amsterdam, the 3rd of June Ao 1631.

June 27, 1632

Mr. Johan de laedt, at Leyden

In Amsterdam, 27 June 1632

Your honor will doubtless have heard how our ship *den walvis* ["the Whale"] which together with the yacht *Teencoorntgen* ["Little Squirrel"] sailed from the Texel on the 24th of May, was on the 26th ditto for nearly two hours tossed about on the banks before Dunkirk, not without great danger of losing the ship and the goods, as most of the people had already left the ship and jumped into the shallops. Nevertheless, it pleased Almighty God to rescue the said ship from the said banks, but as it was very leaky and much damaged they stopped on the 28th at Portsmouth near the Isle of Wight to have her repaired there, the yacht *Teencoorngen* being still with her. Meanwhile Guilliamme lefant, being dissatisfied with the command of David pietersen [David Pietersz de Vries] or according to my opinion rather because he was afraid left the ship and returned over land, to the disgust of the confraters, so that henrij de forest [Hendrik de Forest] will probably be useful to supply the place left vacant by Guilliamine. Said Guilliamme made out that the leak was very large and irreparable, but from the letter of David pietersen to confrater Godyn, dated the 11th of June from Portsmouth, we understand that the same was nearly repaired and that he expected to go to sea at the first opportunity to complete his intended voyage in God's name, drawing on confrater Godyn for 60 pounds sterling on account of the expenses there.[2]

It would be a pity if we missed the whale fishing again, as Director Minuijt, who has come here, assures us that there are quantities of whales in the South River and that the savages of

---

[1] *VRB,* pp. 196-197.

[2] The voyage described in this letter is the one that brought de Vries to the destroyed Swanendael colony in 1632. In his journal, he relates how he ran aground on the Bree-Branck shoals off Dunkirk due to the carelessness of his mates.

those quarters wear on their heads mostly small feathers made of whalebone.[3] So much for matters with which the Company of ten is concerned.[4]

[The remainder of letter does not relate to the South River.]

---

[3] These whalebone decorations call to mind van der Donck's observations that the Indians " are all accustomed to wear a leathern girdle which is usually ornamented with pieces of whale's fins, whale bones or wampum " (*Colls. N.Y. Hist. Soc.*, 2nd Series, 1 : 194).

[4] The "Company of ten" refers to the 10 co-patroons in the Swanendael project (cf. Chapter 4). When he wrote this letter, van Rensselaer should have had information that Swanendael was destroyed, and it is curious that he makes no reference to the massacre. It is also of interest that Minuit, who had been recalled by the Company, encouraged the patroons to persist in their whaling efforts in the Delaware River. Heyes reported that he had arrived too late for the whale season, which explains van Rensselaer's concern about missing the season for the " second time. "

THE VOYAGE WITH THE FIRST SETTLERS TO SWANENDAEL

*Excerpt from Memorial presented by Kiliaen van Rensselaer
to the Assembly of the Nineteen of the West India Company*[1]

November 25, 1633

In December 1630 they equipped a ship of about 150 lasts named
de Walvis, ballasting it with all kinds of materials, such as lime,
brick and tiles, also putting on board four large horses, twelve cows
with calf, also several boats for whaling, all kinds of ammunition,
provisions and merchandise and over 80 persons, costing all together,
including the yacht *de Salm* of which mention will hereafter be
made, over 50,000 guilders, which indeed is ten times more than the
f5,600 which in the beginning they received for their returns, upon
which all their calumnies were founded.

With this ship and people, they, the remonstrants, took possession
of settled, and peopled the fertile and well wooded island of
Tortuga, located on the northwestern side of Hispanola [in the West
Indies] placing thereon over 25 able-bodied men, well fitted out . . . .

With this aforesaid ship *de Walvis,* they also in 1631 [on the same
voyage] took possession of the bay of the South River in New
Netherland, occupying the place of their colony with 28 persons
engaged in whaling and farming, and made suitable fortifications,
so that in July of the same year their cows calved and their lands
were seeded and covered with a fine crop, until finally by the error
of their commis all the people and the animals were lamentably
killed, whereby they suffered incalculable damage etc. . . . for
instance, during the two years when the late Mr. Godijn and his
people were trading in Swanendael the Company received from the
South River through their servants a no less quantity of skins than
in former or later years, but he obtained his furs in addition to
these by bartering with other tribes. This caused so much jealousy

---

[1] *VRB,* pp. 241-247.

that the Company ordered their director to send a commis there, which was done[2] [with the result that the Company's servants] trading close by the people of Godijn deprived him in one year of over 500 skins in Swanendael alone, for which the Company is justly bound to pay, since they had never obtained more than 20 to 30 skins a year in that region before this colony was started. It is maintained with insufferable impertinence that the Company has excluded all but themselves not only from the fur trade, but even from the whale fishery, etc.

---

[2] This seems to mean that the Company sent their own commis to Swanendael when it was learned that the patroons' settlers were profitably engaged in the fur trade. The fact that the patroons had sent twenty-eight men but de Vries found the remains of thirty-two indicates that other individuals joined the original group. Whether these were Company employees is not known. Peter Lourenson deposed that he was en route to Swanendael in 1632 from Manhattan with five men and two horses "for the sd Companie" when, learning of the Indian massacre, he returned to Manhattan. This is further indication that the Company did not want to give the colonists free reign, especially in the Indian trade. In a letter to the States General, June, 1634, the patroons complained that the " Director in New Netherland was ordered to appoint commissaries and assistants in all the patroonships, to affix the placard and in no wise to suffer any of the Patroons to interfere in the fur trade. The Director had no sooner arrived in New Netherland [Kieft ?] than he proceeded against the patroons pursuant to the orders given him " (*NYCD*, 1 : 85).

EXCERPTS FROM TWO LETTERS WRITTEN BY KILIAEN VAN RENSSELAER

To Johannes de Laet, July 21, 1634[1]

I hope that all our shortages in Swanendael (which has too many rulers) will be made up by my colony.

To Jacob Albertsz Planck, May 24, 1635[2]

I can nevertheless not refrain from notifying you by this speedily departing ship, which now sails so hurriedly, while at other times it has lain ready for six months, that the respective patroons of the colonies of Swanendael and Pavonia[3] have sold and transferred their colonies to the West India Company.

---

[1] *VRB*, p. 313.

[2] *Ibid.*, p. 314. On the next page is the account of the transfer of the Swanendael colony to the West India Company.

[3] Pavonia was the name of the colony owned by the patroon Michiael Pauw. It lay on the west side of the Hudson River from the Narrows to Hoboken, including Staten Island, which was bought for him by Minuit (*Narratives, Jameson,* p. 197).

TRANSFER OF SWANENDAEL BY PATROONS TO WEST INDIA COMPANY

February 7, 1635

Another Extract, or Authentic Copy, from a bundle of papers relating to New Netherland, beginning 7th February, 1635, and ending 2d June, 1653[1]

Whereas, Directors of the General West India Company were commissioned on the 22nd August, 1634, by the Assembly of the XIX., to treat and transact with all the Patroons and colonists in New Netherland, for the purchase of the Patroonships, Colonies, dignities, houses, buildings, lands, merchandises, and all the rights, effects, appendages, and dependencies thereof, which they were in possession of there, Therefore the aforesaid commissioners, having reported, have, with the approbation of the Chamber at Amsterdam, dated 27th November, 1634, agreed and concluded with Samuel Bloemmaert, Kilian van Rensselaer, Jacques de la Miue, Hendrick Hamel, Nicholaus van Setterich, Johan van Harinckhouck, and the heirs of Samuel Godyn, deceased, each for their contingent, and they further representing Johan de Laet, *(endehaer vorden sterk maeckende voor J. de L.,)* that they conjointly, and each for himself in particular, for the behoof of the aforesaid company, shall surrender, as they do hereby, their two colonies, named SWAEN-ENDAEL in New Netherland, together with the jurisdictions, dignitaries, lands, rights, appendages, and dependencies thereunto belonging, which they there, by virtue of their two distinct sealed patents obtained before the Council of New Netherland, resident on the island Manhattes, dated the 15th July, 1630, and 3rd June, 1631, in pursuance of letters of conveyance passed by Queskakous and Ensanckes, Sickonesyns, and inhabitants of their villages, and the other by sawotbouc, Wiewyt, Pemhacky, and others appearing on the aforesaid date, both situate on the South River, as well on the south hook of the Bay, as on the east side of the said river, with all

---

[1] This document is quoted from E. B. O'Callaghan, *History of New Netherland,* New York, 1845, 1: 479-481.

such houses, buildings, outhouses, as they or their servants may have purchased, erected, or brought there, none excepted to trade with there, together with their own free goods, without reserving therein any right of action, placing such property from now henceforward in full possession of the aforesaid company, according to the aforesaid original letters, which they do hereby deliver over, consenting at all times to grant to the aforesaid Company, before the Director and Council of New Netherland, when required, further conveyance, acknowledgment, and discharge, and to give therefor suitable authority, without their being bound for any further indemnity.

Likewise, they promise and deliver over, besides these, to the said company, all charters, maps, and papers, concerning the aforesaid colonies and affairs of New Netherland, as far as it remains with them, and moreover to let them remain to the company as their free property, without claiming thereunto any right, action, or pretension. And that for the sum of fifteen thousand, six hundred guilders to be paid — one third part six months after the aforesaid 27th November, 1634, to wit, on the 27th May, anno 1635, and fifteen months after that, to wit, on the 27th August, 1636, the second third part, and fifteen months afterwards, to wit, the 27th November, 1637, the last third part.

For which sum, the company shall deliver to each participant [partner] of the said colonie, according to their quota and rata, by the said comparants surrendered, its particular [special] obligation, without the one being for all that holden to wait on the other for his money.

It being well understood that they conjointly, for the good of the company, shall take care that no man, henceforward, shall claim anything on account of the aforesaid colonie under penalty according to law, as they hereby agree to.

It shall be lawful to the sellers, or any of them, for the sum to which their obligation amounts — to wit, each according to estimation, for the sum of nineteen hundred and fifty guilders, to purchase, or cause to be purchased, goods from the company, in conformity to the Octroy or amplification thereof, and to deduct in whole or in part, at the rate of 6 per cent per annum, from the time the bill is due according to the bargain to be made by them, or from the day that they shall notify the discount to the day of payment.

And all claims and accounts which the aforesaid sellers and the company, on account of the aforesaid Colonies, or other transactions in New Netherland, both as to receipts and expenses, with other outstanding odd accounts, without pretending any other claims or actions in the world, shall be included in this sale, and shall hereby remain discharged, and stand erased on the books.

Only that the aforesaid sellers or their assigns shall, moreover, be free and exempt from the duties on the cargo of timber which the ship West Friesland, whereof Jan Symonz is skipper, shall bring back on this voyage.

And that the lawsuit between the Patroons of Swanendael and the company, depending before the court of Amsterdam, is not included in this transaction, and the parties on both sides, so far as concerns that, remain wholly free to pursue their right as they shall think proper.

And the aforesaid contracting parties shall observe, and allow each other peaceably and freely to enjoy the effect of this contract, under bond of law, namely, that those of the company shall pledge only the effects and goods of the company, moveable and immoveable, present and future, and the aforesaid sellers, their persons and goods in manner aforesaid, all without fraud or guile. In testimony whereof, two instruments only being made, are signed by the respective parties, in Amsterdam, this 7th February, 1635. Was subscribed, Albert Kounraetsburgh, Daniel van Libergen, Jean Raye, F. de Vries, Marcus van Valckenburgh, S. Bloemmaert, Henrick Hamel, N. van Setterich, J. van Harinckhouck ; Hendrick Crip, for the heirs of Samuel Godyn ; Jacques de la Miue, Kiliaen van Rensselaer, for his part in the Colonie of Swaenendael aforesaid, and no more.

ADDITIONAL EXCERPTS FROM LETTERS WRITTEN BY KILIAEN VAN
RENSSELAER PERTAINING TO SWANENDAEL

To Johannes de Laet, October 6, 1636[1]

However, I fear that if we expand too much [at Rensselaerswyck] we may become the counterpart of Swanendael, as the large number often causes confusion and, one pulling this way and another that way, hinder one another and are in one another's way, so that I should conclude the fewer in number the better; but your honor must do as he pleases. When we got so many participants in Swanendael, then came our confusion.

To Toussaint Muyssart, May 7, 1640[2]

There is, there should be and there must be but one head to rule the colony or we shall be in each other's way. Each one will think he knows what is best and meanwhile nothing but quarreling can be expected, as in the colony of Swanendael, which was placed under a board of directors, this is proved by experience.

To Johannes de Laet, February 4, 1641[3]

What difference can it make to me that others make a change herein, as for instance that Mr. Godyn, retaining but the bare name of patroon, permitted as many as ten people to share in the management, [of Swanendael] whereupon the business ran into great expense on account of the many directors, one wanting this and another something else, and had to be sold at a loss of f40,000? What difference does it make to me that the Hon. Coenradus also sold and ceded his colony with its appurtenances; or what difference can it make to me that Mr. blommart never began or developed his? Shall I, who have usually been vigilant and diligent in my management, be deprived of my powers, and do my partners who have either sold or not cared for their rights now want to enter upon mine?

---

[1] *VRB*, p. 334-335.
[2] *Ibid.*, p. 470.
[3] *Ibid.*, pp. 528-29.

IMPORTANT REFERENCES TO THE SWANENDAEL MASSACRE

Before sailing out of the Texel [May 4, 1632] we understood that our little fort had been destroyed by the Indians, and the people killed—two and thirty men—who were outside the fort working the land.[1]

. . . . .

An Indian remained on board of the yacht at night, whom we asked why they had slain our people, and how it happened. He then showed us the place where our people had set up a column, to which was fastened a piece of tin, whereon the arms of Holland were painted. One of their chiefs took this off for the purpose of making tobacco pipes, not knowing that he was doing amiss. Those in command at the house made such an ado about it, that the Indians, not knowing how it was, went away and slew the chief who had done it, and brought a token of the dead to the house to those in command, who told them that they wished they had not done it, that they should have brought him to them, as they wished to have forbidden him to do the like again. They then went away, and the friends of the murdered chief incited their friends—as they are a people like the Italians who are very revengeful—to set about the work of vengeance.[2]

. . . . .

. . . and when we were erecting a colony in 1630 on South River at Swanendael, on the Hoeren creek, and all our people were murdered by the Indians, occasioned by some trifling quarrels of our commander, Gilles Osset, as I have narrated in the beginning of this my journal—it was then requested of the West India Company to be allowed to war against the Indians; but the Company did not permit it, and gave as a reason that we must live in good harmony with the natives.[3]

---

[1] De Vries, *Narratives, Myers,* p. 9.
[2] De Vries, *Narratives, Myers,* pp. 16-17.
[3] De Vries, *Colls, N.Y. Hist. Soc.,* 2nd Series, 1 : 266.

Consider once, sir, said I, what good it will do—knowing that we lost our settlements by mere jangling with the Indians at Swanendael, in the Hoeren Creek in 1630 when thirty-two of our men were murdered, etc.[4]

As the Hollanders were the first discoverers of this river, they were also the first residents, settling themselves down in small numbers at the Hoerekil, and thereabouts, and at Santhoeck, [present New Castle] though the most people and the capital of the country were at the Manhatans, under the rule and authority of the West India Company. The Indians killed many of them because they did not live well with them, especially with their women, from which circumstances this kil derives its name [Hoerenkil].[5]

. . . . .

The third set is at Roymont, a strong, rich and fit place for a Fort. Sir Walter Rawley left there thirty men, and four guns [an inaccurate claim] the Dutch seated there fifteen men and a Fort, both to plant in that rich five miles neck to Roymont river (which runneth down into Chisapoack Bay) choice Tobacco, and thereby to prejudice and undersell Virginia, as to keep up a fishing Stage for Whales these proved but Grampus, and they killing basely an Indian refusing quarter or ransome, were by the Indians killed and expelled twenty years since.[6]

. . . . .

Two leagues from Cape Cornelius, where you enter on the west side, lies a certain creek, which might be taken for an ordinary river or stream, being navigable far up, and affording a beautiful roadstead for ships of all burdens. There is no other like it in the whole bay for safety and convenience. The main channel for navigation

---

[4] *Ibid.,* p. 268.
[5] *Journal of a Voyage to New York in 1679–1680* (Danckers and Sluyter), Memoirs, Long Island Historical Society, 1 (1867) 240.
[6] *A Description of the Province of New Albion,* 1648 edition, p. 24.

runs close by it; this place we call the Hoere-kil. From whence this name is derived we do not know; it is certain that this place was taken and colonized by Netherlanders, years before any English or Swedes came there. The States' arms were also set up at this place in copper, but as they were thrown down by some mischievous savages, the commissary there very firmly insisted upon, and demanded, the head of the offender. The Indians not knowing otherwise brought a head, saying it was his; and the affair was supposed to be all settled, but some time afterwards, when our people were working unsuspectingly in their fields, the Indians came in the guise of friendship, and distributing themselves among the Dutch in proportionate numbers, surprised and murdered them. By this means the colony was again reduced to nothing; but it was nevertheless sealed with blood and dearly enough bought.[7]

---

[7] Representation of New Netherland (1650), *Narratives, Jameson*, pp. 313-14.

SURVIVOR (?) AT SWANENDAEL

In a " List of the men on the farms " in the colony of Rensselaerswyck, under date of July 20, 1632,[1] appears the following:

N.B. If the laborers of Bylevelt [who had returned to Holland from Manhattan after selling some of his livestock to van Rensselaer] should not be willing to serve me or not be satisfactory to me, you may engage *theunis willemsen* who was left over in Swanendael to serve out the rest of his term as farmer up the river.

---

[1] *VRB,* pp. 222-223. Van Laer, translator of the above passage from the Dutch, says this " may mean either that Theunis Willems was engaged in excess of the men required in Swanendael or that he survived the massacre " (*VRB,* fn. 46, p. 223). Johnson (*Swedish Settlements,* 1 : 170, 171) interprets it to mean that Willemsen was a colonist at Swanendael who escaped the massacre. Van Rensselaer is authority that there were twenty-eight men in the original Swanendael colony, but de Vries stated that thirty-two men were killed. Johnson, therefore, surmises that at the time of the massacre, the population numbered thirty-three, five colonists presumably from Manhattan having joined the original twenty-eight. There can be no question of the logic here, because Laurenson in 1632 stated he was making a *second* voyage to Swanendael, with five men as reinforcements, when he encountered another sloop who forewarned him of the massacre and he turned back. That part of his deposition reads, " in order to bring there for the sd Companie five men and two horses, but being at Sea, another sloop of the West India Companie met the sloop where this deponant was in ; and forewarned them not to go to sd Hoorekill, by reason al the Christians were cut of there, by the Indians, whereuppon they did not proceed, but returned bake againe for New Yorke, and further saith not. " The question at issue was whether at the time of the massacre the population numbered thirty-two or thirty-three, and whether one of them, i.e., Willemsen, escaped. The present authors would like to suggest that Willemsen may not have been an original Swanendael colonist, but may have been one of the reinforcements, carried by Lourenson on his second voyage, who never reached his destination.

JACOB ALRICKS' LETTERS, RELATING TO SWANENDAEL (HOERENKIL),
TO THE COMMISSIONERS OF THE CITY'S COLONY

August 13, 1657[1]

. . . I have already stated that there is a very fine and excellent country called the Whorekill abounding very much in wild animals, birds, fish, etc., and the land is so good and fertile that the like is nowhere to be found. It lies at the entrance of the Bay, about two leagues up from Cape Hinlopen. I shall send a draft of it by the next opportunity. Please to keep it recommended; the place can be conveniently visited with a yacht of 8 or 10 lasts, but some people must be there for security. This can be regularly done, or set about in course of time, after numbers are sent and have arrived here, and more of the place is taken up.

October 10, 1658[2]

. . . I have appointed Mr. Inojossa to go to the Manhattans; I shall, by this occasion, demand the original deeds of this Place [New Amstel] also, learn what is to be done for the purchase of the lands at the Whorekill . . . .

October 10, 1658[3]

. . . The wise resolution which has been adopted to annex to this place the Whorekill and the country from *Boomtiens hook* [now Bombay Hook] to Cape Hinloopen is advantageous and excellent. It will be no sooner purchased than I shall hasten the conveyance, and take immediate possession of it; but send then in the spring or in the ships sailing in December, a good number of strong and hard working men. Should they not be forthcoming so speedily or promptly at the time they can be supplied by boys of 15, 16 or 17 years and over, bearing in mind, particularly that they be robust.

---

[1] *NYCD*, 2: 19.
[2] *Ibid.,* p. 50.
[3] *Ibid.,* p. 51.

Whatever is to be accomplished here must be expected from labor. I shall take care to build a redoubt or stronghold in the most favorable position . . . .

August 16, 1659 [4]

. . . The enlargement of this Colonie has been attended to according to order; besides that, a new fortification and settlement were made at the Whore or *Sickoneysincks kill,* which have been daily visited . . . .

---

[4] *Ibid.,* p. 71.

INDIAN DEED FOR LAND AT THE HOERENKIL

*Contemporary English translation of missing original in the
Dutch language*[1]

June 7, 1659

Wee Unther Written Owners of the Landes Lyinge between
Boempies Hook and Cape Hinlopen doe acknolidge this : Neckosmus
or Teotacken Great Upperhed, Meoppitas & Meas Brothers Unto
ye Sd Upperhed Kocketoteka Lyckewys Great Upperhed and Owner
of the Hoerekil (Called in the Indian Lingo Siconece) & the Land
thar aboud, Mocktowekon, Sawappone and Mettomemeckas his
Neare Relations and also Upperhed Katenacku Esippens & Sappeton
Sackemakers (the Land is Called Quistin) Pochocton Queogkamen
and Hohatagkon also Upperheds (ther Land Lys Next Unto Boempies Hook — Mameckus & Honkarkus Upperheds of Tarackus ther
Land is Called Peskamohot, Hemmagkomeck also Upperhed his
Land is Called [K?] wickenesse — Matapagisckan his Land is Cald
Seckatackomeck — Wee doe declare hereby In the Psence of a Great
Quantite of Indians and the Following witnisses that we have Sold
and Transported and Made over unto the Honorble Direct.
Ginneral and Counsils of New Holland as beings fully empowered
by the Reight Honorable West India Company off Amsterdam (and
to all those that shall here after obtain ther Interests by Vertu here
of) all the Above Mensioned Land, Viz : the Land between Cape
Hinlopen and Boempies Hook Lyinge in the South River of New
Holland, stritsing 2 or 3 days Walking up Into the Country or
about therty Myls, Wee doe Transport the Said Parsell of Land fri
and Without Incomberance and doe desist here by off ower Reights
& Properties for Ever, Withoud Reservation off any Reight part
Interest or Dominion thar in, Oblidging Ower Selfs to keep this
ower Transport Irrevocable and to perform the Same Acordinge
to Law Thar for provided, forthermore We doe promise When
these Lands shall be possessed and Cultivated, then as well the Men

---

[1] *BASD*, 4, No. 5 (January, 1949), 10-11.

as beast shall dwell and Live in Unity and peace; and Iff by axsident any dammith should happen; Such shall be Communicated Unto the Upperheds or Sackemakers And they Will take care that Reparation shall be Made, We the disposers off this Landes doe forthermore Own and Confes to have Received full Satisfaction for the Prmisses and Quarters here of this Whas Acted and dun in the Psence off the Interpeter, Sander Boyer Mr. Peter Alrich, Schipper Michiel Poulussen, Jan Broersen, Henrick van Bylevelt and Jacob Jacobsen as Witnesses Requyerd here unto Dated the Kill of Siconece Upon the South River in New Holland this 7 day of June 1659 (Whas Seingned)

As Witnessis	Mark of Neckakosmus
Alixander Boeyer	Mark of Meoppitas
Pieter Alrichs	Mark of Meas
Michel Poulussen	Mark of Koketotoka
Jan Broersen	Mark of Mocktotockas
Hendrick van Bylevelts	Mark of Sawappone
Jacob Jacobsen	Mark of Mettomemeckas
	Mark of Katenagka
	Mark of Esipens
	Mark of Sappataon
(Unthestoot)	Mark of Pochoeton
In my presence	Mark of Ouegkamen
Willm Beeckman, Commissioner	Mark of Hoatagkony
& Vice Director in ye [?]	Mark of Mameckus
Companies Service	Mark of Hockarus
Alixander d : 'Hinojossa	Mark of Matapagsikan

PETER CORNELIS PLOCKHOY'S CONTRACT WITH THE BURGOMASTERS
AND CITY MAGISTRATES OF THE CITY OF AMSTERDAM [1]

June 9, 1662

Because we are at all times disposed to advance this city's Colony in New Netherland, therefore have we, with the knowledge and consent of the thirty-six Councillors, concluded to that end the following agreement with Pieter Cornelisz. Plockhoy of Zierikzee :

That he, Pieter Cornelisz. Plockhoy, undertakes to present to us, as soon as possible, the names of twenty-four men, who, with him, will make a Society of twenty-five persons who will agree to depart by the first ship or ships to the aforesaid colony of this city, to reside there and to work at farming, fishing, handicraft, etc., and to be as diligent as possible not only to live comfortably themselves, but also that provision may thereby be made for others to come.

The aforesaid Society of twenty-five male persons (more or less as they may increase or decrease) shall, for the common welfare and for each individually, take up as much land, provided it belongs to nobody else, at the Horekil [Swanendael] or another part of the Colony, as they are willing and able to cultivate and pasture. These lands, divided and undivided, shall be the property of the aforesaid Society and Colonists to use in whichever way seems best.

The aforesaid Colonists shall enact such rules and laws as they think proper for the peace, harmony, and welfare of the Society with the provisions that each person who feels an injustice can appeal to the higher Magistrates, here or there.

The aforesaid Society, and each member individually, shall be exempt from all tithes and taxes, however they may be named, for twenty years.

To the aforesaid twenty-five persons shall be paid in loan one hundred guilders to provide the needs of each individually, and also to cover the cost of transportation (the wives and children being

---

[1] Leland Harder, " Plockhoy and His Settlement at Zwanendael, "*Del. History,* 3, No. 3 (March, 1949), 138-154. A slightly different version of Plockhoy's contract appears in *NYCD,* 2 : 176-177.

transported at the expense of this city according to the printed Conditions).

The aforesaid twenty-five Colonists shall bind themselves as a group to repay the aforesaid 2,500 guilders to this city, according to article 21 and 22 of the Conditions recently printed concerning this city's colony.

If one of the twenty-five aforesaid persons should decide to leave the Society and return to this country, he shall be free to do so, provided he takes only his own personal property and leaves to the Society the undivided land, cattle, and other common property, so the other Colonists can effect the aforesaid repayment. The transportation costs of such an individual shall be paid by the Society from the common treasury as a compensation to him for his labor.

And if any person should decide to move elsewhere at his own expense and retain or sell his share in the common stock, he shall be free to do so, provided he has someone to replace him, or he sells to someone whom the Society will approve and who will participate and help in common activities.

The aforesaid Society and each member thereof shall further abide in all matters by the aforesaid printed laws, the interpretation of which remains the prerogative of the Burgomasters of this city.

In testimony whereof, we — the Burgomasters and Magistrates aforesaid — affix the seal of this city to these presents, the 9th of June, 1662.

Signed Wigbolt Slicher

Having a seal impressed in Green Wax

Two leagues from Cape Cornelius, or Cape Hinlopen, which runs
in on the west side, lies a safe kill named the Hoeren Kill, which
may well be called an ordinary, or lesser, river : for it is fully
navigable far up, and a beautiful roadstead for ships of all burdens;
there is no other to compare, in the entire bay, for usefulness and
convenience. The direct channel for going up [the bay] runs here
close by.

A reliable person who had been stationed in the fort there for
several years, one after the other,[2] gave us an account of this Hoeren
Kill about the month of June in the year 1662, having just come
from there ; how that it lay from the cape, going along the sea, a
distance of about an hour and a half; and how that it was, in the
vicinity of the fort, about 200 paces broad and from the mouth
upward, for a distance of about half an hour, navigable and suitably[3]
deep. The pilots speak of the water at the entrance as usually about
six feet in depth. With canoes it is possible to go up for a distance of
about two hours. Within lie two small islands, the first quite small,
the second about a half hour in circumference, lying a distance of
half an hour from one another and the latter a distance of about an

---

[1] *Kort Verhael van Niew-Nederlants Gelgentheit* (anonymous), Amsterdam,
1662, in which the above passage appears, pp. 10-11, is one in a series of
accounts containing glowing descriptions of New Netherland. Dunlap's
translation above may be compared with an earlier, though incomplete,
rendition in Samuel Smith's *History of New Jersey*, 2nd ed., Burlington,
1877, pp. 57–58. Smith gives the date incorrectly as 1669, and for unknown
reasons says the account is of Swedish origin. Harder recently advanced the
theory (which agrees with the present authors' thinking) that the author
of this anonymous work was Peter Cornelis Plockhoy (Harder, *op. cit.*, p.
139). Murphy stated that the *Kort Verhael* was published by the burgomasters of Amsterdam on the occasion of the transfer of the Delaware
River territory to the City. He adds that it was intended to invite the
attention of emigrants to the new acquisition, described in flattering terms
at the expense of the Hudson River (*Colls. N.Y. Hist Soc.*, 2 : Part 1, p.
259).

[2] In the original, *aen malkander*.

[3] The Dutch word is *vry*, which literally means " free " or " freely. "

hour from the mouth of the kill, both overgrown with beautiful grass, especially the latter. Around the aforesaid two small islands, in a muddy soil, grow the very finest oysters, the muddy soil beginning about the first little island; whereas before in the kill is sandy bottom, and also very deep, for which reason no oysters are, or grow, there.[4] In the neighborhood of the first little island the water is more than once as wide as mentioned earlier at and around the fort. The kill stretches a good way along the sea, and high-dune-land lies between the kill and the sea, about 1200 paces in breadth. Close by the fort is a glorious fountain-head of fresh water.[5] A small rivulet taking its rise out of the land to the southeast, comes through dune-covered land, flowing down from an elevation into the estuary of the Hoeren Kill. And still nearer the fort, about a half hour away from the aforesaid little rivulet, another kill of about four hours in length comes out of the land through a valley, which, together with the kill, ends at and in the Hoeren Kill.

The land lying far and near around this Hoeren Kill was extolled and praised because of its excellence and fruitfulness before the very best of New Netherland. There are found also exceedingly beautiful, large, and fruitful valleys, extending a good seven to eight

---

[4] Natural and man-made changes in the configuration of the land have obliterated islands, but the possibility is that Canary Creek and Wolfes Creek formerly encircled land areas, making them "islands" in the strict meaning of "land surrounded by water." See D. G. Beers' *Atlas,* Philadelphia, 1868; also Lewes, Rehoboth Beach, Cape Henlopen, and Fairmount quadrangle maps of U.S. Geologic Survey.

[5] It cannot be said with certainty that the fort built in 1659, which is the one referred to above, was on the site of the earlier fort destroyed by Indians, but that possibility must not be overlooked. From a study of land patents the approximate location of the 1659 fort, referred to as "The Company's Fort," has been inferred (see David Marine, "Duke of York Patents on Pilottown Road," *The Archaeolog* (mimeographed), 7, No. 2 (September, 1955), 1-4. "The fountainhead of fresh water" may have been an important consideration in selecting the site, and in this connection, a spring on Pilottown Road, known locally today as "The Fountain of Youth," is thus described : " . . . an ancient spring believed for more than 250 years to possess the virtue of restoring or preserving youth, especially if the water is drunk from that rarity, a right-handed conch shell" (*Delaware —A Guide to the First State,* Federal Writers Project, 1938, p. 206).

leagues up the South Bay and River; and in addition everything about which, on behalf of New Netherland, justifiable praise can be given is to be found there.

The name of Hoeren Kill was reported to us to have originated from the liberality of the Indians (there in places by design)[6] in generously volunteering their wives or daughters to our Netherlanders at that place. It was otherwise, by David Pietersz de Vries, who first about the year 1630 tried to people it, named Swanendal.[7]

---

[6] In the original: *voornementlijk daer ter plaetzen.*

[7] On p. 44 of *Kort Verhael* the name of the stream is mentioned again. A note in the margin may be translated as follows : " Otherwise named Sinkenesse (*sic*), or Swanen-dal." The document above, "Gillis Hossett's Purchase of Lands, etc.," June 1, 1629, gives the name Swanendale, an English translation of the Dutch form. At the time the document was written de Vries was not yet a co-patroon in Godyn's venture; therefore it is unlikely he had anything to do with selecting the name.

PHILEMON LLOYD'S DEPOSITION — THE BURNING OF THE HOERENKIL [1]

April 6, 1728

The Deposition of Philemon Lloyd of Queen Ann's County in the Province of Maryland Esq. Deputy Secretary and keeper of the Land Records of the Province aforesaid Aged fifty five years or thereabouts being first Sworn on the Holy Evangelists of Almight God. Saith.

That having carefully Examined and compared the Transcript hereunto Annexed with the record thereof in Lib. No. 17 folio 89 (one of the Land Record Books now in his Lordship's Land Office) he found the Same to be a true Copy therefrom. And further Saith that Some time in October One Thousand Seven hundred Twenty and Seven, being at the house of Mrs. Elizabeth Jenkins, widow and Relict of Francis Jenkins, late of Summerset County Esq. he was then Shewed his Lordship's Letters patent, Sealed with the Great Seale of this province, for Six hundred acres of Land called Pershore Granted unto the said Jenkins, as by the Transcript hereunto Annexed is Set forth; And that haveing Caused an Exact Copy to be taken thereof, he this Deponent did afterwards Deliver the Same to John Lawson, the present Register of the Land office, who Examined and compared it with the Record thereof which, as he told this Deponent, did Correspond Exactly with that Copy taken from the Letters Patent aforesaid. And further that in Conversation with the Said Elizabeth She told this Deponent, that her late husband (who was one of the Council of State within this Province to their late Majestys King William and Queen Ann, and heretofore Intermarried with the widow of a certain James Weedon,[2] his Lordship's Deputy Surveyor for Woster, now called Sussex, County upon Deleware) had frequently told her, That he dwelt for Some time under the Government of Maryland, at the place then called

---

[1] This document is No. 39 in the manuscripts collected by Dr. Hugh Hampton Young and presented to the Enoch Pratt Library, to whom the author acknowledges permission to reprint.

[2] James Weedon was living at the Hoerenkil May 8, 1671, where he had a wife, one daughter, one son, and four servants (*NYCD*, 12 : 522).

Whorekill; Now Lewis Town; But that afterward certain Soldiers by order from the Lord Baltemore, had burnt the Dutch out; And that her husband's house was burnt down at the Same time also.

This Deponent further Saith, that being Some few days after in Lewis Town aforesaid, The most Interested Proprietors therein, as well as of the Lands adjacent thereunto Informed this Deponent, That they had knowledge of Coll. Jenkins's Letters Patent aforesaid, which by them was distinguisht by the Denomination of a Maryland right : And Confessed Likewise to this Deponent That the Said Lewis Town with the Greatest part of the adjacent Cultivated Land, were Included within the Limitts and Discription thereof, as Indeed it appeared very manifest to the Deponent ; who (upon viewing the Scituation of the place; at the mouth of Deleware bay; open to the main Ocean; and near adjoyning to the South Cape thereof, called Cape Henlopen) discovered that the South west and by west lines in the Patent, from the Whorekill to Pagan Creek bounded by that Survey to the Landward; and Enclosed the whole Neck of land. So that all the other parts of the Survey, are Encompassed with water, vizt. on the Eastward by the Whorekill Creek on the Westward by Pagan Creek now called Broad Creek and on the Northward respecting both the Bay and the main Ocean.

And further Saith that a Certain Gideon Tilman an Inhabitant of Summerset County, told this Deponent, about the Same Time, and that his father [blank] Tilman, had been an Overseer to Coll. Francis Jenkins; and in that capacity lived upon and cultivated the aforesaid Tract of Land at the Whorekill called Pershore, And that he had heard his father often times Say, That the Soldiers Sent by the Lord Baltemore, to keep off the Dutch (who Some time before as this Deponent hath understood from History, had retaken New Yorke &c from the English) from Seteling there; Continued at the Whorekill aforesaid, for almost Three months; But that the poor Circumstances of the people; Incapable of furnishing them with Provisions; Together with the Great Severity of a Cold Season then come on; Oblidged the Said Soldiers to think of Leaveing the place. And upon New Orders Sent, as the said Tilman's father did Suppose, the Commanding officer Ordered all the Houses, not Excepting Coll. Jenkins, wherein the Said Tilman then Lived (for preventing the Dutch from Setleing there) to be burnt down which was done accordingly,[3] And the Soldiers Returned into Summerset County, about the Later End of December, but as to the particular year of our Lord, the Said Gideon could not Charge his memory, Tho he was well assured it was Something above fifty Years ago—And further this Deponent Saith not

Annapolis April sixth 1728   Phile Lloyd

Then Came before me the abovementioned Deponent and made Oath on the Holy Evangelists of Almighty God, to the truth of the Deposition above written and Signed by him, the following words in the transcript of the Patents, vizt the said sum for a fine, being first Interlined, In witness Whereof I have hereunto Set my hand and Caused the Great seal of this Province to be hereunto Affixed the Day and year above written.   [signature]

---

[3] The burning of the Hoerenkil by Lord Baltimore's soldiers occurred after the recapture of New Castle by the Dutch, August 8, 1673. Another reference to this incident occurs in Colve's placard dated January 14, 1674, reading in part : " As some English of Maryland have driven some of the subjects of this government out of their dwelling-houses in a very strange and cruel manner and have ruined the same by burning their houses, whereby several have doubtlessly been deprived of all their means of subsistence, therefore I consider it necessary to proclaim hereby, that all such exiles, Dutch as well as English, who may come here with certificates from Commander Alrigs [Peter Alricks], that they were among the sufferers shall be provided with means of support . . . " (*NYCD*, 12: 511). It is not known how many dwelling houses were there when the settlement was burned, but in 1671 there were forty-seven residents, representing ten or eleven households (*ibid.*, p. 522).

See also van Sweringen's deposition (*ibid.*, 3 :345), wherein he states the City of Amsterdam was about to quit the Hoerenkil when some Englishmen from Somerset County, Maryland began to trade with the Indians and "build and settle in that parte of the country." See also *ibid.*, 12 :497, 503.

During the burning of the homes the soldiers spared one " thatch barn, " which caught fire three times but each time the fire went out. Evidently some of the survivors, including expectant mothers, sought shelter from the cold in this barn (see Leon de Valinger, Jr., " The Burning of the Whorekill, 1673, " *Penna. Magazine*, 74, No. 4 [October, 1950], 476).

PATENT OF SIX-HUNDRED ACRES AT THE WHOREKILL TO
FRANCIS JENKINS — 1672[1]

Caecilius &c Know ye that we for and in Consideration that Henry Smith of the County of Sommerset in our Said Province of Maryland Gent hath due unto him Six hundred acres of Land within our Said Province part of a warrant for Two Thousand one hundred and ninety acres of Land to the said Smith Granted the Eighth day of May 1672 as appears upon record whose right Title and Interest of in an to the Same the Said Henry Smith hath assigned Sold and made over unto Francis Jenkins of our Said County of Sommerset in our Said province of Maryland Gent, And upon Such Conditions and Termes as are Expected in our Conditions of plantations of our Said province of Maryland under our Greater Seale at Armes bearing date at London the 2 d of July in the year of our Lord one thousand Six hundred forty nine with Such alterations as in them is made by our Declaration bearing date the Two and Twentieth day of September Anno one Thousand Six hundred fifty eight and remaining upon record in our Said Province of Marylaand, Do Hereby Grant unto him the Said Francis Jenkins all that parcell of Land called Pershore, Scituate Lying and being on the west Side of a Creek known by the Name of Whorekill near the South Cape of Deleware bay bounded as followeth,

Beginning at a marked Cedar Standing in the Edge of the Branch of the Whorekill by a Spring thence running for breadth South west by South to the main branch of Pagan Creek to a marked white oake Standing by a marsh Side one hundred and Eighty perches thence bounding upon the Said Pagan Creek for Length North west by west five hundred thirty three and one-third perches to the mouth of the Said Creek — thence with a line drawn North East by North one hundred and Eighty perches to the Whorekill point of Land at the mouth of the Creek thence bounding upon the Said Whorekill running up the Said Creek South East by East five hundred thirty three and one-third perches to the first bounder

---

[1] This is a copy of " the Transcript hereunto Annexed " referred to in the Philemon Lloyd deposition of April 6, 1728, above.

Containing Six hundred acres more or Less, Together with all rights profitts and benefitts thereunto belonging Royall mines Excepted To have and to hold the Same unto him the Said Francis Jenkins his heirs and assigns for ever To be holden of us and our heirs as of our Inanno of Worcester in ffree and Common Soccage by ffealty only for all manner of Services Yeilding and paying therefore Yearly unto us and our heirs at our Receipt at our City if St. Maries at the two most usuall ffeasts in the year, vizt. at the ffeast of Annunciation of the Blessed virgin Mary And at the ffeast of St, Michaell the Arch Angell by even and Equall portions of the rent of Twelve Shillings Sterling in Silver or Gold, And for a fine upon every Alienation of the Said Land or any part or parcell thereon one whole years rent in Silver or Gold or the full Value thereof in Such Commodities as we or our heirs or Such officer or officers appointed by us or our heirs from time to time to Collect and receive the Same Shall accept in discharge thereof at the Choice of us and our heirs or Such officer or officers as aforesaid Provided that if the Said Francis Jenkins his heirs or Assigns Shall not pay unto us or our heirs or Such officer or officers as aforesaid the said Same for a ffine before Such Alienation and enter the Said Alienation upon record either in the Provinciall Court or in the County Court where the Said parcell of Land Lyeth within one month next after Such alienation, the Said Alienation Shall be void and of none Effect Given at our City of St. Maries under the Great Seale of our Said province of Maryland the 41th Year of our Dominion over our Said province Annoq Domini 1672. Wittness our Dear Son Charles Calvert Esqour Capt. Generall and Chief Governour of our Said province of Maryland.

APPENDIX B

DEPOSITION OF JAMES WAYE, A QUAKER, CONCERNING YE SETTLEMENT OF ENGLISH AND DUTCH IN DELAWARE [1]

New Yorke SS

James Waye aged 66 years or thereabout deposes a[s] foll[owing] That as this Deponent hath been informed forty three years since that the first Settlement that ever was in Delaware river was made by one Peter Holmes an Englishman near fifty years since brought thither by one Captain Young at a place called Arrowamex a Little above Schoolekil[2] And the said Holmes not being acquainted with the Indians and the Indians gathering together (at which time the Dutch had some Trade in the said river not as owners or Proprietors of the said Land but as merchants or dealers there) the English inquiring of the Dutch what was the great concourse or meeting of the Indians, it was replied by the Dutch that it was undoubtedly to cut them of (meaning the English that were then seated) Then the English for fear of the Indians p[ro]cured the Dutch to carry them away & The next year the Dutch having that opportunity by the English being forced to forsake the place came themselves & seated it[3] And this Deponent further saith & averreth upon his own certain knowledge that in the year 1641 this deponent with others came to a place called Wattseson a little below Newcastle in Delaware river the number 14 or thereabout

---

[1] This deposition was evidently made at the instigation of Lord Charles Baltimore in connection with the dispute with the Penns over the boundaries of Maryland and Pennsylvania. The original Ms is No. 31 of the Hugh Hampton Young collection of documents now in possession of the Enoch Pratt Free Library of Baltimore, with whose permission it is here published for the first time.

[2] " Peter Holmes " may well have been intended for George Holmes who, with a party from Virginia, attempted to seat Fort Nassau, as discussed in Chapter 6. If so, it has not previously been known that he originally accompanied Thomas Yong to the Delaware.

[3] Waye's facts are pro-English and garbled. The Dutch had long been in possession of Fort Nassau at "Arrowamex," and Holmes' party were the intruders.

all Englishmen[4] The next year following this Deponent together with the rest of them went and purchased Land of the Indians at the Schoolkill[5] and Settled there accordingly afterward the Dutch came in and burnt our houses or Garrison & carried us away prisoners to New Haven in New England from whence this Deponent with the rest of the aforementioned company came from[6] And further saith that this Deponent being then under the command of some of the aforementioned company was present when they purchased all the Lands from the Schoolkill to the Minquois habitation & so along Delaware River [to] the great Sea for which there was near 40 lb. Sterling given to the Indians for the purchase thereof And for which said purchase there were writings drawn and presented on the pte of the Indians And further deposeth not The marke of James Way[7]

---

[4] Waye imparts here an important point of information from personal experience ; namely that he was one of fourteen Englishmen (known to have come from New Haven) who in 1641 settled at " Wattseson " (*Watcessit, Oijtsessingh, Wattsesinge,* etc.), Indian name for land near the site of present Salem, New Jersey. The Swedes had been informed in 1641 that "several English families perhaps about sixty persons strong have settled and begun to build and cultivate the land ... " (*Inst. for Printz*, p. 68). It is possible that Waye was a member of an advance party of English who came to the Delaware and were followed shortly by additional settlers.

[5] Amandus Johnson published an English document dated April 19, 1642, which supports Waye's claim that land was purchased on the Schuylkill from the Indians (*Inst. for Printz*, p. 231, fn. 14a). Winthrop wrote that the Indians did not want to sell their land, but a Pequod chief, who had fled his country and was then living on the Delaware, interceded for the English with the Delaware Indians (*Winthrop's Journal 1630–1649,* ed. J. K. Hosmer, New York, 1908, 2 : 56).

[6] On May 22, 1642, Jan Jansen, commis at Fort Nassau, received instructions to compel the English settled on the Schuylkill " in a polite manner to remove, so that no blood may be shed " (*Narratives, Myers,* p. 76). Cf. Chapter 6.

[7] An inaccurate abstract of this deposition appears on p. 18 of *Bernard Quaritch's Catalogue No. 427,* part of which was reproduced in 1929, by the Sun Book & Job Printing Office in Baltimore for the Enoch Pratt Free Library, with a printed cover entitled, *Descriptive Catalog of the Exhibition of Documents Relating to the Early Days of The Colony of Maryland.*

New Yorke SS. April the 18th 1684

Then appeared before me John Spragg Esquire Secretary of the Province of New Yorke the Deponent James Waye and affirmeth under the penalty of Perjury that the within mentioned Deposition is the trueth the whole trueth and nothing else but the trueth Which I certifie

John Spragge

CAPTAIN THOMAS YONG'S LETTER TO SIR FRANCIS WINDEBANKE[1]

May it please your Honour,

I have herewith sent to your Honour a relation of the occurrents of my voyage from Virginia, till this bearer, my Lieutenant's [Robert Evelyn] departure from me, in Charles River; (for that name I have presumed to give the same, in honour of his Majesties name) Nevertheless, I thought fit to give your Honour a particular account of my endeavors and purposes concerning the [northwest] passage, apart; and what reasons I have to hope and prosecute further further the discoveries thereof, whereby I trust your Honour will perceive the great probabilities, I have to attayne the same.

I passed by the great [Delaware] River, which I mention to your honour, with purpose to have pursued the discovery thereof till I had found the great lake, from which I am enformed this great River issueth; and from thence I have particular reason to believe there doth also issue some branch, one or more, by which I mought have passed into that mediteranean [inland] Sea, which the Indian relateth to be four days journey beyond the Mountains,[2] but having

---

[1] Thomas Yong's " Relation " in *Narratives, Myers,* pp. 37-49, describes his explorations in the Delaware River,[1] starting the latter part of July, 1634. Yong wrote the " Relation " while he was still on the Delaware and sent it back to England with his lieutenant and nephew, Robert Evelyn. Yong then continued with his explorations, but evidently left no account of events subsequent to October 20, although he remained on the Delaware for some months. Myers did not publish Yong's letter that accompanied and supplemented his " Relation, " probably because it had been previously published, the most recent being in Fund Publication No. 9, *Papers Relating to the Early History of Maryland,* ed. Sebastian F. Streeter, Maryland Historical Society (January, 1876), pp. 312-214. The following is a transcript of the original letter, now in possession of the Virginia State Library, Richmond, with whose permission it is printed ; it differs only slightly from Streeter's transcript. The footnotes and words in brackets have been added by the present authors.

[2] In the " Relation " (*Narratives, Myers,* p. 47), Yong states that this informant was an Indian King, brother to the Mohegan king, who lived five miles above the rocks. The Indian had been twenty days above his home by canoe, and he said that five additional days' journey beyond, the river issued from a lake. Moreover, he told Yong that four days' journey from the river, over certain mountains, lay the mediterranean sea.

passed near fifteen leagues up the River, I was stopped from further proceeding by a ledge of rocks which crosseth the River over, so as that, I could not get over with my vessel, by reason of the shallowness of the water, which at high water riseth not above a foot and a half over the rocks, and at low water the rocks are discovered five or six foot deep, so that I determined against the next summer to build a vessel which I will launch above the rocks, in which I purpose to go up to the Lake, from whence I hope to find a way that leadeth into that mediteranean Sea, and from the Lake, I judge that it cannot be less than 150 or 200 leagues to the North Ocean, and from thence I purpose to discover the mouths thereof, which discharge themselves both into the north and South Seas. But if I shall fayle of arriving at the Lake, which I am confident I shall not, I will then take with me out of my vessel both workmen and provisions, which shall be portable, for the building of a small vessel, which I will carry those four days journey over Land (whereof the Indian speakes in the Relation), with a competent number of men, and then I purpose to cutt downe wood, and fitt up a vessel upon the bankes of that Sea, and from thence make my discovery. And I am confident that this which I propose is feasible, for I am informed by the Indian who offereth to accompany mee, and is and will bee in my power, that beyond these rocks there are no more rocks nor falls to hinder my passage, so far as he hath been. This River I conceive to be the most probable place for the discovery thereof in regard it runneth so far southerly, and I for my part shall most willingly undergo all hazards and dangers, and be at much charge for the service of his Majesty and honour of my Country : and I hope to give your Honour good satisfaction of my endeavors therein the next winter. In the meantime, I humbly desire your honour to cast me at his Majesties feet, and to be a means that his Majesty may continue his goodness and protection of mee, and that I may not be hindered in the prosecution thereof by any persons either abroad or at home; and moreover, that according to his Majesties gracious grant, I may enjoy those trades I discover in my voyage and that the passage being once found, as I presented it to his Majesty, I may also have the benefitt of his Majesties Articles, whereof I nothing doubt, since I have proceeded so cheerely, and do undertake all, without putting his Majesty to any charge. Only because I may have occasion *to fortefie in some few places as I goe, and especially on the River where I now am,*[3] which is broad, if he will be graciously pleased to lend, if not bestow on me, some ten or twelve pieces of Iron ordinaunce; whereof I wish that some were half culvering at the least, I shall acknowledge myself infinitely bound to his Majesty and whether he favour me with this or no, I will yet be sure to serve him, and love him, and venture my life for him, and for the honour of my Country, with the same alacrity; and will, by God's grace, both live and die an honest man. To your Honour, I am most particularly bound for your great favours and dispatch, and will thinke myself happy in being able to do you ever all humble service, and so I most humbly Kiss your Honour's hands this 20th of October, 1634, from Charles River.

> Your honour's most humble
> and most obedient servant
>
> Thomas Yong[4]

---

[3] Evelyn, in his letter to Mme. Plowden, referred to Eriwoneck as the place "where we sate down." In *A Description of the Province of New Albion*, Beauchamp Plantagenet, 1648 edition, there is reference on p. 17 to the "Fort begun at Eriwomeck" by Captain Yong and Master Evelyn. On the Domina Virginia Farrar Map, 1651 (*Iconography*, 2: Pl. C. 47) the fort is shown at "Eriwoms."

[4] Yong evidently went from the Delaware to New England waters in further search of the passage, and the following note about him is found in Samuel Maverick's description of New England, c. 1660 : "One Captaine Young and 3 men with him in the Yeare 1636 went up the River [Kennebec] upon discovery and only by Carying their Canoes some few times, and not farr by Land came into Canada River very neare Kebeck Fort were by the French Captain Young was taken, and carried for ffrance but his Company returned safe" (*Proceedings,* Massachusetts Historical Society, 2nd Series (1884-1885), 1 : 231).

The following, quoted by Streeter, is from the king's order which was issued to Yong after receipt of his application made in 1633 :[5]

" His Majesty having satisfied himself of the fidelity of Capt. Thomas Young, hath employed him, together with his nephew, Robert Evelin of London, gent, whom Mr. Young has chosen to accompany him as his Deputy, into America, on special occasions of his Majesty's service, which his Majesty thinks fit to remain private to himself, and whereof his Majesty expects speedy and particular accounts from them : He therefore commands all officers to permit them to pass in all his dominion without hindrance, and to give them if needed," etc.

---

[5] For a thorough understanding of the Yong expedition, the reader should consult two letters written by Yong *before* he left England (*The Evelyns in America, 1608-1805,* edited and annotated by G. D. Scull, Oxford, 1881, pp. 55-59).

ANDRIES HUDDE'S PURCHASE OF LAND AT PRESENT-DAY PHILADELPHIA
FROM THE INDIANS [1]

September 25, 1646

Wee, that are named in the end of this, do declare and attest, that on this day and in the date mentioned below before the Commissioner Andres Hudden (because of the general geoctroiide West-Indische Company unto the Command or Government of the Noble Sir Wm Kieft Dr. General concerning the places of New Netherland dwelling upon the South River in their own persons and in Our presence did appear and have been present Sheghire [Meghire] Honden Saeckmaecker of Pemipagka and proprietor [,] and Colonel or the Chiefest of Ackehooren Saeckmaecker of Mattekamikon, and Rinnowyhy brother of Meghire Hondon aforementioned and do declare willingly and with good Consideration, and also with acknowledgment and approbation of the people thereabout for a Certain Summ of Cargesoenen [cargason] which those do confess to have received there with their full Satisfaction and gratefull mind in their hands (as the Same have had declared before that these parcels of Land never have been Sold to anybody that they have transported credit over given and to hold Such Lands to a Right and free propriety and So they do Transport, credit overgive and

---

[1] This document is one of two Mss bearing the identification No. 11 in the Hugh Hampton Young collection at the Enoch Pratt Free Library, Baltimore, Maryland. It is an English copy of a missing Dutch document, the translation having been made for Lord Baltimore's private use. Hudde refers to this purchase in one of his reports as follows :

" As on the 7th of September [1646] following, a letter was delivered to me in which I was strictly ordered to purchase some land from the Savages, situated on the west shore, about a mile distant from Fort Nassau to the north, I accordingly took possession of that spot on the 8th, following, and erected on it the arms of the Hon. Company, and, as the owner was absent hunting, I was obliged, to delay the purchase till the 25th of the same month. After the purchase was accomplished, the proprietor went with me to the spot and assisted in fixing the arms of the Hon. Company to a pole, which was put into the ground on the extreme boundary. Shortly after this, several freemen made preparations to build on this newly-acquired possession . . . " (*Inst. for Printz,* p. 264).

to hold with those the Same in respect of the N. West Indische Company a Certain piece of Land that these men do call Wigquachkoing[2] Scituated in the South River of New Netherland Stretching from the South end of a Vally that runneth between t'vupebol and t'vassebos along the River Verby [*voorby*, meaning "beyond"] t'vogels Sand about New Netherland and to a kill having there a Round and Somewhat high Corner lying over against the South Corner of Seutters Island in the Land about 5 or 6 miles, or So far as it will please the mentioned Company and that withall actions, Rights and Priviledges beforementioned, and the quality that may peratin to them, constituting and Surrogating in their place the mentioned Company in a real and actual possession of it, and do give the like herewith a full and irrevocable Power and Authority and Special Commandment, Such Land tanquam Actor & procurator in rem Suam et propriam of the Said Company or those that hereafter their act may receive to take to use it in peace to dwell, purge and hold and also therewith to doe, to act and to dispose as They with their own well and by Lawfull title obtained Land can doeth without reserving of the Sellers or cedents any part, Right, Action or pretense in the less of it, it may be by way of propriety, Commandement or jurisdiction reserving an[d] holding only concerning as before, now and for ever desisting of all that and renouncing by these, promising not only that this Transport and the Said Land through the Strength of these letters may be fulfilled, done, perpetually kept in his vigour unalterable and irrevocable but also the Same part of Land against every one to Deliver and to hold free of pretensions [blank] and Burden of any to invate [invade] it, All that in good Fidelity without deceit and to a Testimony of the Truth of it have wee the Sellers and resignators of it with us as Witnesses Subscribed Actum in the House of Nassau [Fort Nassau] upon the South River of New Netherland 25 September Ano 1646 Stilo Roma.

---

[2] For other forms, e.g. *Wiccaco, Wickakoe,* etc., see George P. Donehoo, *A History of the Indian Villages and Place Names in Pennsylvania,* Harrisburg, 1928, p. 252.

Index

An analytical index of topics was believed unnecessary because of the construction of the chapters as more or less separate entities, each dealing with a different subject. It did seem desirable, however, to include the following index of names and places, including the names of vessels.